# MY GUARDIAN DEMON

*My Guardian Demon* tells the story of two remarkable artists. Separated by the Iron Curtain, their twenty-five year correspondence, occasionally censored, gives an intimate view of their unique bond. In their letters that were funny and sometimes brutally honest Halina and André shared a consuming love of music and literature and a fascination with the foibles of human nature.

Arthur Rubinstein said of André, 'I think André Tchaikowsky is one of the finest pianists of his generation – he is even better than that – he is a wonderful musician.' Yet André's professional passion was composition. In 2013, three decades after his death, André's opera *The Merchant of Venice* was premiered by David Pountney at the Bregenz Festival gaining international recognition.

'You know that Rimbaud is my guardian demon'… were André's words in a letter of 9 October 1978. André's homage to his alter ego and their shared dark side led him four years later with sardonic wit to donate his skull to the Royal Shakespeare Company. It was subsequently used in performances of *Hamlet* starring David Tennant.

Author Anita Halina Janowska has journeyed from musical conservatoire to a PhD in criminology and a career as a writer. In Poland *My Guardian Demon* (*…mój diabeł stróż*) has achieved three editions and cult status making André Tchaikowsky a household name.

For an account of André Tchaikowsky's musical career, including the recent posthumous acclaim for his opera *The Merchant of Venice,* see *André Tchaikowsky: A Musician Divided* edited by Anastasia Belina-Johnson with foreword by David Pountney (London: Toccata Press, 2013).

*André Tchaikowsky* (1935-1982) studied piano with Emma Altberg, Stanisław Szpinalski, Lazare Lévy and Stefan Askenase, and composition with Kazimierz Sikorski, Hans Keller and Nadia Boulanger. In 1955 he was admired as the youngest laureate of the Fryderyk Chopin Piano Competition and a year later won the third prize at the Queen Elisabeth International Music Competition in Brussels. He was subsequently in great demand throughout his short life as a solo concert pianist and also played with the world's great orchestras and conductors, performing with them extensively throughout Europe, North and South America, Asia and Australia. André Tchaikowsky lived most of his adult life and died in England where he is remembered as an exceptionally gifted pianist and an artistic personality of wit and erudition.

Composition was his true vocation, so in his later years Tchaikowsky limited his concert activity to concentrate on writing music. His most important works include: the Shakespearian opera *The Merchant of Venice,* premiered in 2013 at the Bregenz International Festival, two piano concertos, two string quartets, *Seven Shakespeare Sonnets*, a sonata for clarinet and piano, *Inventions for Piano* and *Trio Notturno.*


The musician, sociologist and writer *Anita Halina Janowska* was born Halina Wahlmann in Łodź, Poland in 1933. She has also written under the pen-name Halina Sander. After graduating from the Fryderyk Chopin Conservatoire in Warsaw with a degree in piano performance, she read sociology at Warsaw University and later worked as criminologist for the Polish Academy of Sciences. Janowska wrote her PhD thesis: 'Murders and their perpetrators' in 1974. She has published numerous scientific books and articles, and since 1997 has been a member of the Association of Polish Writers. Her literary output includes an autobiographical novel *Krzyżówka (My Problems with Hitler and Stalin)*, for which she received the Warsaw Bookseller's Award (July, 1997). Her last novel *The Autumn Variations* was published in 2011. Anita Halina Janowska lives in Warsaw.

ANITA HALINA JANOWSKA

# My Guardian Demon

Letters of André Tchaikowsky and Halina Janowska 1956-1982
Translated from the Polish by Jacek Laskowski

SMITH-GORDON

# Contents

# Acknowledgements

The photographs on the cover were kindly supplied by the Polish publisher Grupa Wydawnicza Foksal and by Anita Halina Janowska. The cover was designed by Designers Collective (d-collective.com). The assistance of Grupa Wydawnicza Foksal and Ewa Krzak is gratefully acknowledged.

Anita Halina Janowska wishes to acknowledge her heart-felt special gratitude to Piotr Goldstein for his help with the editing of the English text.

The publishers warmly thank Jacek Laskowski for his fine translation and for his help and encouragement throughout.

We are grateful to the original publishers of poems published here in translation, as shown on the reverse of the title page.

David Ferré's website, www.andretchaikowsky.com, contains copious information he has compiled over several decades about every aspect of André's career. Ferré is also author of *The Other Tchaikowsky – A Biographical Sketch*. He has been a constant friend and adviser.

# By way of introduction

## *How we met*
## *Warsaw in 1953*

Everything that happened between us was either funny or sad.

The beginning was very funny, at a fancy dress party at the Warsaw Conservatoire. I was not in disguise. I wore a long black dress; and André was in a dark suit. Someone introduced us: 'André, this is Halina, our new student, and, Halina, this is André Tchaikowsky.'

André was already famous. He had come back from France with gold medals from the Paris Conservatoire, was only seventeen, and was to participate in the Chopin Piano Competition in 1955, etc. I was very shy and he looked at me in a strange way, like a tailor, who tries to determine the size of his client. Suddenly he grabbed my hand and took me to a classroom. There was a piano. I was very scared. I thought: 'Oh my God, he will make me play!' And he said: 'Take off your clothes!' I was stupefied. He repeated: 'Take off your clothes!' I still could not understand, so he explained, like an old patient professor: 'It is a fancy dress party. Let's swap our clothes.'

And so we did, behind the piano. Everything fitted him perfectly, even my sandals. In this silk dress, long earrings and a red scarf on his head he resembled Carmen from Bizet's opera. He was beautiful. We came back to the ballroom and… You will not understand how funny it was. Remember these were still the Stalin years. Then the First Secretary of the Warsaw Section of the Communist Party started to dance with André. He embraced him and kissed his hand. He believed André to be a beautiful girl studying singing at the Academy. All our fellow students giggled and André enjoyed it a lot.

And then we met again… in a trolleybus, on our way to school. It was very crowded.

Suddenly I heard a voice from the other side of the bus: 'Halinka, is that you? Where have you been? I thought you were dead!' People were staring at us curiously, and started to grin and whisper.

André, as if that was not enough, continued with: 'Halinka! Would you like to have many children?' I blushed and said nothing. Everyone around laughed louder and louder. I got off quickly.

On the street he took my hand and in all seriousness repeated the question: 'I mean it: would you like to have many children?'. I felt extremely uncomfortable and could hardly speak. 'I think so…,' I said. And he replied in a sad voice: 'What a pity! I wanted to marry you but now I can't. I will be a composer, a great composer, so it has to be quiet at home. No children!' He dropped my hand and went to a lecture.

I was angry with myself. I could have said: 'I want just one child!' Or: 'We could live separately.'

Was he joking, was this just for fun? Maybe I should have reminded him that Bach had twenty children!

After the Chopin Competition André felt lonely and sad – the reason was an unrequited love for a young man. He asked me whether I would like to move in with him. We lived together for nearly one year. It was a good time for us: we were close friends and really understood each other.

That time probably inspired him to invite me to Paris and to write letters about marriage and children.

The correspondence between us started after he was awarded the 3rd prize at the Queen Elisabeth Competition in 1956 in Brussels and decided not to return to Poland.

*Anita Halina Janowska*

*The labyrinth from which it is most difficult, maybe impossible,
to get out is – for the man – the man himself.*

Graffiti beneath Casanova's last portrait.

# Part One
# 1956 – 1962

From the Polish newspaper 'Warsaw Life', 3.6.56

'Polish Pianist's Achievement At The Brussels Competition'. Brussels: Polish Press Agency. In the late hours of yesterday evening the Queen Elisabeth International Music Competition was concluded in Brussels. The prize-giving ceremony took place in the presence of Her Majesty Queen Elisabeth of the Belgians, in a packed concert hall.

The Competition's first prize was won by the young Soviet pianist Vladimir Ashkenazy, second prize went to John Browning (USA), the third prize winner was the Polish pianist André Tchaikowsky – one of the winners at the recent Fryderyk Chopin Competition, fourth prize went to Cécile Ousset (France), fifth was L. Berman (USSR), sixth was T. Vásáry (Hungary) and seventh S. Knor (Czechoslovakia) (…).

Brussels, 12.10.56*

Halinka, my Darling, why haven't you written to me for so long? Whenever I get a postcard from Poland, I always hope it's from you. Surely you cannot forget so quickly! I beg you, write, sort me out a little – if I'm writing letters then things must be very bad. I love you like I've never loved you before, I cry like a baby, I don't so much think about you as feel you. The only memories I'm not afraid of digging up are our mutual ones. The only hope which doesn't seem nonsensical is OURS.

Don't be lazy, write – write quickly and make it long, and make it delicious and, at the same time, slightly foolish, as only you can. Most of all I'd like to bring you over here or go back to you myself. I'm not sure I won't even do that. Halinka, I am so sad here – how good that you're in this world.

Your Andrzej.
Write at once!

---

* In July 1956 Andrzej returned to Poland; in September he left for Brussels on a scholarship from the Belgian government.

Radiogram from Brussels, 21.10.56

We'll call our son Gaspard – what do you think?

Write soon, kisses Andrzej.

Telegram from Warsaw, 21.10.56

I want him to be called Daniel.

Kisses, Halinka.

Warsaw, 26.10.56

To the presumed father of our putative children!
    Thanks for the touching radiogram, but where did you get GASPARD from?* Are you aiming, creatively speaking, to compete with Ravel himself? I'd prefer Daniel because there's a prophet, and a writer, and a defender of the oppressed, and on top of that a biblical figure, so the heritage is right!
    It's hard to believe that Daniel will leap out of your head like Pallas Athene from that of Zeus, so you'll have to come back, Darling. One swallow doesn't make a summer. (…)

Warsaw, 27.10.56

My Darling, I didn't send the letter because it was short and silly.
    Quite extraordinary things are happening here. You'll know about them from the press no worse than we do. You've probably been informed that in the last few days you've become the son of a Free Fatherland, of which you should be as proud as the Fatherland is of you. Joking apart, things are very serious here, and very emotional. Even people who are indifferent to politics are overcome by a furious enthusiasm. Everyone is terribly involved. Me, too.
    Write soon, tell me what's happening to you.
    I'm listening to Oistrakh here and weeping with longing.
    Kisses and more kisses,

Your H.

---

* The idea was inspired by Ravel's *Gaspard de la nuit*

Letter from Aunt Mala*, Paris, 11.12.56

My Darling, dear Halinka.

I was very pleased to receive your postcard with the beautiful view of the Łazienki Palace, which reminds me of the era of my youth. I received the card after a considerable delay (…) during our stay in Paris. Dearest Halinka, first and foremost thank you for Maria Dąbrowska's excellent book *Noce i dnie* [Nights and Days]. Reading it gave me great pleasure. But to move on to the things that interest you most: (1) I assure you that we talk about Halinka very often, and what is most fascinating is that when Andrzej wants to pay me a compliment, he claims that I am completely like Halinka instead of saying that Halinka is like me. Don't you think so? Why, I'm old enough to be my Darling Halinka's grandmother! (2) Andrzej worked, as usual, for two to three hours each day, when all the other prize winners worked eight to ten hours, yet despite that the notices of his last concerts and his last recital, when he played Bach's *Goldberg Variations*, were fantastic! They regard him as the best artist of the present day. He is great already! At present he's not practising at all, he has taken to composition and for the last three days he has worked at night and slept in the day. He is tired, often irritable, but I hope that this will shortly pass. John Browning is leaving for America in four months which makes me very glad. As you know Andrzej is crazy about him which makes him (Andrzej) anxious and sad. My dearest Halinka, what a pity that you can't come and stay with us even for a short time. Maybe you can? I could send you an invitation to come here to Paris where we'll be spending Christmas. On 11 January Andrzej will be playing in the largest concert hall here.

John is undoubtedly jealous that Andrzej has had so much success recently. Music and his career are more important than anything else to John, but I have grave doubts about John having a great career. So far, Andrzej is invited everywhere, people are fighting over him, while John is being ignored. That's how it was in Paris, in Italy, and in America. Artistic jealousy has always existed, does still, and always will. Andrzej alone is not jealous because he has that confidence in himself. Besides, Halinka, you are a very talented pianist as Andrzej tells me, so you understand all this.

Well, let me kiss you warmly,

Your Auntie Mala.

---

* Aunt Mala, sister of Andrzej's grandmother, addressed her letter to 'Madame Halina Tchaikowsky'

Part of a letter from Andrzej to the pianist Halina Musiałówna
(Andrzejewska), a fellow-student and friend, January 1957

Darling, you probably know by now that I intend to bring Halinka here with so-called 'serious intentions', because I have reached the conclusion that permanent things can be built only on great friendship, not on passion. You can deduce from that what kind of lesson I've just received because during the vacation I was still cock-a-hoop.

John ditched me on the day of my 21st birthday, so it was the first of November, and I still can't get over it. The days are normal, but the nights are impossible. To begin with it was even worse… Luckily, I had a lot of concerts then. I worked like a packhorse, I got up to 10 hours' practice a day. I longed for revenge. I wanted to show him that I hadn't been done. I did more in 2 weeks than I had done in the previous 3 years. Just imagine: Prokofiev's 2nd Concerto played in the same evening with Beethoven's 4th and Chopin's F minor! John played Beethoven's 4th Concerto 3 days before me, and the press all compared us to my advantage. Bach's *Goldberg Variations* brought the critics to a frenzy of rapture. John wasn't at the concerts, but everyone told him so much about them that he couldn't stand it and went and listened to the tapes. He said afterwards that there was no one who could play Bach like me. For many weeks I sat at the piano constantly, I swallowed piece after piece, treated music like morphine – without that I'd have probably gone mad or done something stupid. My musical victory gave me no satisfaction, I'd have exchanged a hundred victories like that for his love.

Since John's departure I've let myself go completely, I don't go to the piano and content myself with signing contracts for the coming season. The only thing that really does interest me is my own concerto. I'll be playing it on 14th March 1958 in Brussels. For my performances with Mitropoulos I'm planning Prokofiev's 2nd or 3rd Concerto, and for the recital – 4 Ballades and 24 Preludes by Chopin. I like playing Chopin very much now. When you love him, he's not all that difficult. Rubinstein recently said that the only Chopin which didn't irritate him was mine, yet just a year ago he was crying with despair over my *Barcarolle* and Nocturne in E flat major. Oh, God, I'm running out of paper. (…)

Stay well, Darling, many kisses,

Your friend – Andrzej.

Paris*, 12.2.57

Halinka my Darling!

Your letter is a literary masterpiece – if you write a novella like that you're certain to go down in the history of world literature. Then you'll get the Nobel Prize, and I'll get an Oscar – for interpreting it. You're probably smiling to see me mention that telling name. Yes, it's true, but do I really have to be the same kind of clown and buffoon as him?

I'm drunk now, and I've recently become acquainted with hashish and cocaine. I'm horribly sad, even though I'm getting over it, or maybe because I'm getting over it. That fact is objectively sadder than the wild distress and confusion I felt earlier. It is, of course, practical that one should forget... .

My only way out is for you to write me lots – don't imagine I'm bored by it, or even entertained by it: understand that you can help me. My Darling, you can see for yourself how all those 'grandiloquent' fantasies turn out, but we keep on. Of all the people I know, you are the one I treat most seriously. Maybe it's because you are the only one I never promised anything?

Forgive me, I wanted to write you something, but nothing seems to come out. Give Halina [Musiałówna] a hug and, taking advantage of the pretext, throw yourself at Ryszard [Olszer] – you are my best friends in Poland. Write to: 149, rue de Rennes, Paris VI (chez Monsieur Charles Fortier)**

Kiss you,

Your Andrzej.

Paris, 18.6.57

Beloved Pussycat,

I've finally managed to get that authentication of the document out of the Commissariat: five days the wretches kept it! (...)

Funnyface, I'm very uneasy about you, and this isn't a good time for me, either, having to do everything at once: finish my concerto by the first of August, record three commissioned LPs (*Gaspard de la nuit* and *Visions fugitives*; the *Goldberg Variations*; three preludes and fugues by Bach and six sonatas by Scarlatti), sort out some passport problems at the prefecture, undergo a kind of cross-eyed nostalgia (the left ventricle of the heart longing for Warsaw, the right for New York), and pay daily visits to Mr and Mrs Rubinstein, which is a lot less entertaining than it sounds. Mr Rubinstein is very interested in my concerto and says it will be Bartók's 4th (he dislikes Bartók). He advised

---

* The envelope of this letter was addressed to 'Dear Halinka Tchaikowsky'
** Kazik, Andrzej's cousin, Aunt Mala's son

me to: 'Open yourself up! Let your soul sing. You have a talent, my child, a golden talent, you should write to make the whole audience dissolve in tears.' But I doubt if I'll follow his advice: I might end up writing Rakhmaninov's 5th! My conductor, the handsome André Vandernoot, gives me diametrically opposite advice: 'Oy, such a pretty theme, isn't it a waste for the piano? Who needs that typewriter? Turn it into a symphony! The piano was fashionable in the salons; another ten years and hardly anyone will be playing it any more. Listen, dear boy, the orchestra plays so much better when there's no pat-pat-pat getting in the way.' Under Rubinstein's influence I wrote a theme that all my friends judged to be horribly sweet and maudlin; under Vandernoot's influence I gave it an accompaniment straight out of a post-dodecaphonic series with 'concrete' rustlings in the percussion, kettledrum glissandos pianissimo and quarter-tone trills. Heaven knows how it will all end up. But I'm already looking forward to the first performance and I feel that we'll all have a good time. I can just imagine the faces of the orchestra at the first rehearsal (where, incidentally, I expect to see you). It will be a veritable Sinfonia Zoologica: drums growling, clarinets miaowing, brass roaring and flutes barking with their flutter-tonguing; the real menagerie, however, will be out in the auditorium. Darling, it's 25 past 4 already, and the recording starts at 5. God help me, because I don't know what I'll be doing (I'm not the only one. A couple of days ago I went to a concert given by Cortot who plays and looks like a worn-out old condom. The erudite Staszek Kołodziejczyk sees a similarity with Ramses II, but I must say that, this far, Egyptian civilisation is better preserved. No one thought to embalm Cortot when there was still time to do it; and now, I greatly fear, it is too late, both for him and for Mrs Marguerite Long whose face greatly resembles that of Moby Dick. Only King Artur is in more or less reasonable shape).

Take care of yourself (…) Auntie is hurrying me along terribly, thwacking me on the back and yanking my hair to get me going. I should, perhaps, have mentioned that I'm still in my pyjamas.

A thousand kisses to my Darling from

Your Andrzej.


Warsaw, 25.6.57


My dearest Andrzej, what's happened to you? Even Tristan did not conduct such a lively correspondence with Isolde as you're doing with me… If I join you for ever, then Polish literature will suffer irrevocable harm. I've read the letters of the great Bolesław Prus to Miss L. – they do not compare with yours! I am bewitched!

My broken finger has grown back and I'm preparing my diploma recital for September (the Bach Partita in B flat major, the Beethoven *Appassionata*,

Schumann's *Kinderszenen* and Prokofiev's Sonata No. 3). Just before the vacation, I played part of the partita for Maria* while my finger was in plaster. I thought she would be charmed, but she said: 'This, my child, is a conservatory, not a circus.'

Next month I'm off to Malbork (accompanying at a choreographic summer school for young people). Yes, yes – you will be playing New York, and I will be playing Malbork.

Many, many kisses,

Your H.

Malbork, 15.7.57

Beloved Andrzej!

I'm in Malbork, playing from dawn to night. It's an easier day because they're all on an outing leaving me behind as the camp warden. Before they went there was an accident – one of the boys broke his leg and I had to call the ambulance. By mistake, however, I went to the wrong room where a teacher from the village was sleeping, and I took him for the lad with the broken leg. I had to find out his identity to give to the emergency services.

'What is your name?' I asked, slightly surprised that the little lad's legs sticking out from under the duvet were so monstrously hairy. Only half-awake, he retorted: 'Zygmunt Springer, why?' I, still concerned, went on: 'Does it hurt very much?'

'No, nothing hurts,' he replied, truthfully.

'You're a brave lad!' I praised him. 'I'm sure you're hungry. I'll fetch you something to eat.' And I ran to the kitchen for some milk soup.

'To what do I owe such bliss?' asked the astonished teacher, eating his soup.

'It's only natural. I'll just bring you some sandwiches.'

When I came back with the sandwiches, he kissed my hand. Embarrassed, I ran out quickly and phoned for the ambulance. It arrived soon afterwards. I walked into the room, I looked…, and there was Springer (nomen omen) springing round the room in his briefs. Seeing me, he shouts: 'Oh, there you are! You've surely fallen in love with me!?' And he stretches his arms out to me: they are just as hairy as his legs. I stand there, pole-axed, and say sharply: 'Kindly get dressed, the ambulance has come for you.' And he says: 'God Almighty! I knew she was a nutcase, I knew it.'

Meanwhile, in the next room, lay the tearful and hungry seven-year-old Tommy. The ambulance took him away. The teacher has locked himself in his room just in case, and I'm sitting alone in my room, looking through the

---

* Wiłkomirska, pianist, professor at the Academy of Music

window into the cemetery. The cemetery here is our garden, our beach, even the pasture for the local cattle. It's a Lutheran cemetery. Yesterday, an old man carrying a staff shouted at me: 'Graves should be respected! Whether they're Polish, or Jewish, or German!' He thought I had been grazing cows on the graves…

I'm writing all this nonsense because you're so horribly far away and you're not writing at all.

Kiss you. H.

PS. As for John (if you've still not got over it), I recently read this in Flaubert's Letters: 'When you want to put the sun in your trousers, you burn your trousers and you piss on the sun.'

Łódź, 20.8.57

Andrzej, Darling, I've just received a letter from Paris; unfortunately it's the one I wrote and sent you in July, from Malbork. I hope the one about the hospital reached you. Janek* cut out my appendix and now everyone's gone away on holiday.

I'm alone and feeling rotten. I'm being looked after a bit by this friend of Ryszard Olszer, a mathematician called Marek. I have to spend hours discussing open circles and one sphere divided into three spheres with him. He's trying hard to persuade me to join Ryszard and Ryszard's fiancée Krysia Serejska in Wisła. Maybe I'll let myself be tempted, or maybe I won't.

In the mean time I'll kiss you and not give up hope that you'll write again sometime.

H.

PS. Yes, my feelings for you are the greatest and saddest thing in my life.

Postcard, Wisła, 26.8.57

Darling, I succumbed to temptation because I was going mad with sorrow. Before I left I had a phone call from your grandmother's friend Mr R. telling me you owe him 15 thousand. Should I sell the radiola and pay back the debt? Write. It's pleasant and jolly here. Marek is touchingly solicitous and gentle. He recently said: 'You'll probably go to Andrzej and you'll probably come back. That's what I'm counting on.' (Counting is his profession).

Bye, Darling, kiss you. H.

---

* Halinka's brother-in-law, a surgeon

In Flight with Eastern Air Lines, 1.9.57

Funnyface, Mr R. has gone mad! (It's a shame, he was a good soul). You'd be a sucker to give him the radiola when there's no reason to; I should think that a neck-tie would be more than enough even if it was his birthday. I don't owe Mr R. one drachma, let alone the 15 000 drachmas he mentions. Yet to think he was always so sniffy about surrealism.

Hide the radiola well; swallow it, but don't let him have it (unless you want to). I must finish up because the plane is reaching New York and I'm reaching for the sick-bag. It's landing – landing – God Almighty!

You can sell yourself to Mr R., if you want to. But I'd prefer Kazuro*.

Kisses, Darling, Your Λ.


POSTCARD: LA GRANDE CÔTÉ – L'OURS POLAIRE

1.9.57

The last snap of your teddy bear.

Andrzej.


Letter addressed to 'Halina Czajkowska (Pianoforte)', New York, 17.9.57

Halinka! Help me! I'm at my wits' end. Maybe these are inauspicious times for old mythomaniacs but even so, it's hard to deny that you're hellishly, hellishly far away. And these last ten days I've needed you terribly. There are so many situations when no one can help me like you… Consequently, no one did help me, or rather, which was worse, they all helped me as best THEY COULD…

It all started like this. First, there was no concert. The orchestra went on strike, and I was struck down by Asian flu (to distinguish it from ordinary flu – apart from the name there is no difference). I was supposed to be playing Prokofiev's 3rd on Friday and Saturday, and on Sunday the Schumann; but on Tuesday I discovered that the concerts were cancelled so I could afford to suffer with the flu. On Thursday they phoned me and said the strike was off and the orchestra, better paid now, had agreed to play with me on Sunday. I injected myself with penicillin for three days, while taking six aspirins daily and devouring vitamins and steak tartare to get my strength and fitness back. Throughout all this, my Friends-and-Relations** called me 30 times a day to wish me luck. Exhausted by the aspirins, invigorated by the raw steaks, terrified

---

* A 75-year-old professor at the Warsaw Conservatoire
** Rabbit's phrase from *Winnie-the-Pooh*

by good wishes not to mention the news (passed to me at the last moment 'to give me strength'), that Mr Horowitz would be listening to me on the radio, I went out on stage and gave a middling performance. Just that: middling. It was neither good enough nor bad enough to be at all memorable. Nobody there knew me so nobody was particularly disappointed. Later, they wrote me up in the papers and all agreed dispassionately that I am a good pianist. But I'm not a good pianist: I'm either something much more or something much less than that. But to show them that, I must have someone to play for: someone in the audience I want to convince. For a long time now – a year? Longer? – I haven't found anyone I would want to play or write for, and I've become hopelessly banal. My playing is very lucid and it's always exactly the same. The critics like it very much, praising me for 'the mature artistic restraint astonishing in someone of [my] youth.' Halinka, let me confess. I'm suffering from an Eeyore complex.

I called John in Los Angeles. 'I've finished the concerto and I'd like to know what you think of it.' This is what I heard: 'Oh, how charming. That's really nice. And are you dedicating it to me? Great! I'm very busy at the moment, but I'll have a look at it sometime. Is everything else all right? No news? Take care, old man.'

HALINKA, I WANT YOU HERE! When you come over in the spring we'll buy ourselves a small apartment and we'll live together in Paris. Most important of all, we must have children. I so want someone who will be mine – always. Then all this playing and everything else will have some point.

Write and tell me what needs to be done so you can come over. Did Kazik send the invitation? Write soon!

There's one other thing that worries me: I've been losing a terrible amount of hair lately (…) there are more and more clearings in this forest. My dad was completely bald by the time he was my age – just like all the men on his side of the family. And now it's my turn. You can't be exceptional in everything, I suppose. Our son Daniel will probably go bald in time, too.

I have no idea what you're doing and when you're getting your diploma. What didn't you want to write about? Is your life meaningless, too? Do you still want to see me? When you come, I'll show you some wonderful fingering for the hardest part of the Chopin Ballade in F major. But you probably play it far better than I do anyway. Write about anything that interests you, let me live in your aura again for a while – we'll be together soon. (…)

Many long, passionate and matrimonial kisses.

Your Andrzej.

GREAT NORTHERN HOTEL, NEW YORK

3.10.57

My Darling – Halinka – mon amour – meine ferne Geliebte!

I've been sitting here for what must be 20 minutes and I just don't know how to start: that's what my inability to write is all about. Maybe the best thing would be to begin with my morning meeting with Mitropoulos. It was the first time I'd seen him and his appearance reminded me of Żurawlew*, but most of all he reminded me of myself. The first thing he said was: 'My God, such a pretty boy and he can't even knot his tie properly. I must teach you how it's done.' 'I'm certain I'll learn a thousand things from you, sir,' your handsome husband replied. 'By all means, let's start with knotting ties.'

This scene was being watched by old Mr Steinway, who must be New York's only ancient monument. The renowned pianoforte manufacturer is now as old as the harpsichord, and in silhouette looks like a flat**. He's been busy for years now, working on the invention of a third leg to justify the existence of the third pedal on the piano; he keeps the public informed of his progress at regular intervals. Oh, the futility of life! Darling! You know me better than anyone else does, so tell me: what do I really think of Sophia Loren? Everyone here keeps asking me that. But let's talk seriously (…). It would be best if Kazik sent you the invitation. He's longing to meet you anyway, and he's promised to help us get settled in Paris. (…) If you received the invitation from me, you'd be seen as a second Scarlett Panufnik***.

If you come to Paris for the first of March we'll arrange a Belgian visa for you and one for England where you'll hear the world premiere of Chopin's F minor on 24 March. Bye, bye, my azure angel, my scarlet vamp, my melodramatic black pearl, my honey-soaked serpent (from a 'literary flirtation' of 1947)****.

Kissing you long and passionately, A.

---

* Jerzy Żurawlew, professor at the Warsaw Conservatoire, initiator of the Chopin competition

** In musical notation the symbol for 'flat' is ♭ suggesting Mr Steinway's shape

*** Andrzej Panufnik (1914–91), the prominent Polish composer, took refuge in England in 1954 having fallen out with the Polish authorities of the day. He was married to (and later divorced from) an Irish woman nicknamed 'Scarlett' who resembled the heroine of *Gone With The Wind*. She played a dramatic part in his life about which she wrote a book. Panufnik was knighted and died in England

**** 'Literary flirtation' was a parlour game with cards each containing a slightly erotic phrase for the player to present

ERNEST ALLEN RANCH, FORT WORTH, TEXAS

20.10.57

Darling little Halinka,

Would you be so good as to have a very good photo done of yourself and send it to me in New York horribly quickly? It's very, and I mean very, important; my life depends on it, I really don't know what I'll do if you don't send it to me. In the next few days I'll send you my first record – Ravel's *Gaspard de la nuit* and Prokofiev's *Visions fugitives*. The record's so-so, but there's quite a good photograph on the sleeve. And *Le Gibet* and *Scarbo* are very good – only *Ondine* is… old, wrinkled, chaste, dull and bookish. There is, fatally, nothing womanly about her – an *Ondine* like that from me is a virtual confession, let's hope no one suspects.

I'm drunk and I'm finding it hard to write. Halinka, really, send me that photograph. Absolutely! Sweetie! Can you hear me?

Take care and don't practise too much. And don't write too much. Nor too little. And never, for God's sake, just enough or I'll say you've grown old.

See you, Funnyface, look after yourself.

Kisses, lots and lots, A.

POSTCARD FROM FLORIDA: HARIDA FLAMINGOS, FLORIDA

1.11.57

Funnyface,

I'm sending you a thousand kisses and an alligator handbag. I've decided to send you a card on *my* birthday because I never know when yours is. It's very nice and hot here – but it would be nicer for me to be in Kalisz with you than in Florida alone. But nicest of all would be Florida with you.

Which will happen – meanwhile bye –

Your Andrzej.

New York, 8.11.57

My poor little Funnyface,

I came back to New York the day before yesterday and received your three letters. I read them in the wrong order and got everything mixed up. Truth to tell I cried when I saw the muddle and 'what's become of us'. Then I picked my nose and drew some conclusions. Halinka, it's quite simple: you can't leave Marek now. You wouldn't have agreed to stay with me anyway – that's not 'real life'. Even if we'd spent 50 years together, had more children than Haydn wrote symphonies and made love in every possible position, it would still not be as good for you as one hour with Marek. You would feel that even more strongly now than you would have done earlier (…). And Marek, too, would be very unhappy. Halinka, enough of this play-acting – it's time to start living. You're exceptionally lucky that you're succeeding in doing so at last.

So, do marry Marek, but that doesn't mean that you shouldn't come to Paris with us in the summer. On the contrary, it could be a dream honeymoon for you both. Marek will surely demonstrate how much he trusts me and not raise any objections – besides, it will be to his advantage. Let us suppose that Halinka's love for Andrzej has survived the test of time and the test of absence; but what about the test of presence? When you see me as I am, an old, bald, wrinkled mummy, then, with a shriek of terror, you'll throw yourself into Marek's embrace – and serve me right! As Sacha Guitry puts it: 'If you want to punish your wife's seducer, the greatest revenge would be to let him keep her.' Joking aside: will you come, or not? There is the question of our would-be child Daniel outstanding. Have you spoken to Marek about it, and does he agree? As far as I'm concerned, I'm ready for anything and I await your joint decision patiently.

Halinka, if I've insisted that I wanted you here it was because I could see nothing better for you in Poland. Despite that Auntie Mala always reproached me, saying: 'You're heartless. You'll tear the girl away from everything she knows and likes, and what will you give her in return? A de luxe edition of Shakespeare? Will she comfort you each time you get punched on the nose, will she knot your bow-tie for you with maternal concern before you go out to play?' 'I am everything she knows and likes,' I told Auntie Mala proudly; but that has changed, and everything she said is coming true – luckily for you. I have an urge to hug you both and to give you my blessing – I am very moved: to think that I came within a whisker of ruining your life. We'll see each other this summer in Paris.

Write back soon. (…) Your old Andrzej.

PS. I was at Horowitz's. He's old, sick and sad. His wife's eyes follow him, and they're filled with love. They have not said a word to each other in four years.
I'd really like to die young. A.

Trieste, 22.1.58

Darling, crazy, surely happy little Funnyface,
I'm being shaken about so much I can't write anything, for God's sake. I'm in a train between Venice and Trieste. I'm playing in a different place every night and spending my days in trains. I'll always love you very much, whether

it's allowed or not. I hope that you'll be happy together, but if you're not – come to me! Now or in a hundred years – I'll always feel the same towards you.

Last night I wrote to Marek. I'll send both letters together from Trieste. Read Marek's first, and if you don't like it, don't show it to him.

Stay well.

Your Andrzej.
Write!

Letter to Marek

My dear, ginger Marek, I've decided to write to you because I like myself and everything which reminds me of myself. And we are very alike. We are both ugly (though very nice), we are both balding, and we are both madly in love with Halinka. I see just one difference: you love women, whereas I know them. An exchange of experiences would be mutually beneficial.

Listen! I'll tell you the story of Little Katie. Katie had a handsome husband and I visited them often. Unfortunately, this husband – Lanky Mietek – had stomach ulcers which made him over-sensitive and grotesquely jealous. Once, when a salad with mayonnaise made him feel more ill than usual, he created a terrible scene in front of Katie – about me. The result was devastating. Katie, who had never till then imagined that anyone could be jealous of me, suddenly noticed me and within half an hour had fallen madly in love with me. Both Mietek and I were quite simply terrified by this.

But worse was to come. I don't know what Katie's father told his ancient lady wife about me, but the fact is that a few days later Katie's mother started revealing unambiguous symptoms of a pathological, all-consuming passion. Within three weeks she greeted me with a kiss on the lips and the offer of a double helping of salmon with garnish. That was just too much. I left Poland and have lived abroad ever since.

Now judge for yourself what women are like. Forbid Halinka something, and you'll give your rival his greatest weapon: a myth. I warn you: if you say 'no' to Halinka it will be the same as giving her to me. You'll turn me into someone distant, forbidden, unreachable, and she'll close her eyes and think of me at the moment she is giving herself to you. Say 'yes', and you'll suddenly deprive me of any glamour I may have.

Hoping you'll appreciate the sincerity of my intentions, I embrace you and wish you both the fulfilment of all your desires. Keep warm.

Andrzej.

Marek's letter to Andrzej,
Warsaw, 10.2.58

My dear Andrzej!

Thank you heartily for the amusing letter, but above all for the charming compliments you shower on me. Writing that I am as ugly as you, you compare me almost with Valentino, and calling me 'ginger' you let me forget I'm bald – thank you, my dear friend. Let's not nurse complexes about it – baldness is, apparently, evidence of masculinity though it's hard to prove. But back to the letter! I liked your entertaining story about Little Katie very much and I'll try to draw the right conclusions from it. I trust your good intentions completely, and believe that the feelings which Halinka has towards you terrify you every bit as much as they do me, but if they don't, then listen to my cautionary tale.

One morning I was visiting Tworki [a hospital for the mentally ill]. I was being shown round by a friend – a psychiatrist. I was particularly interested in the melancholics and cholerics, since they were the most striking. My friend opened the door to one of the isolation wards and pointed to a man sitting on a bed – he was pale, sad, and he was holding a pink pillow in his hand and talking to it softly. 'What's this?' I asked. 'A romantic story', my friend said gloomily. 'He loved a woman who married someone else. Now he imagines she had a child by him and he hugs and cuddles the tiny pillow for days on end.' In the next isolation ward some madman was jumping like a man possessed, tearing his hair out, and shouting in a voice that wasn't human: 'I'm a cretin! I'm a buffoon! I'm an idiot!' 'What's that?' I asked, terrified. 'Ah, that,' replied my friend, nodding his head meaningfully, '…That's the one she married…'

I think, dear friend, that you will believe the sincerity of my intentions.

Let me hug you.

Marek.

Brussels, 16.7.58

How are you, little Monkey? You are so far away and we probably can't help each other at all, but we both need to – don't we, little Monkey?

I am in mid-air, somewhere between London and Brussels – they released me from hospital in London yesterday where they were cutting out my tonsils and injecting me with streptomycin for seven whole weeks. (…) But, it's all over now. Unfortunately, the family funds – i.e. mine, Auntie Mala's and in the end even Kazik's are gone, too. Hospitals in the West are immensely expensive and I am not, as yet, insured. In other words, I've ruined the family and I don't know what's going to happen next.

I spent two days in Brussels and now I'm travelling to Paris by train. I visited Stefan Askenase – his place is a madhouse at the moment – his wife's entire family is staying (one brother with wife from Tel Aviv, another brother and wife from Buenos Aires, a nephew and wife from New York, five children belonging to the above mentioned, a cousin of Stefan's from Turin, two cats and a dog). The whole caboodle sits in his home eating, drinking and smoking cigarettes. They're staying there for another three weeks. God's teeth!

Darling, write soon, I'm staying in Paris for the time being. (…) Where are you and Marek-the-Cat going on holiday? How is he? I hope that the three of us will meet in a year or two (…). Write and tell me how Halinka M. and Michal Wesołowski* are getting on. How's Darling Ryszard? He's the most splendid person I know. I'd rather have a half-hour conversation with him than a whole night with John – until, that is, I see John.

Are you still writing? Send me one of your pieces, Pussycat.

Kiss you, Andrzej.


BRITANNIA HOTEL

Trondheim, 25.9.58

Funnyface,

I'm in Trondheim, on the west coast of Norway, and this evening I'm playing the Brahms Concerto in B flat major. It's truly a joke: you wouldn't believe how many false notes one man is capable of playing in one concert. But as Stefan Askenase says: 'One has to muck it up now and again so the public realises how difficult it is.'

I'm becoming a diplomat in my old age and it's proving to be very useful. A reporter in Oslo asked me: 'Who is your favourite composer?' and I answered: 'Bach and Grieg.' Then I played the Beethoven G major like a booby and was a huge success… I haven't played in Stockholm yet, but the Swedish papers are full of the news that I'm young and very gifted, and my favourite writer is Strindberg. In Finland I'll be full of admiration for Sibelius, in Bulgaria for Vladigerov, and in Poland probably for Józik Kański**.

(…) But we must see each other. I'm counting on seeing you both in Paris next year. I'll be returning from America at the beginning of July – we'll meet in Paris and we'll all go away on holiday together: you, Marek, Auntie Mala, Kazik, Kazik's wife and Misha.

---

* Fellow student of Andrzej's. A pianist, professor and editor living in Sweden
** Fellow student of Andrzej's. A renowned music critic, author of *The Opera Guide* and contributer to *Opera*, the English monthly review, since 1962

Oh, yes, Misha. You don't know anything about him yet. He's a young doctor, charming, exceptionally musical (heaven only knows why doctors are all so musical: maybe it's because, compared with ordinary people, they know so little about medicine). Misha plays the clarinet, the piano, the violin and the French horn a little; but his real vocation is conducting. When he was still at medical school he formed an orchestra consisting entirely of doctors and medical students which won first prize in an amateur competition in England (…). Currently, partly under my influence, he is planning to give up medicine and devote himself entirely to music (this I persuaded him to do because I was deeply concerned for the English: ever since Misha started at the hospital the mortality rate in England has just about doubled and life expectancy has dropped by ten years: let's hope that his playing will cause less harm). (…)

Oh, mother, I have to rush to the rehearsal!

Bye, Darling. Andrzej.


Letter from Lili, Halinka's sister, London, 25.2.60

Halinka, beloved little sister,

Yesterday I spoke with Andrzej. We met in a café, and then went for a walk. I thought how unjust it was that it was I who was walking with him. I was 15 minutes late; he was waiting for me and he was so nervous he got his tongue in a twist. But I'd better begin at the beginning. Yesterday I went to his concert at the Queen Elizabeth Hall. I bought him a beautiful bouquet, 18 tulips as white as snow; they wouldn't present them to him on stage because only women are given flowers here. They sent the flowers to his room during the interval. He played beautifully at times, but his playing isn't quite finished; it's as if he hasn't become independent of the piano yet. He looks like a little boy. He's thin, his hair is close-cropped, and he is very good-looking.

When I went to him after the concert, he locked us in his room and was furiously disappointed that you weren't there. 'I nearly went berserk during the interval, I thought that Halinka was in the auditorium.' So it worked. He was so excited that I couldn't stand it and gave him the card you had coloured for him. We agreed to meet in the café. He's as poor as a church mouse: he's constantly giving charity performances. He wants to move from Paris, which he can't bear, and live permanently in London. He's renting an apartment here. He worships the English. He's become more serious. He said that, after the concert, he didn't sleep all night. He'd dearly like to see you. It doesn't in the least look as if he doesn't care a hoot for you. (…) Write soon.

Hugs and kisses.

Your Lili.

Letter to Marek,
London, 8.3.61

My dear Marek,

Yesterday I found out from Halinka's letter that she's suffering from tuberculosis of the kidneys and that the doctors were incapable of diagnosing it for more than three years. It's an awful and very dangerous disease (that's why I'm writing to you and not her); I am very anxious about her and you. This morning I went to a doctor acquaintance of mine and found out what I could. (1) You cannot donate your kidney; however Lili or someone else from her immediate family can. (2) It just so happens that the best specialists and the most modern clinic for kidney disease in Europe is here in London in Hammersmith. They have artificial kidneys there which keep a patient alive in emergencies during even the riskiest operations, and my doctor friend would do his best to get her admitted. I am certain that in a situation like this she'll get a passport; I also hope that you will be able to come with her. (If you couldn't, I beseech you not to be jealous: Halinka worships you). I'll try to arrange visas for you both and I'll send you tickets, but we must act quickly! Remember, Halinka is a scatter-brained little girl and doesn't appreciate the gravity of the situation; it's better that she shouldn't, but that makes it harder to persuade her. My dear Marek, I beg you, write back immediately, and start collecting all the medical data the clinic here needs before they can admit her. I've moved, so write to my new address: 25 Clarendon Gardens, London, W9.

Do you have a telephone? Please give me the number! Is H. in Zakopane* already?

I embrace you with all my heart.

Andrzej.

London, 4.61

Little Monkey,

I can see for myself that you're ill because you've never before written so much nonsense. You can't possibly ruin me because I've been broke for a long time, and besides all medical treatment in England is paid for by the government. People come here from as far away as the Philippines to treat themselves to a free pneumothorax or electrohypnosis (the latter, I'm afraid, doesn't exist yet). You say that you're not 'that' ill yet; I must warn you that if you die it could be too late to do anything. Anyway, I hope that you'll shortly have a turn for the worse and that I'll see you, at least, or even all three of you, in London. Thank Marek-the-Cat for his letter and remind him that he promised

---

* A mountain resort

to send me the results of all your tests, X-rays etc. I'm no Hans Castorp* and I won't have them framed and hung on my walls, but I'll send them to the doctor who's interested in your case and who would, if the need arose, easily shove you into that clinic. Get thoroughly bored at the sanatorium (boredom is excellent for one's health) and write soon to tell me if you're alive and where I should send my letters. I'm relying on the Cat to send them on to you in the mean time.

Just to cheer you up – apparently, La Callas has got liver cancer.

Kisses, if I'm allowed to

Andrzej.

PS. To the Cat: I'm not writing to you because Halinka will show you this letter anyway.

19.10.61

Halinka,

You have no idea how much pleasure your last, enchanting letter gave me, but especially the *bewitching* photographs. You sent them just in time because I could remember virtually everything you had ever said, but not what you looked like. I must admit that you look quite magnificent. Either you've grown enormously beautiful in the last few years, or I must have been blind when I left you in Warsaw five years ago. You were pleasant and pretty then, now you are *beautiful* – and yours is the best kind of beauty which comes from within. Auntie Mala, Misha and Zamira are as enchanted by you as I am (I'm sure you must have heard of Zamira, Yehudi Menuhin's daughter and Fou Ts'ong's wife; Ts'ong and she are, apart from Misha, my best friends in London. I've told her a lot about you and showed her your photographs with great pride).

Basia is a delightful, enormously feminine little devil; she could give lessons in refined flirtation to Marilyn Monroe herself.

I wonder what you'll say when I send you a picture of my own misshapen mug – I've been meaning to for sometime, but I can't find one – Misha promised he'd come round and look for one, so I might still enclose it. Shall I send you my publicity leaflet? There's a photograph and a frightful text in which they extol my virtues as if I was some kind of anti-inflammatory suppository – that's the decadent West.

As to our meeting, I'm ready to greet you in any country you care to mention. You, however, prefer to have me a long way away, in some poetic, rosy mist and that's why you keep finding reasons for not coming. Being so far

---

* Hero of Thomas Mann's novel *The Magic Mountain*

away is more literary, of course, but this game is no longer enough for me, I'd rather have photographs than letters, and I'd rather have you than photographs. So tell me: where and when? Maybe Stockholm at the end of March, or London in May?

Send your reply to Tokyo where I'll be from 30 October till the end of November; I know no one there and I'm sure I'll feel very lonely. This is my address: A.T. c/o Kambara Music Office 5, 6-chome Ginza, Chuo ku, Tokyo, Japan.

Hug you tight even if I'm not allowed to,

Your Andrzej.

PS. I didn't find a photograph, so I'm sending you the work of my German pimp instead – only don't show anyone this nonsense!

### BERLINER KONZERTDIREKTION HERMAN GAIL

Worldwide triumphs of the 26-year-old pianist.
Soloist with: The New York Philharmonic (conductor: Mitropoulos); Chicago Symphony Orchestra (cond. Reiner); Los Angeles Symphony Orchestra (cond. Martinon)
Artur Rubinstein: 'I believe that André Tchaikowsky is the best pianist of his generation, and that he is something even better than that: he is a miraculous musician.'

André Tchaikowsky:
Born in Warsaw in 1935. Started his studies at the Łódź Conservatoire under the direction of Professor Emma Altberg. In 1948 went to Paris where he continued his studies under Professor Lazare Lévy at the Paris Conservatoire where, two years later, he won first prize as the school's best pupil. On his return to Warsaw he joined Stanislaw Szpinalski's class at the Warsaw Conservatoire. André Tchaikowsky was a prize-winner at the Chopin Competition in Warsaw and at the Queen Elisabeth Competition in Brussels, where he won third prize in 1956; Artur Rubinstein was a member of the jury and he expressed the highest regard for Tchaikowsky. André Tchaikowsky has played concerts in Paris, Brussels, Lisbon, Madrid, Oslo and London.

From the autumn of 1956, thanks to a scholarship from the Belgian government, he participated in Stefan Askenase's master class.

In 1957 he made his debut in the United States with the New York Philharmonic under the baton of Dimitri Mitropoulos, then with the Chicago Symphony Orchestra conducted by Reiner and the Los Angeles Symphony Orchestra under Martinon. These concerts were a huge success. In 1959 A. Tchaikowsky received a second invitation to the United States; this time his performances included Canada and South America. The following concert season saw him appearing with the best conductors and orchestras in France, Spain, Portugal, Belgium and Switzerland. In 1960 he appeared in South America and in the same year performed with the London Mozart Players in Western Europe. In the 1960/61 season he started an extended tour with the Hallé Orchestra; in 1961/62 he appeared in West Germany for the first time.

As a composer he has performed his own Piano Concerto No. 1 with enormous success.

*Press notices*
North America
> Prokofiev's Second Piano Concerto, played with the Chicago Symphony Orchestra conducted by Fritz Reiner, was the high point of the season. Tchaikowsky's playing is exceptional, passionate, suggestive, authoritative. His full, richly textured tone is evidence of an unusual sensitivity; an interpretation full of intuitive expression, there is nothing 'bookish', everything is natural. Exceptional achievements! (Chicago: *Daily Tribune*)

> Tchaikowsky created musical beauty. His art is pure. We have not heard a pianist like this all year. (*Denver Post*)

> Astonishing maturity and musical richness. (*St Louis Globe Democrat*)

> The interpretation of Beethoven's Concerto No. 4 was infinitely beautiful and filled with inner richness. We have not heard such a perfect performance of the second movement in years. (*Rocky Mountain News*)

South America
> A pianist endowed with a great talent, with an unprecedented ability to recreate various musical styles. There is no doubt that he is perfectly capable of interpreting everything from the baroque to contemporary music. (Buenos Aires. *La Nacion*)

> You can sense in him both a great pianist and a great musician. (Caracas: *El Nacional*)
> Tchaikowsky deserves an honoured place amongst the greatest of contemporary pianists. (Caracas: *El Universal*)

Europe
> The great event of the evening was his interpretation of Chopin's Concerto in F minor. It was a remarkable example of exceptional playing and a

highly intelligent interpretation. It was an unusual joy for us to hear this performance in which magnificent technique was allied to enormous sensitivity. (London: *The Times*)

His appearance caused a sensation. An inspired, magnificent interpretation. What maturity for a 25-year-old! How profoundly he can reach into the depths of a piece. (Stockholm: *Svenska Dagbladet*)

London, 4.12.61

Funnyface,

I have lots to tell you and little time, so I'll limit myself to what's most important. Bravo, encore, and hurray for your wonderful idea that we meet in Stockholm. It can be arranged, but we'll have to consider and organise the meeting in order to maximise our enjoyment of one another.

There are numerous difficulties. It's not a question of cash which will have to be found even if I have to knock it off (I also have debts: it's the psychoanalysis that's costing me so much). When I received your letter I started to save seriously and I'll carry on all through the winter. Whatever happens, you'll come, and we can have great fun in Stockholm, and if the worst comes to the worst we'll just eat bread and soup! So let's not worry about that.

Time is more of a problem. I'll tell you frankly that I'm a bit frightened of meeting you during a concert tour. We'll talk and mooch around all night long, play bridge and on the piano, argue and tenderly make up, go crazy with happiness, and meanwhile I'll be playing like an arsehole! Don't tell me we're older now, wiser, more mature. You may be, but I'm not. I know when I see you I'll lose my head completely. So you could come at the beginning of April, towards the end of my tour, hear a couple of my last concerts and stay with me somewhere through Easter till the end of the month. (...)

I apologise, funnyface, for this boring and matter-of-fact letter. You know that this meeting is very important to me, and when you come we'll be able to discuss Gałczyński* again.

For the sake of fairness, I hope that Marek-the-Cat will have time to service all those females for which he's been granted a dispensation (his balls will surely fall off), and that you get a visa for this trip from him, too.

You're talking nonsense when you say I don't love you. I love you *very much* indeed, and you're just sulking about the 'very'. But we'll discuss that in Stockholm. For now it's bye and kisses, rape the Marek-the-Cat for me, and

---

* Konstanty Ildefons Gałczyński (1905-53) was a poet whose work included satire and the 'absurd'. Many popular composers set his poems to music

Basia, and give nice Michał my heartfelt regards. I'm unlucky with his address, I've lost it again, but I think of him often. Keep warm (the heat here is making me faint).

Your own, as always,

Andrzej.

PS. I am indeed playing the Brahms concertos, but if you heard them you'd stop being surprised.

[This letter, in which significant passages have been destroyed, was the reply to the proposition that steps should be taken to bring 'Daniel' into being.]

London, 3.62

Halinka, funnyface,

This is my saddest and last letter. Although you asked me to reply immediately, I couldn't bring myself to do it for a whole week, and even now I'm finding it a great effort to write. Darling, we can't meet in Stockholm this spring. We can't meet anywhere, ever. The pain I'm causing you by writing this is nothing compared with the terrible wrong I've done you over the last seven years and which I became aware of only after your last letter. The most experienced sadist couldn't have done you more harm. For years I've been undermining your sense of reality for just one reason, apparently to ruin your life. Without giving you anything myself, I took away, or poisoned, everything you have (…).

Before your letter, and despite your silence, I did prepare everything for your arrival – especially the financial matters. I thought everything between us was settled, and there was no point in writing and thereby irritating Marek. It was so hard for me to give all this up that even after your letter I wanted you to come over despite everything. But now I no longer want you to, because I've understood a lot of things. (…) I've understood the *unreality* of our whole situation. Marek is what he is but he is *real*, Basia is *real*, whereas I'm what? One shouldn't fool around with the imagination because when it hurts it *really* hurts. The only real thing between us is pain – and enormous friendship.

You say that Marek is lifeless and cold. You'll see what he's like when you and I stop writing to each other. There isn't a man who would be gentle with his wife in a situation like this. Momentary misdemeanours can be forgiven, but something which drags on for years can't. You say women don't interest him. I know one woman who interested him so much he wanted to give her one of his own kidneys.

Take care of yourself, Halinka, our friendship *was always real*, and so passionate, and so mutual, that it could almost, but not quite, have replaced love. A friend like you were to me is very hard to find in this world, and it's as that friend I shall always remember you. But you must forget about me as quickly as possible.

Andrzej.

POSTCARD FROM ANDRZEJ: THE ACROPOLIS IN ATHENS SOUND AND LIGHT,
SENT IN AN ENVELOPE – NO MESSAGE, BLANK

31.3.62

[This was the blank postcard sent by Andrzej at Halinka's request to indicate confirmation of his decision that the severing of contact should be final.]

# *Part Two*
# **1966 – 1969**

London, 19.10.66

Unforgettable Halinka,

Many, many thanks for the consignment (I can scarcely call it a letter). Judging by it you're just as I remember you: imaginative, disarming, entertaining, bewitching; and yet (or maybe therefore) I still think we should back out of our correspondence. I don't even know if, after all these years, we still know, let alone like, one another! I've changed a lot, I've grown old, I've become selfish and a hermit – I live alone and cook for myself so as not to have to go out; I've limited my social life to a minimum and my sex life is close to non-existent. That's nothing like as sad as it might appear: I've got books, records, I'm never bored and I don't even feel lonely. I'm now living for myself and not for other people, and my friends have come to realise that 'you can't count on me', and they rarely write or phone.

But the main reason why I prefer not to write to you is my present conviction that one has to live in the real world and not in an imaginary one (see now how much I've aged?). Not just because we can't run away from reality anyway, or because we are condemned to it – that's a pessimistic reason, and I'm now teaching myself optimism – but because reality is a great deal *more interesting* than fantasy – it's changeable, it's astonishing, it's full of surprises. In your life I have always been the Imagination and thereby done you much harm; who knows – Marek might have treated you very differently if it hadn't been for our 'adulterous correspondence'? At least he entered your life, while I entered only your head. Am I still sitting there in your head?

If we could *meet*, then I would agree to that despite the feeling that such a meeting would prove mutually disappointing (not because I would be disappointed by you or you by me, but because we would certainly have no point of contact). Last year I saw Michał in Paris; we had dinner together, we went for a walk, but we had nothing much to talk about…

Halinka, I know that this letter will hurt you; but I will send it – one must write the truth.

All the very best,
Your old

Andrzej.

Warsaw, 5.11.66

Darling, I must write back. Even if it's only to assure you that I won't write. Otherwise you'll live in a state of constant anxiety that one day, years from now, when I'm old and decaying, I'll send off yet another fiery letter entitled: 'What about our child? Will there be no child!?' Darling, I've stopped thinking about it. Our child would have been very unhappy. He would certainly have suffered from an obsessive neurosis (you are neurotic, I'm obsessive). If I'm writing to you it's because I miss you. I miss your chatter, music, your climate. And I know I still like you very much, more than anyone. And I know you haven't changed at all. And wanting to have some contact with you is a 'flight from reality'. Ever since I became a criminologist, I've had whole lots of a reality that's interesting, not daft and I can't run away from it. Nor do I want to. I also write a little, and of course I have Basia (who is pleasant, witty and makes up funny verses). Oh yes, and there's the so-called emotional life whose mood has lately been reminiscent of the Etude in E flat minor, Op. 10 (he has countless children and at least one wife). In the evenings, like you, I read books and listen to records. The latest book was about tolerance, *Gantenbein* by Frisch, the latest records: Berg's *Wozzeck* with the New York Orchestra and Mitropoulos (the man who taught you to tie a bow tie). My forthcoming travel plans: in January it's Berlin definitely, in August, not at all definitely, it's London. I know why you agree to see me: you'll come to the meeting trying to be fat, bald, and arrogant. It won't help. To me you'll always remain the same: with a splendid head of hair, slim, and delightful.

    Kisses. Or better not!

Your H.

PS. That lady with the little dog in the photograph is Basia.

London, 14.11.66

My dear Halinka,

    You must have laughed out loud when you saw my handwriting on the envelope. First I wrote that I would no longer write to you (as if I'd written such a lot before); then you wrote that you wouldn't, either; one couldn't wish for a better beginning to a correspondence. What makes it more amusing is that I *hardly ever* write letters, so now I'm corresponding exclusively with a woman to whom I have resolved not to write.

    Why am I writing? Two reasons: the first – because I fancy it, and the second because I simply can't stay silent about your possibly coming to London! You'll be the first to agree it would be silly for us to be in the same town at the same time and not see each other. No, it's a rare opportunity and we have to seize it; otherwise we'll never know if such a meeting will enchant us or disappoint us. Only *afterwards,* maybe, will we have something to write about to one another.

So if you can come, let me know when and where you'll be. And meanwhile? Write or don't write, as you want; don't be angry if I don't reply; and rest assured that if there is an opportunity to meet, I'll not let it slip.

Your old

Andrzej (fat, bald and arrogant)

PS. I'm giving you my private address: 29 Waterlow Court, Heath Close, London NW11. Don't let anyone else have it!

London, 9.3.67

Halinka, I'm ashamed that I haven't thanked you for the Penderecki. But you, too, should be ashamed too, for dazzling and spoiling me with impressive presents – I beg you, don't do it any more, even without them I know you think of me often and with affection. (…)

I'm also pleased that I saw Janek [Halina's brother-in-law]. He told me a few things about you and your life (with subtle comments, of course), and then intrigued me because it turned out he knew my mother! By the way, you remember that photograph of my mother which used to hang on the wall of our apartment, above the desk? Do you, by any chance, know what happened to it? It's almost impossible after all these years but if by some miracle you found it, then it would be the most beautiful present I could possibly have (see how sentimental I am?). I have no photographs of her here, in fact I have seen only that which belongs to my aunt in Paris; it shows a plump, thirteen-year-old calf, completely unlike the woman I knew. Maybe, despite everything, you could still find that photograph…

Talking of mothers, I wonder what you tell Basia about me. She sends me kisses, she draws flowers for me… At least I know her from her photographs (she looks like Lolita), but she doesn't know me at all. Do you spin her yarns about a deranged uncle in London    'God says you should love your uncle…'? No, that doesn't sound like you. Far more likely is: 'Basia, it's time for you to know about the men in my life…' Yes?

Do you feel like writing back? Then don't hesitate, don't deny yourself – now we are corresponding it's nothing to be ashamed of! I prefer letters to records, it's so much more personal somehow. (…)

All the best to you and to Basia,

Andrzej.

PS. Do you know yet if you're coming here in the summer?

Warsaw, 20.3.67

Andrzej, Darling. I was so pleased that you'd written! I do indeed have your mother's picture, and I'll send it to you.

You disconcerted me when you mentioned Janek's 'subtle comments'. We lead such separated lives now that he knows little about mine. He probably told you my life with Marek, who can't stand me, is a torment. My work makes me concentrate on the corpses left by my murderers instead of dealing with the living, and I'm spoiling Basia who rules me and the entire home.

It's not quite like that. Firstly – Marek doesn't torment me because we haven't spoken to one another for years; furthermore – it's untrue that he can't stand me because he is incapable of any lively emotions. As for my research on homicides – it's a great lesson in life: if people die earlier than they need to then it's always for important reasons. I might eventually discover what is really important to people. As for Basia – I don't know if I'm spoiling her, but I've certainly made her a bit crazy. This is a fairy-tale she made up: 'There was an old man and his old wife. They loved each other very much and then they died. The old man went to hell, and the old woman to heaven. The old woman longed for the old man and she asked God: 'Please, Lord God, let the old man visit me here.' 'Very well,' said God, 'but first the old man has to entertain the Devil so the Devil stops doing evil things.' And the old man started to play cards with the Devil. They played and they played, and they didn't stop. The Devil forgot to do evil things, and the old man forgot about the old woman. And the old man never came to visit the old woman again. But the old woman didn't care, because she didn't love the old man any more.'

As you can see, eight-year-old Basia already has her views about the permanence of feelings. She longs for a little brother: 'Mummy, can you have a child without a daddy?' 'No, you can't.' 'What about a half-orphan?' A few days ago she told me a dream she'd had: 'I dreamt you'd given birth to a baby. You were very busy and you kept going out. The baby cried. I didn't know what to do so I took the baby and put it into a book as a book-mark. You came home and you asked: "Where's the baby?" I said: "It's in a book as a book-mark." "Which book?" "I've forgotten." You shout: "You messy girl, you never know where you put things!" And we started to look for this baby in the books, but it was never found again.'

Basia knows you, of course, and adores you. Recently there was a programme on the radio about Tchaikovsky. Basia heard that he was dead. 'What?' she shouted. 'He died?' 'A long time ago,' I replied calmly. Terrified, she yelled: 'OUR ONE?!'

Yes, there is something like a cult of you in this home. One can't forget you your photograph is on the record sleeve which stands on your bookcase surrounded by your couch, your piano and your radiola. And you kidded yourself that in these circumstances I could forget you! Added to which I wear the wristwatch you gave me, the watch which stops when I sleep with it.

Lately I've been writing a bit. Not just about homicides. In my next letter I'll send you my two latest stories. M. (my latest love) liked one, the other I wrote yesterday and it made me laugh, so maybe it will do the same for you. The one for which I won a prize in the contest I'll send you in its book form – it's due out any day now.

I kiss you very briefly, carefully, and just once.

H.

PS. I'm sending you a picture of my home bedecked with flowers (the home where your piano stands and your cult reigns). Those flowers are for you.

London, 9.4.67

Darling Halinka (see, I'm not afraid), Why pretend? I'm pleased, I'm unashamedly pleased, that we've renewed contact. Many, many thanks for the stories, letters, the little dog and my mother's photograph (I'm very moved that you kept it).

I'll reply as soon as I find some time. And you continue to write, don't deny us the pleasure.

Kisses,

Your Andrzej.

Postcard: Hamburg, Binnenalster (inner Alster Lake) and the city
18.5.67

Darling, I've been meaning to write to you all week while you, despite my protests, continue to shower me with presents. Of the *Authentic Stories**, I've so far read only yours. Is it really authentic, or merely true?

I'm amused to see how rapidly your demands are growing. A couple of weeks ago it was: 'I want only to write to you, regardless of whether or not you reply'. Now *you'll go mad* if I don't write – and about myself, too! That's women… I'm amused by it, but not surprised. Keep writing, please.

I'm thrilled by your stories. Do you know more about your visit to England yet?

Kisses,

Your Andrzej.

---

* A selection of stories from a competition run by the weekly magazine *Świat*, edited by Kazimierz Dziewanowski, published by Iskry in 1967

London, 3.7.67

Darling,

Today, I received two letters: one from you, the other from the prime minister of Israel (to whom I wrote, asking him to help the Arab refugees). Yours was much more interesting. But full of nonsense.

Firstly, it's untrue that your stories bore me. I agree the suicide episode is less successful: your guy knows himself too well and speaks of himself too well – as a rule people are not like that, with the exception, of course, of you and me, and maybe Hamlet. (…) *The Love of an Honest Man* however is very entertaining. As for *Pages from Court Records*, the style is marvellously well done, but I'm not sure what you were aiming for in the story, laughter or sympathy?

And now a few words about Matt. Forgive me if I'm butting in, but I think that since you write about him it's surely because you want me to say something. Darling, judging by the last exchange you reported, I sense that you're irritating him a little. Men hate it very much when they feel pressurised by questions or by other means. After all, he's asking you, he's coming round to see you, so you must mean something to him – isn't that enough? But he doesn't like to, and can't, talk about it. When he was a child he fell out of a window and from then on he's incapable of talking about love. Someone who hadn't fallen out of a window might feel less but could talk about it infinitely more. What you call 'using' someone is the only love that the most people are capable of, because most people simply don't love anyone. It's not even their fault because Love – that's love with a capital L, the kind you have in mind – is a rare and unfortunately completely non-infectious disease. Besides, tell the truth: do you love him? No, you don't. But you don't love me, either. What you're feeling is not love at all; it's a painful lack of, and longing for, love.

You'll say I'm arrogant because I've virtually given you a sermon though I've not seen you for 11 years, and I've never seen him. So what, you know I'm arrogant! But I write what I really believe. I embrace you and Basia,

Your Andrzej.

Edinburgh, 3.9.67

Funnyface,

At the moment, I am in the most beautiful city in Europe – when you come over, we must take a trip to Edinburgh. I've time for only a few words, because tomorrow I'm playing at 11 in the morning – just right for me, isn't it? Lately I've been rushed off my feet and I didn't have time to reply, but don't be put off and keep writing! On Thursday I'm playing with the orchestra – Stravinsky's

*Capriccio* – and then I go to Stratford to see *Macbeth*. I'll be in London on the 14th so I'll be just in time to meet Piotr before he leaves. Lilka and I have talked about your visit. It won't be possible before April because I'm doing a tour to New Zealand, Japan etc. I'll give you a few addresses in my next letter, and in the mean time I'm expecting a word from you in London. (I'll write, too, just as soon as I'm a bit more free.)

What's Piotr got to do with Hercules, Archimedes and Francis of Assisi? Kisses,

Your Andrzej.

London, 10.9.67

Darling, you wrote to say that your apartment has changed into a museum devoted to me, so I'm contributing the enclosed to the collection. The Clarinet Sonata is very old, composed in 1959, but I have no other recordings (even private ones), and I want to repay you for the stories!

Kiss you, write quickly so I get it before I fly out!

Bye, Darling, A.

QANTAS, AUSTRALIA'S ROUND-THE-WORLD AIRLINES
between San Francisco and Honolulu

9.10.67

Darling, At last I've got time to write you a few words. To start with, a couple of addresses.

I'll be in New Zealand till the end of the month – c/o New Zealand Broadcasting Corporation, P.O.Box 98, Wellington, New Zealand.

The first few days of November (till the morning of the 4th) in the Philippines at the Tower Hotel; between the 4th and the 12th I'll be in Hong Kong – Repulse Bay Hotel. From the 12th November to the 4th December at the Hotel New Otani, Tokyo, Japan. I don't know where I'll be between the 4th and 14th December.

From the 14th to 19th December I'll be in Holland, Park Hotel, Amsterdam. And from 20th December I'll be home.

Please, write to me often – when I'm home I generally feel excellent, but on trips, in hotels, I'm often lonely even, or maybe especially, when I'm surrounded by a lot of strangers! I'll write, too, mostly in aeroplanes where nobody bothers me and I have masses of time.

I'm glad you like my records, but I'd like to know precisely what you like in them, and what you don't, and why. If you like the Sonata for Clarinet then you'll be pleased to hear that after long endeavours I've just finished a song cycle (*Seven Shakespeare Sonnets*) which Margaret Cable, a young English singer, is interested in, and English radio has asked us to record the cycle for them in the spring, maybe when you're there! It took me nearly three years to write the songs (I write only when I don't have any concerts, otherwise I'd never be able to play anything decently), so I'm pleased I've finished them and they work. The string quartet is nearly finished, too; I think I'll get it done around the New Year.

And now for your postcard. 'God bless you for such fucking letters'. Don't take offence, it's a quotation from your story! It's not true that nobody likes you (everyone likes you), nor that nobody loves you (Basia loves you in any case).

I spent a very pleasant evening with Lili and Piotr. He is very pleasant but why, according to him, am I 'fantastic'? He already knows what he has to say to get round you. Bye for now, write soon (…).

Kisses, don't be miserable, thank everyone who doesn't love you because people who are in love are horribly bothersome.

Give Basia and Piotr a hug from me.

Your Andrzej.

REPULSE BAY HOTEL, HONG KONG

6.11.67

Darling,

My letter wandered for 17 days, while yours took only a week! I'm writing back straight away, hoping that you'll receive it in time to reply while I'm still in Tokyo. It's very important because Tokyo is the ugliest, noisiest, most irritating town I know. Keep my spirits up there a little so I don't fall into a neurotic depression.

I am in an excellent mood at last, a little tired, which isn't surprising! In the last week of October I played five concerts in New Zealand, repeating only one programme (Beethoven's Sonata in E minor Op. 90, Liszt's Sonata in B minor, Ravel's *Valses nobles et sentimentales* and Stravinsky's *Petrushka*); apart from that I had rehearsals with the orchestra (Brahms's D minor and Mozart's K 503). I travelled through the day and played in the evening; on November 1st I was in Sydney, the 2nd in Manila; and in Manila a typhoon hit me unexpectedly. It was fascinating – roofs and trees were falling, shop signs were flying, telegraph poles were toppling. The last was the worst, because electric cables hung in the air and the hurricane beat furiously against them, and all you needed was to touch one of those severed cables and you could be poured into an ash-tray! Like an idiot I went for a walk because I was very interested in the typhoon. I was accompanied by another madman, an Indian, whom I met in the plane from Sydney. As you can see, no harm came to us, but the police came after us and took us back to the hotel by force.

You'll certainly hear the song cycle when you come over. Talking of which, stop worrying about the cash; I want to see you, and if I didn't want to no one could make me. Really, there are times when I simply can't wait for you to come! There are others, too, when I want to run away from England so as not to see you. Both feelings are completely irrational; you must come first – there'll always be time to run away later. I'm intrigued by our forthcoming meeting and I think about it and you a lot.

Bye for now, I'll write you again about Tokyo. Give Basia a hug and yourself, too (use a mirror).

Your Andrzej.

PS. If you really want to send me something, I'd be most grateful for a good Russian novel (e.g. *War and Peace* or *The Brothers Karamazov*) in a Polish translation. They don't work in French, and in English they're even worse!

Warsaw, 16.11.67

My Darling Andrzej,

I'm writing back immediately, even though it's midnight again and once again I'm going mad with exhaustion. You're right about my clever-clogsing on the subject of your sonata (…). But I really do believe in your writing, and I know what it means to you. (…)

Maybe this will surprise you, but I'm not frightened by the prospect of our meeting. We'll come to an understanding somehow, unless you make me speak English. But what are you so afraid of? That I'll start my old hysteria from years gone by? That will never happen again. Yes, I did want your child, I fought, and I lost. I had to lose because I was out of touch with reality. You were right, it was too late. The idea of bringing up both Basia and Daniel, alone, without Marek or you, could have been born only of a sick imagination. But I did desire it very much. Now I don't desire anything very much. I'm writing so openly and superfluously because I don't want you to be afraid or to run away.

I completely forgot that this letter was supposed to 'keep your spirits up'. So I'm sending you a little poem* which ought to help you: 'When you're bored of everything make yourself a little angel and a little old man, you play it like this: you trip the little old man up so he smashes his mug on the pavement – the angel lowers its head. You give the old man five pence, the angel lifts up its head. You smash the old man's glasses with a stone, the angel lowers its head. You give

---

* Andrzej Bursa's *From Children's Games*

the old man your seat on the tram, the angel lifts up its head. You empty your potty onto the old man's head, the angel lowers its head. And so on. Then go to sleep. You'll dream either of a little angel or a little devil. If it's an angel – you've won, if it's a devil – you've lost. If you don't dream at all – a draw.'

When you're sad, or feeling bad, or bored – try playing that. It helps me. I must finish off because I'm falling asleep. This time I'm sure I'll dream of you and think I've won.

I'll send you everything you ask for (a new edition of *War and Peace* has come out in the last few days), and something you didn't ask for – my story called *That poor liar* is nearly ready. It tired me out because it's the correspondence of four people all of whom write in a different style.

I'm falling asleep, kisses, goodnight.

H.

NEW OTANI HOTEL, TOKYO

18.11.67

My Haletchka,

Your letter moved me greatly. Of course Matt is right to say that I'm a kind of myth in your life and our meeting will be something like a Götterdämmerung – the whole of Valhalla will burn down. You write a lot about what I've given you. But what Darling, what will happen if I take it away? It wouldn't be so bad if I really did 'kick you and throw you out of the window.' That would be *something*, but my fear is that *nothing* at all will happen – the only outcome you'd not be able to take.

It's not just that, honestly, I'm fat and bald now (I was always arrogant), nor that I care for no one but myself – that's how I was in the past, too; you surely know I am an egotist. It's that my *inner* life, which means so much to you, is truly internal – I share it with no one. It comes out only in my music, and particularly in my compositions, and that's why I was so furious (yes, furious) when you tried to write a down-to-earth critique of my sonata. If I'd given you my diary to read – would you have written an essay on it too?

And life? Sometimes I talk, more often I'm silent, but most of all I like to be alone. My friends have learned that I shouldn't be invited out, and that they shouldn't phone me. You complain about Matt, but I won't see you for days on end, either – and what will you do with yourself? You'll have no one here apart from me. I fear for you, Halinka.

Stay well,

Your Andrzej.

PS. Darling, send your next letter to London. Do you know how much I like your letters?

Warsaw, 13.12.67

Andrzej dear, I don't know how much you like my letters, but I have a faint suspicion, so I'm writing though I feel terrible.

Whenever I'm ill, I'm suddenly molested by a crowd of people. So in the morning – the telephone rings, it's my supervisor, Professor Adam P. 'Good morning.' 'Good morning.' 'You have a cold.' 'I have.' 'Excellent. I'll pop in to see you this afternoon.' He appears, sits in the armchair, and says: 'The whole of sociology is a sham, it's boring, and it's unreal. Personally I acknowledge only love, music and gossip.' And then about women: 'Happily married women go daft, divorcées write doctorates and treatises. None of them is ever read, so they go around frustrated and ill. With a cold in the head, for instance…' Adam leaves and in comes my beloved friend Rysia. Rysia used to be a charming, crazy girl, but since she married she's constantly tidying things or sewing something. She soon notices there are two buttons missing on my duvet. She sews the buttons on and confesses: 'He's so big, isn't he? So I call him: Elephant.' 'Yes, Rysia, if you want something big and pure in your life it's best to have an elephant and to give him baths.' Rysia leaves, and in comes Teddy Bear (the tiny, plump director). Teddy Bear brings a rose. He recites his verses: '… at opposite ends of a curved line, at opposite ends of the world we live, we don't know each other's lips, we don't know each other's hands, we wait for each other in others…' 'The reason my poems are good', says Teddy Bear, 'is because I am full of sincerity and simplicity, I don't have a facade self' (that's all we need, I think quietly). Teddy-Bear leaves, in drops another friend, Anka. She's always loving or hating someone dreadfully. As a consequence she's grown pale and fragile, like a wafer. 'Halinka!' she shouts. 'Save me! Do you know what my daughter said? My daughter said: "I hate you! I want you to die just like grandpa!" '

'And what did you say to her?'

'Nothing. I shouted: "I hate you," too.'

'What did she say to that?'

'She kept on shouting.'

'What about you?'

'I did, too.'

'What was it all about?'

'She said: "I won't go to school!" And I said: "You will, idiot!", and she said: "I swear, I won't!" And she threw a potato at me. A potato! Do you hear? A potato at her own mother! Halinka, save me!'

Then in comes Joanna. She's one of the most beautiful and saddest women in this town. She suffers from tanatophobia. She wakes in the night and shouts: 'I'm dying! I'm dying!' In the daytime she can't stop talking. Her face is like a wise, very sick madonna's. She adores Rilke: 'I am Malte…' she says. Today, she's feeling worse, she wants to sleep at my place. 'You'll catch my cold.' 'I'd rather have a cold than die of fear.'

Marek P. phones in the evening. He's a charming boy, a talented painter, except that he's a whoremonger and a drunkard. For years on end his wife had the patience of a saint, everyone admired her. Marek: 'Oh, Halinka! Danka has left!' 'But that's what you always longed for.' 'True, but when Mrs Cervantes walked out on Cervantes she left him one little daughter, whereas Danka has left me three! I have to marry someone immediately. What about you?' 'I have a cold.' 'What a pity! I'll have to marry someone else. This is urgent. The little daughters could start dying any day now. I've no idea what little daughters eat. Well then, bye, Darling.'

Then the postman brings me a letter from you. Before I have time to read it, Professor Batawia phones. 'Dear colleague', he asks, 'what was Harry Stack Sullivan's assessment of therapy for schizophrenics? D'you no' ken?'

Oooph, that's it. As you can see, everyone wants to have a chat – and so do I. I kiss you, Darling, lots and lots because it seems I'm beginning to miss you.

H.

PS. On the subject of nostalgia. When Basia was four years' old, we received a visit from Adam P. (the same Adam P.), and he showed off in a most charming way. When he was leaving, Basia said: 'You're nice, you're great, when you go away I'll try to miss you.'

Oslo, 10.1.68

My Haletshka,

I'll jot down just a few words because I'm very tired. I also have to fly to rehearsal (I'm playing Mozart's C minor, the most beautiful of all his concertos). But I want to thank you for the Tolstoy which came just before my departure, and even more for the delightful letter. You know, you really do write marvellously – Anka's dialogue with her daughter was, if authentic, marvellously captured and conveyed, and if imagined, then all the more laudable! I understand what writing is for you – write as much as possible! To me, too – I always wait for your letters with eager anticipation. What about the passport and visa? If you don't manage to arrange things for April, come over in July – I'm free then, too. They've come for me, I have to stop now! Write to Pension Biederstein in Munich where I'll be from the 24th. Bye for now and a Happy New Year to both you and Basia.

Hugs,

Your Andrzej.

Warsaw, 4.2.68

Darling, your telephone call on my birthday touched me, and so did the fact that you worry about my health. But don't worry, I'm not paralysed, it's just a dislocated disc; one leg walks and the other leg won't. But it hurts. If you only knew how much you'd kiss me better. No, I'm not depressed, in fact today I really did laugh. My friends brought a Bulgarian sculptor called Volodya to see me. I didn't know him, but what I saw was extraordinary! Volodya's face is Christ-like, and the rest of him is just hair – black and wavy, down to his waist from all four sides because he wears a beard at the front. That's what Volodya is like from the waist up; from the waist down he looks like the Bird of the Apocalypse: following an operation his legs bend forward at the knees, instead of backwards! So now imagine me hopping as I greeted this Volodya! I wanted to laugh even then, but I was too frightened by the sight of him). My friends said: 'Look after Volodya, he is a Christian believer.' And they went. Volodya and I were left with these legs of ours and he talked to me about life beyond the grave. Then this friend of mine arrived: he'd been shot in the leg during the Uprising and now has a limp. It was like something out of Beckett and I got an attack of the giggles.

Your friend Sylvia Rosenberg rang. Somehow I dragged myself to her concert at the Philharmonia. I sent her flowers with a card but she gave them to the pianist. After the concert she was besieged by ecstatic listeners, so not wanting to interfere, I slipped away. She played Bach wonderfully! (…)

Generally, though, there's a lot happening. (…)

Did you, by any chance, read Jeanne Moreau's *Confessions*? Do you remember the ending?

'Above all else I value personal freedom. Freedom to me means the possibility of choosing a partner who is worthy of depriving me of that freedom. Each time I believe that I am choosing for the last time, for ever. Apparently there is some kind of fault in this method, isn't there?'

See you, Darling. Kisses.

Write anything… absolutely anything

H.

20.2.68

Darling Andrzej,

Hearty thanks for the letter. It came at the same time as a letter from Witek Jedlicki. Did you know him? He wrote a book which everyone talked about, he used to go to all the concerts, he's very wise, loves Bartók. He's also in some sense your 'double' friend through friends of our friends…, and he's friends not only with me but also with your friend Staszek Kołodziejczyk. I'll write you about him one day because he's an extraordinary guy.

You know, somehow I can't believe in our meeting, but I'm learning English just in case. Won't you be amazed if, right after my arrival, I shout: 'Nelson's column stands right in the centre, there are many, many pigeons!'?

At the moment I'm writing a story about you. Very mysterious. No one will know what it's all about. It'll be funny but after reading it one will, for some reason, experience a transcendental sorrow, and even cry a little. I'll send it to you soon, but don't cry too much.

Another idea is for a story about a very sick girl who doesn't know if she'll ever get out of the hospital, or if she'll stay there till the end. She tries to guess the truth from the behaviour of the doctors, the nurses, her relatives, her friends. She also thinks about HIM – constantly, sadly and badly because HE never visits her in hospital. One day he appears, and with a bunch of roses, too. She looks at him in terror: he has never given her as much as a leaf of clover before, so this must mean…

I'm not too jolly lately. Basia says: 'Mummy, you're getting sadder and sadder. What's happening? Are you becoming wise?'

I kiss you, Funnyface.

Your H.

POSTCARD WRITTEN BY ANDRZEJ IN ENGLISH SHOWING<br>NELSON'S COLUMN IN TRAFALGAR SQUARE, LONDON

1.3.68

It doesn't stand right in the middle after all, my pet! Sorry, the pigeons don't show very well in this photograph, but you can see that part of your sentence is quite true. I'll write soon.

Many kisses. A.

London, 3.3.68

Funnyface, what's going on? When decent women walk they always use both legs. I won't console you, I'll stroke you instead wherever you want me to. You can put your stay in hospital to advantage if you manage to write something; but don't write about the girl who was given flowers in hospital because it will only depress you. Write the story about me – that'll entertain you.

Sylvia Rosenberg knows the flowers were from you and she's been trying all week to write you a letter in German! By the way I scribbled a few words from Holland – presumably you didn't get them. Apart from that I was silent, but not because everything was OK – February was a difficult and tiring month for me, maybe things will settle down now. Write as quickly as you can, tell me how you feel and where you are, so I can write to you at the hospital. Get well as fast as you can and come here to convalesce – you could appear as early as the middle of June.

The quotation from Jeanne Moreau's memoirs reminds me of the end of Shelley's *To the Moon*: 'And ever changing, like a joyless eye/That finds no object worth its constancy?'

Kiss you.

Your Andrzej.

London, 23.3.68

Funnyface,

I'm truly mesmerised by your photograph: have you suddenly become pretty, or do I now have better taste? Whatever, I am enraptured. I had a long talk with Lili today and we arranged to meet the day after tomorrow. Lili tells me you're writing your doctorate in hospital, and that's good, but write for fun, too, because hospitals are by nature boring and miserable and it's better to live by one's imagination in them (you don't need anyone to give you this advice, of course). Try to write a play – you have an excellent feeling for dialogue. Darling, I think about you more and more and I truly can't wait till we meet again! Get well as soon as possible and come over! (…) I'll stop now because it's morning already – the night rushed by; first I was writing the quartet, then playing chess… I'll write again when I've seen Lili. You write, too, Darling, even if it's only a few words!

Kiss you,

Your Andrzej.

London, 29.4.68

Funnyface,

I'm enclosing the score for the Sonata for Clarinet. It's the only copy I've been able to find, and it's missing the clarinet part (which will have to be written out). Write and tell me if there's any chance of a recording in Poland?

A week ago there was a performance of my song cycle (*Seven Shakespeare Sonnets*). There were a few musicians there: Andrzej Panufnik, Daniel Barenboim and his wife, Gervase de Peyer (who performed the Clarinet Sonata), and Fou Ts'ong's wife; he himself was playing somewhere that evening. What came out was that the song cycle really is first class, incomparably better than the rest of my output so far. As a result, Andrzej Panufnik's wife gave birth (two weeks early). I hope the baby's normal. (…)

I'm writing to your home address because I feel you must have returned from the sanatorium. I like your last admirer very much (no surprise there). Write and tell me if the disc is back where it belongs! (…)

Leave everything and come here. Thank you for the book, which arrived safely and has given me great pleasure.

I must end up because I'm playing four pieces on Thursday of which I once knew one (Beethoven's Op. 28, Schumann's *Phantasie*, six Études by Debussy and Chopin's fourth Ballade). In addition, I'm learning the *Diabelli Variations* – a wonderful piece.

Bye, Darling. Write quickly.

Your Andrzej.

Warsaw, 30.5.68

Darling, today I'm going to tell you the story of a murder. This was seven volumes of court papers which I was working on. For the first time I cried over court papers like a fool. I don't even know why.

It all started perfectly normally. A popular magazine published a letter from a 25-year-old typist. 'I am lonely, my handicap will not let me believe that anyone will ever love me.' A boy of 22 from the other end of Poland replied to this letter.

I saw their photos. She was pleasant, pretty, charming (her complexes the result of a slight distortion of a shoulder-blade); he was small, stout, hunchbacked with a face like a subnormal horse. He'd had a woman once – a prostitute who'd infected him with syphilis. The disease of the spine started when he was at school, and he spent seven years in hospitals and sanatoriums. He didn't go back to the town where his parents lived: he didn't think they wanted him back. He went to live with his uncle, in the country. During the winter he stayed in a small loft, during the summer in a barn. He worked at night – carting manure, guarding the stores. In the daytime he used to run away to the wood 'so people wouldn't see my disgusting shape'. He finished only seven classes at school but read a lot during his illness. The correspondence with the pleasant young lady began very formally: 'Dear Madam! With reference to your letter in today's *Kulisy*…' In time he started writing letters which were prose masterpieces – simple, wise and sad. They were full of all sorts of things: sensitivity, thoughtfulness, lectures on astronomy, legends about the stars, anecdotes, quotes from the *Song of Songs* and Gałczyński. And they were packed with lies: he was a university graduate, he had his own apartment in the country, the state of his health made it impossible for him to return to the town etc. He did not, however, conceal his handicap. The exchange of letters lasted two years. Hers were correct, naive, full of love. He lived happily in the world of emotions he'd invoked by lies. Unfortunately the girl wanted to see him, wanted to sacrifice herself for this crippled man and become his wife. She invited him to visit her many times; he lied. He couldn't come because his father had died. He couldn't because he had to go on a business trip. He couldn't because he'd had an accident and his leg was in plaster. And then she decided to visit him. There was no way out, he had to agree. He asked only that she should arrive on the night train because he had no time during the day, he was so busy.

They met one late frosty evening on a village station.

She thought: he'll be a refined, romantic boy with whom she'll spend the night in his home; she won't be ashamed of her handicap because he is handicapped, too...

She saw: a squat, gloomy hunchback in a torn overcoat. For that he hated her. He'd started to hate her when she wrote that she was coming. He didn't even have a suit he could wear for the meeting. He couldn't take her to a loft full of rubbish. He'd dug several trenches in the wood – he didn't know where he would kill her. In his pocket he had a hammer and a knife. A terrible murder! Twenty-seven knife wounds and her head crushed by the hammer. He buried her along with her suitcase in one of the trenches. Then he tried to commit suicide by using the hammer against his temple. When he regained consciousness he returned to his loft. And there... he wrote her a letter. 'My Darling, I long for you so much...' Maybe he really did long for her; but the court found that he'd been trying to create an alibi. Several months later, when the snows melted, police dogs discovered the trench. He was sentenced to death, later commuted by the Supreme Court to life imprisonment. In the courtroom he said: 'Nobody will believe this, but I loved that woman. Only her, the only time in my life. I owed my happiness to her: two years of constant, true love. And she had to destroy it by her stupidity! Why did she want to see me? I didn't want it. I knew she wouldn't go with me. I killed her out of fear, hatred, and retribution. I was afraid of suffering, of being humiliated. Yes, she was the only one who could humiliate me, she was the only one who could make me suffer. I was afraid. It was more than I could bear...' When the prosecutor asked: 'Why did the accused lie in his letters?' he shouted furiously: 'Be quiet, fool! You'll never understand it!'

They told me (at work) that I should see him: carry out tests on him and similar nonsense. I said no. I think that as soon as he has an opportunity, he'll commit suicide in that prison.

Forgive me this gloomy story. It had a great effect on me; that's why I'm writing about it.

H.

London, 5.6.68

My Halinka,

Thank you for the letter and the photograph. I'm terribly glad you're better – now I can tell you that I was more than a little anxious! Lili, too, was quaking with fear, and I was afraid you'd arrive on a stretcher or in a wheelchair. Thank God you're running around: man does not live by intellect alone.

I was going to write to you anyway today. I didn't write earlier because of the following problems:

1) I lost my glasses. This will surprise you because I didn't use to wear glasses, but now I do and it's hard to cope without them – the world looks like a Monet exhibition.

2) I fell in love. That's all over now. For a few days I was flying, and then I landed on my nose. Then I was a hurt and bitter man in (though that's stupid, because who's to blame?). Now I'm recovering my balance. (…)

3) I'm in turmoil, learning Mendelssohn's idiotic Concerto in G minor (the finale sounds like a third-rate operetta) which I've been forced to play. In fact, over the next three weeks I'm giving seven different programmes (and eight concerts, because I'm playing the wretched Mendelssohn twice).

4) I feel sad, God knows why – my life is pleasant, intense and interesting. But sorrow comes regardless and then it goes away, so it's best to treat it like a cold or the flu – simply wait for it to go away. Waiting, of course, is a very difficult art.

Talking of waiting – Darling, I'm in London only till 4th August, and then I'll be in Australia! Do all you can to catch me before I leave, otherwise we'll have to wait till next spring!

I'll close for now because it's hard for me to write in the dark. (…)

Kisses,

Your Andrzej.

PS. Please send me a picture without the dark glasses.

Warsaw, 11.6.68

My Darling, the question of our meeting has temporarily been decided for us. Professor Batawia will not agree to my going in July; to comfort me he said: 'Dear Colleague, I've visited all over the world and believe me: it's not worth going anywhere.' (…)

Without dark glasses I look like a moronic suckling since not only am I short-sighted but I also suffer from photophobia – that's why I won't send you a picture without the glasses. You're probably better off, so wear your glasses only when you must; after all, remember what Hamlet said: 'To see things as they are is to see them too precisely.' (…)

It's good that you can still do 'flying'; your previous letters suggested you no longer like to, you've grown out of it, you no longer want to. It's true that with each disillusionment one flies lower and less willingly. And often disappointment comes because the person who causes us to start flying turns out to be completely different and hinders our 'flying' on. Which they can do in so many different ways! But one must fly – one simply must – otherwise one becomes static inside and sad. Remember Rådström?* 'She's not actually involved. That's what concerns me and what I'll never be able to comprehend. Not comprehend with my mind nor seize with my hand. It is something which concerns only me. But I intend to call it love.'

I kiss you, Darling.

H.

London, 19.6.68

Darling, What a pity!

*Of course* I'll invite you for next spring. In fact, I'm inviting you now. It'll be best if you come in May or June – all right? But arrange it well in advance and seriously.

As to 'flying', it is of course the most pleasant activity in life; but you must agree it's not a relationship with the person 'who causes us' to fly, but with our own imagination: in other words, it's spiritual onanism. There's nothing you can do to help the other person with such a love, nor can you get close to them – quite the reverse. As you yourself write: 'the other person hinders us in our flying'. But perhaps it's our flying that stops us getting to know and love the other person, stops us being in a true relationship with them?

Forgive this moralising – it's just that I badly want to *learn* something in my life, and not just spend it flying, landing, and constantly being amazed by it all. Maybe it would be better to limit one's imagination in life to let it bloom more abundantly in art?

Darling, I must close: this is the busiest and maybe even the most important week of my year. Yesterday I recorded for radio my song cycle with an excellent young singer: the public premiere takes place on Saturday. I'm enclosing the programme.

Halinka, don't be discouraged by the postponement of your visit; the most important thing is that we're in touch… Keep writing, I will, too, and our meeting will happen one day. I'll send you a recording of the songs as soon as it appears.

Kisses,

Your Andrzej.

---

* Pär Rådström *Murder*, 1968

London, 19.7.68

Darling, what's happening? For God's sake, take care of yourself! Get well quickly, then have a *long* rest, even if you do find it boring: walk slowly (you say you've been running!), don't do any physical work (let someone else do it for you), and return to your previous healthy state *gradually*. I beg you drop me a line so at least I know how you are.

Many thanks for the records which arrived at virtually the same time as the card (...). I'm reading your Tolstoy and I am ENRAPTURED (there are so many exclamation marks and underlinings on this one tiny page that I had to write that in BLOCK CAPITALS; that's called INFLATION).

My cycle went magnificently; the public was overwhelmed, the notices were dreadful, so everything is just as it should be and I am pleased with both. But most important was a quite private matter: I hadn't seen Michael for 3 years (that's what the songs were about), but I knew, I knew months ago, that Michael would be at the concert. Things end like that only in plays and in novels; life is too disordered to provide such *complete* experiences. But that was a complete experience: everything in my life, the personal and musical motifs, came together, my past was fulfilled and closed like the most perfect work of art. And it left a great stillness.

Darling, I still have eight more letters to write and it's 12 already, so bye, kisses, and a million good wishes, especially for your backbone: may it get straight soon. Write quickly even if it has to be brief. (...)

Kiss you again,

Your Andrzej.

Warsaw, 7.68

Dearest Andrzej, I'm leaving for Łódź today, I'm going to hospital. They're digging that cursed disc out. What luck that I didn't go over to see you! I look as if I've escaped from a painting by Picasso: one hip has completely vanished, and the other is of extraordinary proportions. Hopping is one of the more cheerful memories of my past – at present I move along by crawling or rolling. (...)

Darling, I've been thinking about what you wrote: 'Maybe it would be better to limit one's imagination in life to let it bloom more abundantly in art.' I suspect you can't limit your imagination in your contacts with people because it's the same imagination which serves you so valuably in your art. You can merely limit your contacts with people, you can teach yourself solitude. Does that help your creative work? That surely depends on the individual. What's important is what experiences awake the need to create in a person: is it good or bad 'flights', is it other people, is it other people's art, is it solitude – who can tell? Some of the great creators couldn't do without people, others resorted to absolute solitude. So, 'sibi constat', as Horace wrote. That's all.

And hindering? Hindering can depend on the fact that the person we choose doesn't want to be chosen. And then – as you wrote – one cannot blame anyone. But we can also be hindered when the person we're with doesn't fulfil our expectations. Believe me, we are most often hindered not because our expectations are too great, but because they're internally contradictory! Darling, tell me, do you know now why you split up with Michael? Wasn't it because Michael was a strong individual, or at least someone with ambitions, and you were rapacious? Unable to be himself next to you – he fled. Staszek said: 'All the way to another continent.' It must have been emotional; if you run away from someone you don't love you need only to cross to the other side of the street.

Isn't your problem that what you demand from people with a strong individuality is contradictory: both total surrender and the total preservation of their individuality? If they choose total submission – you despise them, just as you did with A.; if they won't surrender – they have to run away, as Michael did. Though of course I don't know, maybe it was completely different, but that's not the point. The point is that we should draw conclusions, understand the nature of the vicious circles in our lives. Does that help? Not always, unfortunately. Our needs, which make us fall into those 'vicious circles', are on the whole impervious to sober arguments. When the desire to fall comes along – we fall right in. (…)

I kiss you, Darling.

Your H.

Łódź, 4.7.68

Darling, I'm in hospital already. I'm waiting for the operation.

Precedence for the knife is given to those who are having something dug out of their skulls. Where are you going to be now, Funnyface? I need you and I don't want to lose you somewhere in the world.

Łódź, 8.7.68

Thank you for your Darling letters. I find it hard to write because I've had my operation and to keep me straight they've wound me onto these cylinders like a mangle. Everything's OK, it's just that I'm lying upside down and I can't write a wise letter, or a pretty one, because I'm also feverish. The fever's not a consequence of illness, it's because I've received six letters and two postcards, added to which I'm reading some Simone de Beauvoir (*Force of Circumstance*) and everything's muddled up. The lady isn't stupid, just boring and lacking in inspiration; her pathetic, un-French seriousness is irritating. There are some nice lines in it, but they were written – in letters to her – by Nelson Algren (that lover of hers in *The Mandarins*); e.g. 'From then on I tried to take back from you my own life. I am attached to my life and I don't want it to belong to some woman who…' There is sorrow and charm in that.

You'll think I'm posing saying these literary problems haunt me in my fever; not at all – it's just that I'm bored by the illness and I'd rather talk about something else.

This is what Basia wrote about her summer camp: 'There are pictures hanging on the walls and there are spoons, forks, and knives in the pictures. Underneath there is writing to tell you how to use a spoon, fork and knife. I think this is silly. If a child doesn't know how to use a spoon, fork and knife, then it certainly can't read.'

Darling, where will you be now? Where shall I write, and where should I long to be?

I kiss you with all my heart and thank you for your concern.

H.

London, 24.7.68

Funnyface, Darling,

Today, I received that most beautiful and wisest letter. What you write about Michael and me is the absolute truth – I am astounded, because you've never seen Michael and you've not seen me in 12 years! But I am completely different now, not in the least possessive – my last encounter was all about my feeling sorry for someone and badly wanting to help. That's something completely new for me.

But what you wrote makes me feel very close to you now. How well you remember and understand me! I think that if we met now, it would be like we had never been apart. Even though I've changed, you would understand those changes, too.

I'm relaxed about your operation. You are very clearly in good hands. (…) I'll be thinking about you a lot, and you must let me know as soon as you're better. I want to be sure that everything's in good shape. Look after yourself, Darling. And don't worry: it will be easier if you don't.

I kiss you and hug you,

Your Andrzej.

MOCAMBO HOTEL, FIJI

14.8.68

Darling,

So everything's fine! Your friend Jagusia*, finally also wrote to tell me the operation was a success and you're walking a little (…).

You once wrote that you play the Ballade in F major like a Melanesian woman. I have to tell you, Funnyface, that they are very laid-back women; everyone here is calm and sleepy; all the planes arrive at three in the morning and the tourists, instead of partying, go straight to bed.

There are the English here to whom, in principle, Fiji belongs; there are the Americans, who are under the impression that the whole world belongs to them; so I make friends only with the natives. They are pleasant and, by and large, do not eat people. But if it weren't for *War and Peace* I'd probably not survive.

I'll be in Australia the day after tomorrow. Write c/o Australian Broadcasting Commission, Sydney, New South Wales. I'll be there till the end of November.

Take care of yourself, rest and don't read Simone de Beauvoir. Write often; it will do you no harm and it will be of exceptional help to me (truly!). If you like masterpieces, read Dickens's *Great Expectations*. Stay bored for a long, long time and don't hurry back to work. It's only a matter of patience – the hardest of the virtues. And now you'll be able to write at home, won't you?

Darling, I'm so glad you're well again. Or nearly. (…)

Kisses, and millions of best wishes.

Your Andrzej.

Warsaw, 16.9.68

Andrzej dear, you'll have guessed that I was silent for a reason. Marek, in joyous certainty that I'll never return from the sanatorium in Polanica, sent your letter on to some non-existent address: instead of the 'Hazel' sanatorium he wrote the 'Heather' sanatorium, and when, dumbfounded, he saw that I had returned, he confessed that he'd sent the letter to the 'Hawthorn' sanatorium. Then I wrote a long and moving letter to the postmaster in Polanica all about the Hazel and the Hawthorn, and he replied by sending me an envelope addressed to the Heather. Now you know everything. Well, not quite everything. I missed you horribly! (…)

I feel so good that I'm surprised. Just two weeks after the operation I was dancing as if I were at a ball, and a week later I was collecting memories (just

---

* Friend of Halinka, staying at that time in London

like André Gide in Algeria). Gide irritates me. First he forces himself to tell the truth about himself, and then he writes such buffooneries about his marriage! He could have written that he liked Emanuelle or that he missed his family, but no – he writes: '… was it virtue that I loved in Emanuelle? That was the heaven my insatiable hell was marrying.' Whenever people are at odds with so-called morality they nearly always start making fools of themselves. They're either consumed by a sense of guilt, go into sack-cloth and ashes, debase themselves, or they start boasting and acting superior – in the name, of course, of a new, personal, better morality. Whereas morality is in life what creativity is in art – you have to remember what you've heard, what you've seen – yet go your own way.

Darling, write more about yourself, and with more details. What happened in San Francisco? How are the concerts in Fiji going? Are they anything like the concerts in Polanica? When Edward Auer* came and no one from the sanatorium wanted to go to the concert, the lady director made the following speech: 'Ladies and gentlemen, I would encourage you most warmly to go to the concert because I think that if Mr Auer has crossed the ocean to play in Polanica, then he has most certainly learned the pieces he intends to play and he will most certainly play them all to you, ladies and gentlemen.' (…)

Funnyface, I'm writing too much. But I want you to follow my example. It doesn't bore me (even when I've read it several times). Corresponding is a kind of living together. In future times, scientific research will prove it's the best kind! So write.

And take off your glasses – I want to kiss your eyes, your ears, and your whole funny face.

Yours, to the last disc, H.

KINGS CROSS MOTEL, SYDNEY

29.9.68

Darling, (…) Be careful when you go memory gathering. It would be sad if some exceptionally extravagant reminiscence should cause you to slip a disc again. (…) Have you ever tried memory-gathering on a ship? It's very pleasant: you just lie quietly and don't stir an inch; it's all done by the sea. It happened to me in 1959 and I still haven't forgotten it! It's worth gathering long-lasting memories which are often the result of very brief encounters.

As for Gide, I can't agree with you. He is not a buffoon: there's something much sadder than that going on. Despite desperate attempts, Gide never freed himself from a terrifying puritanism nor from the constant guilt instilled in him

---

* American pianist who won a prize at the 1965 Chopin Competition

by his Calvinist upbringing. He's endlessly aiming to *vindicate* himself, and he writes about his Arabs not because he is bragging but because he is confessing, *justifying* himself and looking for the blessing which he needs so much. He wanted to screw in *a state of grace*; in fact, he needed two lovers at once, one of whom would screw him and the other bless him. Today it sounds paradoxical, but I'm certain that in 20 years' time, following the gradual liberalisation process which Christianity is being forced to undergo, Gide will be acknowledged as an outstanding *Christian* moralist. Just look at how often and how well he writes about the Gospels. He's always arguing that the main thrust of Jesus of Nazareth's teaching was joy, not penance, and he's constantly proclaiming that joy. But joy came to him only rarely and with great difficulty because in his childhood he was taught only penance; that's why he writes about joy so much, to facilitate it for himself and for others. He had to teach himself joy. Sometimes he does write awful rubbish, but he always does it sincerely and courageously, and you can't call him a buffoon when he lived in a country and a time crawling with buffoons: just compare him, for example, with Jean Cocteau!

I'd better stop this because I'm starting to lecture you. Besides, it's always me you want me to write about. Tomorrow, I'm playing the Brahms Concerto in D minor and apparently this one concert, or one critic's opinion of it, will decide my present and future standing in Australia. That's how it is in our profession. I'm a bit uneasy, especially as at yesterday's first rehearsal I played pretty poorly; I was very tired and over the last two days I've been having the shits (forgive me: my illnesses are far less serious, and far less decent, than yours). I felt weak and the Brahms doesn't allow you to be weak. I did, as it happens, play loudly enough, but I struck the wrong keys. Thank God I've got a day's break today which will let me practise and rest; the second rehearsal and the concert are not till tomorrow. I find that the hardest is starting the finale at the right tempo. At home I play it allegro ma non troppo, and it sounds like Brahms; but at the concert I get excited, it comes out decidedly troppo, and sounds like a csardas out of some Hungarian operetta. In fact, the more tired I am the more unable I am to control myself and the more quickly does it all come out. And more loudly. So often, being in a state of near total exhaustion, I create an impression of unfettered and slightly maniacal energy! But when I really am full of energy, I manage to play much more calmly.

Enough about me for today. And you write about yourself, about me, about anything you want to – I find it all interesting. Write as much as possible, don't wait for a reply, just write whenever you think of me. Your story hasn't reached me yet; I can't wait for it to arrive. Incidentally, my cycle of *Seven Shakespeare Sonnets* is being broadcast on the radio on Friday; my secretary will make a tape of it off the radio and that can be used to make private records later.

I finished reading *War and Peace*. It's wonderful. But why that lecture at the end? It's long, boring, and badly written – in complete contrast to the entire novel which is exceptionally, classically pellucid.

Bye, then. Work, play, but do take care of yourself, rest whenever you can and avoid people whose names begin with the letter M because they don't bring you any luck.

Hug you, Your Andrzej

AIRLINES OF AUSTRALIA

27.10.68

My Darling, I'm so busy at the moment that not only have I not replied to letters, I haven't even had time to read them! (…) Last week I played four concerts, each one at a different corner of Australia (for example, today I'm flying from Rockhampton to Melbourne; that's probably at least 2500 kilometres); worse still, I wasn't alone even for one moment but had with me an official from Australian Radio. I'm alone at last now, but I'm so tired I'll write only a few words.

Your story was delightful; just like Laclos but so convoluted that I was completely lost in it. (…) But it did make me laugh because of the spellbinding way you wrote it!

You know, the Brahms came out rather well after all – the second movement was very nice, and I found the right tempo for the finale. The worst was the coda in the first movement. But it's very hard to concentrate and work in Sydney – too much traffic, noise, anxiety; it's a beautiful city to visit, but not to live in.

It's a strange thing about cities, but it's nothing to do with their beauty, its about the people and the general atmosphere. For instance, I like London best of all though there are more beautiful cities (Rome, Hong Kong, Mexico, Rio de Janeiro). But I could never feel at home in any of them, and I'd go mad within a week in America – a country of fascists and gangsters. If you fainted in Paris they'd trample you underfoot instead of helping you. But in London, even though no one takes any notice of you, all you have to do is to fall ill and you'll see what kind of neighbours you've got. The English are calm, discreet, they don't reveal much of themselves, and that's why you can rely on them (inasmuch as you can 'rely' on anyone, which I suspect you can't). A Frenchman, on the other hand, will kiss your arse one day and won't recognise you in the street the next.

Generally speaking, despite its incredible activity, especially in the arts (five orchestras, three operas, 20 permanent string quartets, several small chamber ensembles, which means that there are at least three concerts taking place every evening; the National Theatre, the Royal Shakespeare Company, about 70 other theatres, 300 cinemas and everything else on the same scale), London is nevertheless still a peaceful town, a town full of parks, squares, and gardens, and quiet corners where one can live as if one were in the country… That's how I live there: in a tiny, carefully concealed apartment which cars can't get to and opposite a huge park.

I've written so much about London because I'm missing it – there are many beautiful things in Australia, but there's no atmosphere or poetry here; the towns here are built along perpendicular lines and you can't wander about and lose yourself in the same enchanting way… The people here are angular, too; so healthy and straight that I can't make them out at all.

Darling, I must finish. (…) Be well and of good cheer and give Basia a hug from me. (…) I'll write again in a few days.

Your old Andrzej.

ANSETT – ANA, THE SYSTEM OF THE GOLDEN JET

3.11.68

My Darling,

I read the story yesterday. I haven't a clue if it's good or bad, and I don't care. All I know is that, as a result, you're closer to me than ever before, that's why I can't think about it objectively. When Christine says: '… one can truly love only out of pity or admiration. Do you not think that is so?' – I'm sure it's you talking and I just want to answer that sad question. In Michael's words I also recognised a line which I myself once wrote to you: 'What you felt was not love, but a painful lack of, a painful longing for, love.' But even without that, I felt I understood his unfinished confession. But will the average reader?

I was most moved by Michael's words: 'And then we bring children into this world to cheat our own deaths.' That, quite simply, terrified me. Well done! That's how one should write: courageously, not flinching from anything, like Proust. (…)

I read the story as an intimate confession. Tell me, Funnyface, how can I help you? I'd like very much to help you psychologically as well as practically. Let me know if you need anything. But don't imagine that I love you out of pity! The fact is, I don't love you, but I like you so very much, so hugely.

Every human being has something for which they can be admired, and something for which they can be pitied. So there's no need for you to play the little orphan or the princess. Just be yourself. It's possible that both those elements are a part of love, but they are not all that there is to love!

Can't one love anyone out of sheer joy? As an equal? Does one really have to extol or denigrate him or her, to love them from below or above? Maybe one loves someone because they are different and yet similar, love them because we have so much in common with a being that is so different. Where would admiration or pity fit into all that?

Darling, I must close, but now I really do feel compelled to have a good talk with you. Write again soon.

Bye, Darling, I hug you with all my heart.

Your Andrzej.

Warsaw, 30.11.68

Andrzej, dear, today a strange and sad conversation between a divorced couple took place. For openers, Marek handed me a book: Ernesto Sabato's *The Tunnel*. He handed it to me and said: 'Read this passage.' I read it, and now I'm copying it out so you can understand. '... only the tunnel existed, it was dark and lonely: my tunnel, through which ran my childhood, my youth, the whole of my life. And on one of these stretches of the stony tunnel I spied this girl, I believed she was walking down another tunnel, one parallel to mine, whereas in fact she belonged to the wide world, to the world of those who do not live in tunnels; out of curiosity maybe she came up to one of my strange windows and saw a picture of my solitude, which could not be retrieved. (...) Sometimes, I could see her in the distance, laughing, dancing carefree or, which was worse, I could not see her at all. So I imagined her in inaccessible and absurd places. Then I comprehended that my fate was a great deal more solitary than I had imagined it to be.'

Then Marek said: 'My life is senseless. I'd like to bring up my child, then I would have something to live for. I'll buy you an apartment; move out of here and leave me Basia. If you refuse – I'll commit suicide. I've thought everything through and that is my final decision.' To which I said: 'For the time being we're living in the same apartment and you can bring your child up to your heart's content. I will not let you have Basia because she'd be unhappy, just like you are.'

Professor Batawia, who is a psychiatrist, said: 'You should get away from that home. He *could well* commit suicide because has a depressive personality. You should run away.'

I won't run away because I have nowhere to run to.

Andrzej dear, don't be angry with me for making you listen to these gloomy confessions, but then you do tell me about your sorrows, don't you?

Kiss you. H.

PS. Do you still want to invite me over?

HOTEL-RESTAURANT, ADR. DE HAAS N.V. AMSTERDAM

26.2.69

Darling, at last! Everything will be all right. Judy* will arrange everything this week. She's crazy about you (a bit like Basia is about me) and says there's nothing she wouldn't do for you and she can't wait for you to come. So it's the middle of June, yes? I'll be relatively free then; after that they'll be starting to chase me again. Try, Darling.

You want me to write about New Zealand. Funnyface, it's not a distaste for confessions that's stopping me, it's a reluctance to write about something which it will be much easier to talk about face to face. On paper it would sound like 'literature', but since you want me to, I'll just give you the situation. Robert lives in Christchurch, works in the university library, and is a baritone in the choir. He's lived, since he was 17, with his former English teacher, a good, charming, older man who gave Robert everything he lacked in his own home. In the early years Robert was in a suicidal state and Lawrence saved his life several times. The first time Robert jumped out of the car when they were going on a trip somewhere: he broke his arm and several ribs. He was in hospital for a long time and Lawrence, naturally, sat with him and read books to him. When he left hospital, Robert tried to commit suicide again. He could be calmed only by years of patient love; it was that love which Lawrence had, and still has, for him. Now that Lawrence is growing old, is he to be left alone? Then he would do exactly what Robert tried to do. Except that there'd be no one to save him... Darling, neither I nor Robert is capable of doing that. It would be simpler and less cruel to whack Lawrence on the head with an axe – can you see me in that role?

Besides, Robert is tied to his house, his work, his surroundings, a sense of security which is essential to him: he has such a passionate, restless, impulsive nature that if it weren't for the atmosphere of domestic peace, permanence and tolerance which Lawrence has created, he'd be completely unhinged. There's only one thing he lacks: a reflection of what he himself is so full of – ROMANTICISM. Lawrence can't give him that because his ideal is the triumph of reason, peace, of what he calls: 'The Mozartian attitude to life'.

I could give him that, of course, but is that enough? You know how volatile I am, jealous, restless, and most difficult with those I love. You can learn a great deal from love, and if Robert were free I'd certainly try to learn everything he needs: patience, goodness. But in the present situation I can learn only resignation.

Come over, Darling, and teach me what you already know only too well, namely that happiness is not necessary to life; that one can be sad and yet live and work, and that's what virtually everyone does... Kiss you, funnyface.

Always your Andrzej.

---

* Judy Arnold, André's friend who acted as his secretary and impresario

London, 14.4.69

Funnyface, So we'll see each other in 6 weeks! Or even sooner, in 5. Take care of yourself, now is not the time to be ill! Judy is looking for an apartment for you somewhere close to mine, and you'll enrol for an English language course as soon as you arrive (and you'll teach me German, all right? Otherwise I'll never get round to making the effort). Unfortunately, you won't be able to listen to me practising because I won't be practising then, only writing; and I do that in secret...

You ask what people in London are wearing? I haven't a clue. You can't see anything under the raincoats anyway. Speaking for myself, I prefer to wear trousers.

Darling, hug you, because I have to continue practising Schumann's *Fantasie*, Chopin's *Barcarolle*, Ravel's *Valses nobles et sentimentales*... On top of that the Beethoven Concerto No.3. The recital's tomorrow, the concert next Tuesday.

Stay well (I mean it!)

Your Andrzej.

Bremen, 20.4.69

Ah, funnyface, what are my worries compared with yours which are like something out of Sartre's *Huis Clos*. You have no idea how concerned I am about you but also how glad I am that you'll have a rest at last with me (staying with me is not, as a rule, regarded as restful, but compared with your present domestic situation, Caligula would be a relief).

So you really are coming at last! I still don't know where I shall put you, my place is so cramped (I have an apartment the size of a letter-box), but I'll arrange it so that you're very close and we'll spend enormous masses of time together. You'll do most of the talking, because I have, over the last few years, learned to listen; anyway – what could I possibly say since, even without my saying anything, you know me inside out! I keep thinking that I've changed so much in the last five years, but your letters show me that it's only my behaviour that's changed; my feelings haven't: I mean, you've not seen me for 13 years yet you still keep hitting the bull's-eye... (...)

I'm on tour in Germany at the moment; yesterday I played Mozart's Concerto in C minor in Gressen and now I'm travelling to Bremen with the Concerto in C major (K 467, the one you were learning when you were living with me). Then come two recitals with the same programme (Beethoven's Sonata Op. 28, Schumann's Fantasie, six Études by Debussy and Chopin's Ballade in F minor), and a recording for radio in Frankfurt (the same Beethoven sonata and the *Valses nobles et sentimentales*). As you can see, quite a comfortable programme except for the Debussy Études which are unexpectedly dangerous but which have recently started to work.

Bye for now or I'll miss the train (that would be the second; I was late for the first). Write back, Darling, at once, so that the letter is waiting for me when I get back; I am rather lonely at present and it will make a great difference. The more you write, the more you'll help me at the moment.

Kisses to you and to Basia,

Your Andrzej.

London, 18.5.69

Darling, Judy says that the fashion is for dresses up to three centimetres above the knee; she herself takes no notice of that (or any other) fashion. As for you, who are you intending to flirt with? Tell me at once so as I know who I'm supposed to be jealous of.

The recital went surprisingly well – you'll hear the tape when you're here. Tomorrow I go to Bremen with Beethoven's Third, and I come back on Wednesday. Perhaps you'll write again…

In any case, you have to tell me where and when I'm to wait for you! I hope I won't be late. You'd better tell me you're arriving a quarter of an hour earlier, then I'll be there on time.

Kisses, as usual,

Your Andrzej.

Sanatorium, Lądek Zdrój, 25.5.69

Darling, thank you very much for both letters. I can't stop writing either, probably because of the panic induced by our forthcoming meeting. I dream that when I arrive you will lock me away in a cellar – like the Collector* – and look in on me from time to time. But you're not the Collector, and I'm no beautiful woman. Besides, he locked her away and waited for her to love him, while you would lock me away and wait for me to stop loving you. Maybe that's an even more interesting idea.

There's no problem with the dresses; it seems I'm already wearing the latest London fashion! I won't tell you who I'll be trying to seduce because it's a secret, so don't even try to guess. My experience here has taught me that to seduce Mr A one has to flirt with Mr B, whereupon Mr A will inevitably fall

---

* Alludes to John Fowles' novel and the film based on it, *The Collector*

for you. I'm surprised Parkinson hasn't written an instructive book on the subject yet.

While on the subject of flirting: when the men here discovered that I work for PAN* there was no end to their chatting me up. I thought they were impressed by the fact that I was a woman who worked for the Polish Academy of Sciences. But it was a misunderstanding: they thought I work for a gentlemen's fashion house called Pan, or Mister, and that I'll be able to get imported suits for them. That's what the men here are like; there's one of them who ends every sentence by adding the word 'yes', and another who ends his by adding the word 'no'. The second one told me of his adventure at the ball, and the story went something like this: 'So at the ball I ask this lady to dance, no, and she says to me: "Stop treading on my slipper with your clumsy foot, no", and I say to her: "I'm not touching your slipper with my foot, no, because I haven't got a foot, no, I've got an artificial leg, no." ' (...)

See you soon! H.

PS. I should be arriving in London on 21.6. at 18:00 hours. I'm not putting the time back a quarter of an hour. You'll just be late, that's all. I've waited 13 years for a meeting with you, I'll wait 13 years and a quarter of an hour if I have to.

---

* Pan is the Polish for man and Mr but PAN stands for Polska Akademia Nauk, the Polish Academy of Sciences

# *Part Three*
# **1969 – 1978**

Warsaw, 20.8.69

Darling, if you only knew how much I owe you, you'd get to like me again. It's not just the trip to England, or the good days with you, or the sun, or the lesson in life, or the lesson in chess, but also: earning money in England (and that by typing in a bathing costume in a meadow in Thurlestone – where I was taken by Z., an old school friend who lives in London), the wonderful journey along the coast, the piano recital at the Methodist chapel and the table-tennis match I won there! Meeting Professor Marvin Wolfgang in Cambridge and the scholarship I was offered in the States. Finally, the trip to Germany where I was unable, unfortunately, to strike up so much as one interesting conversation. I had no contact with young people there, but the Germans of the older generation are pathetic, banal, obsessively preoccupied with mulling over reality. Their words are deprived of smiles, you can sense their constant concern – yet you can't tell what it is that's making them worry: is it the imminent annihilation of the world that's making them worry or simply the stain on the tablecloth. And what personal dignity they have! And how seriously they treat everything... Yet it's probably true to say that the fewer things one takes seriously, the less harm one does.

Darling, I'm writing this letter on the train to Poland, and the train has just moved off and it's shaking horribly, so I must stop. But I want to thank you once again with all my heart and to kiss you like I did that time you were waiting for me at Paddington Station.

H.

London, 15.12.69

Halinka,

I was afraid I'd be getting recriminations, score-settling, but what I do get is presents. And what presents: *Notes from the Underground* is, apparently, Dostoevsky's best novella and *The Eternal Husband* is the second best; I've been longing for them for years. I haven't got down to them yet, but I've swallowed the Chekhov in one go. I am now reading a biography of him.

I'm delighted with the records, too. As for the little mascot, the puppy, you're an incorrigible optimist: an entire zoo would not be enough to help me play even three notes as well as Richter – ever.

Seriously, though, I am disappointed that, despite everything, you haven't decided to forget about me or at least to finish with me. After all, it is HARMFUL to you and it can be of no help to me. If you hadn't known me then perhaps you'd have been happy with someone else long ago.

After you left I wrote you an incredibly vicious letter in which I insisted that you break off relations immediately, but I couldn't bring myself to send it. Maybe I should have done. Just as I once did with that postcard… Though that postcard didn't work either.

Forgive me this idiotic letter. I could have tried to write more interestingly, more happily, to give you some news, in other words to write 'just like before'. But that would make *no sense* – I want to *awaken you*, not to go on rocking you to sleep. Don't you understand how much you've lost, and are losing, in this barren relationship?

Once and for all get angry, take offence, shake yourself free of me. In a few years' time you'll realise that your youth has passed by! And for what? Is it worth it? At present you still have a chance of a real life – maybe alone, maybe with someone who will love you, but not with someone who is indifferent, distant, an apparition resident abroad. No, do not forgive me this letter after all.

Farewell and thank you.

Your Andrzej.

PS. I hadn't meant to write this when I started, but it's good that it's happened…

Warsaw, 6.1.70

My dear Andrzej,

It would be natural if I said nothing about your letter, but that would imply that I agree with what you wrote, that I do hold you responsible for the fact that I'm incapable of living and loving like a normal woman. I am incapable of doing so, it's true, but there is no merit of yours in that, and no fault.

I became convinced of that while I was still in England, during the wonderful two-week trip along the south coast. Z. said: 'Come back here from Germany, everything will sort itself out somehow.' But I was afraid. Afraid of what was immovably, unforgivingly real. And you had nothing to do with that because I knew then that everything between us was lost. So I understood why – in a certain sense – I was always faithful to you and why you always seemed somehow to be the person closest to me.

The reality of my life has been exceptionally gloomy: an Occupation childhood with no school and in a state of constant fear; after the War – tuberculosis and several years spent in a sanatorium, several unhappy loves, an absurd home situation, flight, and then love for you; the realisation that I had to change careers which entailed starting new studies, an unsuccessful marriage, seven years spent living with my husband after our divorce, tuberculosis of the kidneys, a disease of the spine... 'Liebchen, was willst du noch mehr?'* And so for me reality was revolting, I had not a whit of confidence in it and that's why I taught myself to live *outside* reality.

Now I realise that what always most attracted me to you wasn't your beauty, or your talent, or the hope that you might grow truly to love me, but the fact that you, more than any other person I've known or know, can create a fiction, believe in a fiction, and live a fiction. I think that when you realised we were alike what occurred to you was that we are both mythomaniacs nurturing a shamefaced longing for something real and ordinary and yet, at the same time, we are both terrified of it and convinced that the possibility of such an ordinary life is, in fact, a virtual impossibility. (...)

You were always close to me and you probably are still. But you bear no responsibility for the fact that I live the way I do and no differently. That is my own handicap and there is no cure for it. I am, quite simply, a Billy Liar, and you the dispenser of ambrosia.

I'm closing now, Darling,
hugging you warmly,

Your H.

London, 18.1.70

Dear Halinka,

Your letter is very sad and very real. It's only now I understand you as I never have done before (no psychoanalyst would be capable of describing you better). I also understand, for the first time, your attitude towards me. What you say about my penchant for fiction is, of course, absolutely true and I understand it could well have attracted you. Maybe it is abnormal, but in my work it comes in very useful. The basis of composition is, after all, 'what happens if...', and even in playing, the imagination – with a certain dose of discipline – comes in very useful. (...)

But you know what? I have a feeling that you've solved your own problem already. Nobody could say that your last letter was a flight from reality – you wrote about your life in a way that was to the point and pitiless. A disease of which the patient is so well aware has every chance of being cured! You've explained brilliantly that it's not I who am guilty of your mythomania. So we can continue to write to one another without any worries, can't we? But I don't

---

* 'Darling, what more do you want?' – from a poem by Heinrich Heine

know if, now that you've 'grown out' of your mythomania, you'll want to keep writing to me! Well, we'll just see.

I was very ill in the autumn (pneumonia etc.), but I'm feeling very well again. *Ariel*, the cycle of songs which I could no way finish in July, is now finished and, in my opinion, it's quite brilliant! It is undoubtedly my best composition. Now I'm writing a piano concerto – a longer piece but I hope to have it finished by the autumn…

For the moment bye, hugging you and sending you best wishes,

Andrzej.

PS. Hans Keller has seen and studied *Ariel* and is very impressed. It's he who believes the concerto will be ready by the autumn; personally, I'm not sure it will be even then.

ALBANY HOTEL, NOTTINGHAM

20.3.70

Halinka, my dear, I'm crying and you laugh. Can't you write seriously? I don't have a court, so I don't need a jester. I am terribly depressed: my concerto has been put to one side, I have been a pianist again for a whole week and I'm playing *awfully* – it's only now I realise how much I've lost during the three months I've been writing the concerto. I don't know how long this will last; I practise more than I have ever done, but the results are always somewhat delayed. It's so hard for me to believe in myself again. You wrote that you missed your vocation – that's true. But I can't agree that you should have been a psychoanalyst – on the contrary, you should have been a patient. No, don't take offence! After all, the difference is minimal: a psychiatrist is simply a lunatic who is paid, while a patient is a lunatic who pays. There is one other difference: a patient can sometimes be cured, a psychiatrist – never.

For the moment, anyway, write. That's probably the only positive form of mythomania. Soon I'll write to you about mythomania and about why, despite everything, one *ought and must* cure oneself of it.

In the mean time bye, my loyal friend,

Your Andrzej.

Warsaw, 3.4.70

Darling, it's hard for me to reply to your last letter for how can I console you so that you will indeed be consoled? Am I to assure you that you are a uniquely original pianist even when you play somewhat different notes? To tell you again that the music to the *Sonnets* is exceptionally beautiful and the more one listens, the more beautiful it sounds? To concentrate on the wonders of your personality, to talk of the 'set of symptoms which accompany the introversion of the psychic energy of the extrovert personality'? If you heard me giving you such a lecture you'd acknowledge that I am completely mad and that you had long suspected it.

Darling, I do, however, have a really good idea: get rid of your charlatan analysts and go to Eysenck. He is one of the best psychotherapists in the world, a splendid man and very imaginative. Added to which, he lives in London! (…) You haven't dropped off the moon and he will treat you with appropriate interest and care. He'll most certainly help you deal with the insomnia and neurotic insecurities which you are helpless to deal with on your own. That's all I can advise you to do.

Following your advice I, too, went to see an experienced psychiatrist who, however, treats his patients in a decidedly brutal manner, which is against the rules of the art. He explained my *problem* straight off without waiting for me to get there myself. After a longish conversation, in the course of which he spared me no drastic questions, he concluded: 'You are no mythomaniac: you wash, you cook, you bring your child up, earn money, pursue an academic career – where is the flight from reality in all that?' I interrupted: 'Doctor, my personal life is a shambles. I keep waiting for the *last* man in my life. Is that not mythomania?' 'Not at all' he replied, coolly, 'it merely shows that you feel least sure of yourself in that kind of relationship and that you are constantly wanting to *prove* yourself. Even if you slept with Gregory Peck it wouldn't help – you'd start to denigrate Gregory Peck instead of starting to have some faith in yourself (…). It would be wonderful if you were a mythomaniac and you could release all those absurd complexes in your imagination, but your misfortune is that you cling to reality with manic obstinacy, like someone completely *devoid* of imagination.' 'Can anything be done about it, then, doctor?' 'So far you've pretended to be in love to provoke feelings in order to dismiss them. You must put an end to these games. You must love without pretence and without worrying about it being reciprocated, or you must give it up; you must accept that these matters will never bring you happiness, and that you will continue to hurt people just as you hurt your husband – it's because of you that he is now a vicious misanthrope. It simply could not be otherwise.' 'But I sincerely do love Andrzej, my friend in England!' '*Sincerely?* Then why didn't you take the risk of marrying him when he wanted you to? Fear again; lack of faith in yourself. Besides which he has the same complexes as you. That's why you can correspond with one another for years on end, but when it comes to love you can't help each other. Every one of your relationships *must* end in failure, but in your letters you can play at "stoking your imagination". Yesterday, you told me the story of the hunchback who killed his lover. You cried when you were telling me it. Why? Because you *identify* with the hunchback. Just like him you were afraid of meeting the object of your "love"; in order to put off the meeting you even let yourself be operated on!' 'Doctor, surely you're joking…' 'Not entirely; diseases of the spine can also be psychosomatic, they can be tied in with tension, with deep unconscious anxiety.' 'But luckily, doctor, nobody murdered anyone.' 'Only superficially… Don't you understand that it was the death of *hope* – your hope and his?' 'Doctor, you don't like me!' 'Does everyone have to like you? Does everyone *have* to think you're pretty? Yes, even for this meeting with me you had to come straight from the hairdresser. Wake up, woman! Be honest with yourself, act responsibly towards others – cure yourself at your own expense, not other people's!'

This doctor has a reputation of being a crazy monster; he's had three or four wives himself and countless lovers. It's quite possible that he has a similar problem and that that's why he was so brutal. Maybe it's just as well because I've gone off any kind of psychotherapy.

Darling, now let me hug you with all my heart and apologise for this egocentric letter. To finish with I'll give you a golden thought from Basia's journal: 'Few people succeed in doing a lot in life, but then again only a very few achieve nothing at all. Slowly, I shall make discoveries and inventions.'

Kiss you. Your H.

PENSION BIEDERSTEIN, MUNICH

1.5.70

Darling, forgive me, I don't seem able to write to you just now. In fact, I'm not able to do anything, and I don't want to do anything. Your last letter was enormously interesting and I hope that you'll write again. Apologise for me to Janusz Kaczanowski who wrote me a very nice letter – I don't even want to play chess with him, either. You know, I feel as if I've died already, as if everything inside me is finished. I've decided to give up composing, or at least to put it to one side for a longish time. Besides which, I've just broken off with Judy.

So you can see for yourself that there's nothing more to write about, can't you? So you're the one who must keep writing. Write to my London address because I'll be home by evening. I thank you very warmly for the Chekhov plays (…).

Hug you, bye, Andrzej.

London, 30.6.70

Funnyface Darling, don't worry about me at all! I'm in good form again and in a marvellous mood. As for Judy, I'm going to the theatre with her this evening.

Nevertheless, the depression has been very serious and very useful. I've learnt a lot from it but it's very difficult to talk about it.

The thing is to learn simply TO BE, and that means to be oneself, not to try to be something better, not to be making impressive plans, and above all not to be giving oneself grades. 'Thy will be done' is the wisest sentence that I know, even if we don't know who or what 'Thy' refers to.

As soon as I was born almost everyone plotted to turn me into a wonderful child and everyone constantly insisted that I was completely exceptional. Now I'm neither a child nor wonderful and when I realised it I thought I was a complete nothing. 'And what else can I do?' I wondered. 'Just go up onto the platform and pretend that I know something?' But I eventually reconciled myself to the fact that I know nothing, that everyone was wrong, and I'm just a worthy mediocrity after all; and since then not only have I felt better but I've been playing better, too. Now the season is finished and in a few days I'll get down to writing again – and we'll see how that goes. I feel better at the thought that no one can expect masterpieces from a mediocrity!...

And you? How's Basia?

I hug you both – Andrzej.

PS. Yesterday Stephen Bishop came round and we played chess. He told me to give you his best wishes – you'd be surprised how well he remembers you! I accompanied him a few days ago in Bartók's Second Concerto which he plays quite phenomenally.

London, 4.11.70

Darling Halinka,

Many thanks for *The Double* [by Dostoevsky] I know none of the stories in the whole volume. But there's something else I'm even more grateful for.

Quite recently I came across a letter you wrote me about six months ago. In it you write: 'You only *seem* to tolerate your solitude. Solitude gives you a sense of freedom, of doing what you want with your time – playing, composing, thinking. But by being solitary you are stopping other, very important, needs in your nature, from being satisfied... You're imposing upon yourself the role of an introvert, when in fact you are an extreme extrovert.' And so on.

It's only now that I realise how right you are. Not that I entirely agree with your last sentence – my impression is that I am both; my profession demands that

I adopt the role of an extreme extrovert, a performing monkey which has to show off constantly whether it wants to or not. After concerts, receptions, press interviews, solitude becomes essential in order to restore a certain balance… But apart from that, you were absolutely right. I'm sure that soon I'll write and tell you how I came to be convinced of this, but at the moment I'm too afraid of going back to it, I need some distance between it and myself… So, in the mean time, how do I go about distancing myself from it more quickly? There's one way: immerse myself in my work. The famous Piano Concerto is still not ready (I should call it 'Eternal Songs'), but the prognostications are looking good: so far, four people have seen it (Stefan Askenase, Stephen Bishop, Hans Keller and George Lyward – the psychologist I told you so much about), and they are all very impressed. I was most pleased by Mr Lyward's reaction because he is not a professional musician and he responds to what he hears intuitively – so it seems that my music is capable of working on someone who doesn't go into details or musicological analyses; that all it needs is a normal, human sensitivity…

Tomorrow, I'll probably be sitting over the concerto again. Although I'm tired (I've played ten concerts in the last three weeks, and my life's been tossed about like a ship in a storm), I'm incapable of resting at the moment. We all know that exhaustion causes depression, so the first thing to do is to break out of the vicious circle! Anyway, work is far less tiring than so-called 'feelings'.

That's all my news so far. What about yours? Write me about life in your new apartment – I hope you're not missing Marek. And with whom are you falling unrequitedly in love this time? I'm not being sarcastic, Darling – it's just that now I know what it is you need.

Bye, and kisses,

Your Andrzej.

London, 1.1.72

Darling Halinka, thank you for the book which arrived this morning. You've written at last! And I've finished the Piano Concerto at last! I had thought that the day would never come. Now I won't write anything else for another six months because I'm quite dreadfully busy. Among other activities I'm recording 16 Beethoven sonatas for the radio, in November I played all of the Bach *Klavier-Übung* (five different programmes in five days) – and any number of new pieces – Mozart's Double Concerto, Bartók's Third, a dodecaphonic but beautiful concerto by a young English composer called Richard Rodney Bennett; numerous solo pieces, e.g. Bartók's suite *Out of Doors*; quite a bit of chamber music – Fauré's Quartet in A minor, violin sonatas by Mozart and Beethoven, and Bartók. It would take ten pages just to write out the names of the pieces. How am I going to cope with it all?

One good thing is that with all this going on I haven't time to fall in love. It's about time I did something different anyway.

Bye, then, and give us a kiss.

Andrzej.

HOTEL PARMELIA, PERTH, WESTERN AUSTRALIA

1.2.72

Darling,

Even though I haven't time to write I wanted to jot down a few words to you about your feeling 'that life is senseless'. Funnyface, leave all that to Hłasko.* I know that feeling only too well – every time I stop writing or loving, in other words, whenever I'm not doing what matters to me, I get the feeling that life is merely a shoddy imitation The trick is to *make* sense of your life. It's just as Gorky says: 'If you believe in God, there is a God – if you don't believe, then there is no God.' As for God, I don't agree with him because that's fundamentally an objective figure, but that's exactly how it is with the sense of life. I don't know if life 'in general' has any sense, but then 'in general' nothing can have any sense. Your life and mine, though, can have sense and that depends on us. Keep your head up and get down to some writing. (…) A letter from you would really cheer me up. Address it c/o Mr Malcolm Bickard, New Zealand Broadcasting Corporation (Music Department), Wellington.

I hug you and Basia,

Your Andrzej

PS. Is the Erhardt who listened to my records Ludwik Erhardt? I remember him perfectly, give him my regards. Perhaps I'll send the Piano Concerto over for the Warsaw Autumn in '75, but I won't play it myself because I'd die of nerves.

Warsaw, 1.3.72

Andrzej, forgive the hysterical letter. I was simply in a state of ghastly anxiety as a result of a stream of anonymous letters with insulting greetings on the envelopes. They were sent to me at work, to the family, eventually even to Basia. It took me a long time to guess who was sending me these surprises from London. So hear a gloomy story entitled: 'From pleasant beginnings to nasty ends'.

As you know, after the (not very pleasant) parting from you I had to stay in England another two weeks waiting for a German visa (my poor old friend was

---

* Polish writer of pessimistic novels and short stories (d.1969)

dying of cancer in Düsseldorf). Quite unexpectedly, Z., an old school friend who's settled permanently in London, offered me work and a holiday together. He was on his way to a guest house run by a religious sect of sun worshippers. So we arrived at a beautiful little house in Devon. Love could not have been further from our thoughts: I was obsessively recalling my stay with you, he was telling me about his future wife who was coming over to London all the way from Kraków along with her furniture and carpets. We went on excursions, to cinemas, pubs; for a few hours each day he would dictate the text of a book he'd translated into Polish (most often I'd be writing on the lawn where we'd put the typewriter on a collapsible table). In the guest house we were given a shared room (in order to obtain a concession on the prices, Z. was using the membership card of a married couple belonging to the sect). So everyone regarded us as a couple, and as a result of this there were some comic misunderstandings.

One day, a small boy called Michael broke his leg when he fell down the stairs. This happened at dinner time, the guest house manageress was searching for the boy's parents: anxiously, she approached our table of ten and, turning to me, asked: 'Do you have a son called Michael?' Frightened that I had misunderstood, I turned to Z. and asked: 'Do we have a son called Michael?' And he says: 'As far as I know, we haven't, no.' The entire company fell about laughing and the guest-house manageress was speechless with astonishment. There was also a good piano there and a beautiful table-tennis room. When, in the course of a single day, I won the table-tennis championship and then took part in an artistic programme, playing Scarlatti, Chopin, and Albeniz, I suddenly became very popular indeed. Z. was proud of his fictitious wife, who was, after all, regarded as his real wife. And from that moment on, he started to behave like a real husband. I was quite simply enchanted by this charade, probably because it was just a charade. When we returned to London and I picked up my visa, we made our farewells at night, by the Thames. In the distance we could hear a guitar and some singing, and the moon, too, was doing its bit; in a word, the mood was so romantic that Z. suggested that I should return to London from Germany. I don't know whether he intended to halt the transportation of furniture and carpets from Kraków, nor do I know what he was thinking when he wrote to me in Poland saying he would like to have a child with me ('I wonder,' he wrote, 'what a woman feels when a man makes her a proposition like that'). I advised him sweetly that rather than with me he should have his child with his future wife.

Our correspondence flickered slowly until it died away completely. After two years of total silence I started to get these revolting anonymous letters. The lady with the carpets had obviously read the letter in which I gave my blessing to the future conception of her child and fell into a rage. No wonder, especially as (this is something I've only just found out) she left behind in Kraków the young man she really loved; she was living with him at the time Z. was writing the letter to me in which he said: 'At this very moment my plenipotentiary is at the Kraków

Registry Office asking a certain lady if she wants to be my wife… I should think that by now she's had time to say she does. And so, I am a married man.'

Ooph… I've finished my confession, so now quickly to other matters. I've finished writing my thesis, the viva will be soon, after the exams. I'm not in love with anyone except Basia. Basia wants to be a stunt artist. I ask her: 'Aren't you afraid?' She says: 'No, because I'll only be doing the erotic scenes.'

Have you read Hłasko's *Dirty Deeds* and Frisch's *Gantenbein* yet? They are two books with diametrically opposed attitudes to life. I prefer Gantenbein, you probably prefer Abakarov, don't you?

I hug you very tightly,

Your H.

PARKHOTEL, DEN HAAG, HOLLAND

17.3.72

My little Halinka, Why does anyone need novels? Your letters are far more interesting. I'm writing from Holland so you won't be frightened by an English postage stamp. Darling, one must never read anonymous letters on principle because they don't deserve it, and nobody writing such letters can possibly ruin anyone's reputation. Thank God, at least, that you didn't suspect me of writing them!

As usual I have heaps to tell you and, as usual again, I don't have time to write. I'm playing every evening this week: yesterday, today, and tomorrow it's Chopin's F minor and then after that it's Brahms's D minor and two recitals. Then it's Mozart's D minor in Denmark, and a short break during which I'm supposed to learn Bartók's Concerto No 3! And in the middle of all this I have to fly over to London for a day to hear the first public performance in England of my quartet (this quartet has been performed in Germany on Stefan Askenase's birthday, but that was a semi-private thing – in England it has only been broadcast on the radio).

As for the Concerto, I won't be playing it at all for the time being because I've surrendered the rights to the first performance – it will probably be played by Radu Lupu. In case you've not come across his name, I assure you that Radu Lupu is quite simply *the world's greatest pianist* – and not only am I not exaggerating, but it's also the very least one can say about him. From the moment he asked me to let him do this performance I've been feeling like a Walter Mitty and I tremble at the thought that he could change his mind! Just to be on the safe side I'll learn the concerto myself so that, if need be, I can take his place.

Bye, kiss you, and write again whenever you feel like it.

Give Basia a hug,

Andrzej.

London, 17.8.72

My Halinka, Your card cheered me up greatly, but I'd prefer another 57 letters! A visit from your nephew Staś will also cheer me up, no doubt, though of your family I like Piotr best (except you – to our mutual amazement) (…). Perhaps you'd like to start playing chess with me, too? Excellent, then I'll begin right away: 1. e4. That should guarantee us an uninterrupted correspondence. If you don't understand the notation ask Basia – she is more knowledgeable than you in every respect.

Stefan Askenase has married quite a young maiden. When I'm his age I, too, will marry.

Meanwhile, give me a kiss,

Your Andrzej

Warsaw, 30.8.72

Andrzej Darling, dear, 1. … e5. Thanks for the letter. If Staś hasn't appeared yet it must be through an excess of respect for you. (…) Staś is my alter ego to a much greater degree than Basia (incidentally, Basia recently announced: 'You think that you're wise and ugly, but in fact the reverse is true').

Darling, a digression: you once recommended the books of O'Connor. Did you mean Frank or the lady Flannery? I have read collections of stories by both, but I've become quite a fan of hers though what she writes is piercingly sad (…). I am at present alone in Warsaw and I'm writing a bit again. For a year now I've been pretending to be an essayist; so far they've published five silly little stories. I'm incapable of anything bigger than that. When I was little and at death's door, they decided to christen me at home. A pastor arrived (I would swear I can remember this) and, during the christening ceremony, the canary suddenly died. Then my father said: 'She won't die now, the canary's soul has entered her.' It's surely true that, since then, I've had the soul of a canary: I hop about, I chirrup, and I'm incapable of doing more than that.

Kiss you. H.

London, 10.1.73

Darling,

For some time now I've been meaning to thank you for the Witkiewicz plays which are simultaneously incomprehensible and fascinating – just like you. But before Christmas I was horribly busy, and when I got back I sat down to compose for an hour and found *I simply could not stop*. I did nothing else for two whole weeks. Eventually I did stop because I'd finished the first draft of the first movement of a string quartet. Believe it or not, the first quartet is generally considered to be my best composition (personally I prefer the *Songs of Ariel* which have never yet been performed, so I can't prove to anyone that I'm right), and next month it's being performed for the seventh time! That's very encouraging seeing that my compositions are usually played or sung three times at most. And since it is dedicated to Stefan Askenase I want to write another one so I can dedicate it to my steadfast and enthusiastic interpreters, the Lindsay String Quartet. Gratitude is probably the most pleasant of all motives for writing.

Still, I had to stop and get down to rehearsing! In ten days' time I leave for a three month tour to Singapore, Kuala Lumpur, then to Australia and – as usual! – to New Zealand (forgive the errors: I'm listening to Stravinsky's *Apollo* while I'm writing this). My playing gets worse and worse while my compositions, apparently, are getting better and better, and yet I have to play to pay off my debts. Not just for that, either: I really *like* playing the piano, just as one can still like – even after 20 years of marriage – one's wife, with just a trace of resignation and long-suffering. Composition, on the other hand, quite simply consumes me like the great passion of one's life.

For the time being write to me in London because at the moment I don't know where I'll be staying while I'm in New Zealand. (…) Did you hear Fou Ts'ong when he was in Warsaw? He's quite simply in love with Poland – he says it's been years since he felt so good anywhere.

Heartfelt hugs for you and Basia.

Your Andrzej.


London, 10.10.73

Darling,

Many thanks for your fascinating letter and the brilliantly chosen books. Maybe I should send you something for a change. What would you fancy?

In truth I thought you'd died and I even went to a seance to meet you. That's easier than going to Sweden because from the end of February to the end of May I'll be in Australia! The University of Western Australia has booked me for ten recitals – the first five devoted to Bach's *Klavier-Übung*, and the rest under the impressive title of 'The Historical Development of the Variation Form' – nothing but variations starting with Bach and Handel and ending with variations that don't even exist yet. I've commissioned them for this event from a young and completely unknown but very talented Englishman. Then I go to New Zealand, as usual, and I probably won't return to London till some time in July.

Fou Ts'ong recently married a beautiful Korean whom he'd met two weeks earlier and took everyone by surprise. I didn't marry anyone and no one was surprised.

I've recently read two novels by Kosinski: *The Painted Bird* and *Steps*; he writes brilliantly, but is it literature or just a sadist's onanism?

Give me a kiss,

Your Andrzej.
Give Lolita a hug, too.

Warsaw, 27.12.73

My very dear Andrzej,

Once again I haven't written for a very long time because I am very sad and I didn't want to talk about it. I'm going through something for which I wasn't prepared, which I can't afford, for which I haven't the strength. In short, the same damned drama as in *Love Story*. It started with my newest friends telling me for a whole month about this marvellous, enchanting fellow who was coming back to Warsaw and whom I simply had to meet. He's a brilliant cameraman*, has won countless awards 'both here and abroad'; has just divorced his wife, needs to be helped because 'he drinks a little too much'.

I met him by chance, at my neighbours'. He took not the slightest bit of notice of me, vivaciously telling anecdotes about the film world: how the whole film crew had arrived in Skierniewice, gone to the chemist's and asked for 500 condoms and half a litre of vodka (the condoms are used for making 'eruptions', wounds spurting blood, and to protect the camera lens, the alcohol – to clean the cameras). The pharmacist wasn't shocked by the number of condoms, she merely asked: 'Why so little vodka to go with them?…' (…)

I was in a hurry to get home and I was just leaving when Tosio stopped me. He asked me to stay and talk to him, and to tell him where I live because he wanted to pay me a visit.

We live in the same block and Tosio appeared the same evening. He was so charming he immediately won Basia over. Then he asked me to go down to his place, he wanted to change into paratrooper's uniform to show me how good he looks in it. He looks very good.

But Tosio's room is sad. A large, black table, black benches, and hanging on the wall a huge black-and-white abstract picture by Kantor. I sit down; I'm very embarrassed. Tosio pulls out some brandy and says: 'You know, I'm no intellectual but I do feel certain things. I've known you for only a few hours, I know nothing about you, but I *feel* that you are the one who will help me. (…)

---

* Antoni Nurzyński (Tosio)

It's true, I don't know you, but I do know that I want to be with you, and that I will try to cure myself for you...' (...)

I did not know then that he is terminally ill. Now I do know for certain. I found out by sheer chance: Tosio was feeling unwell, and Lili had just arrived; she examined him – just like her – from top to toe even though he resisted, saying it was only a cold.

'You are seriously ill; you should go to hospital.'

He refused, said he prefers to die without any hospitals, would rather not live than vegetate and cause trouble to others.

Then, surprisingly, Lilka agreed with him, but only when she was alone with me: 'It's cancer or, at best, far-advanced cirrhosis of the liver. The choice is between death in hospital or death at home. I, too, would rather die at home.'

I can't accept it. Maybe I'm an idiot, an egotist, but I want him to go to hospital, I want him to have treatment. I believe that he can be saved! I can't reconcile myself to leaving him with no help and simply making his last moments more pleasant. (...)

On a day-to-day basis I manage to feel good, I'm cheerful, I entertain and feed Tosio, I find things to occupy him. But sometimes I break down completely and stupidly, in public, I start to cry so desperately that I'm ashamed.

My friends tell me that it's a punishment from God and that I'm like a butterfly that's been run over by a truck.

Darling, I didn't want to wring my hands in front of you, but in the end I just couldn't keep it in.

Kiss you,

Your H.

London, 12.1.74

My Darling,

There are experiences to which one can find no reply. For what can I say to you – except that I sympathise with you enormously? Advice would be simply impertinent.

Nevertheless, I will tell you what I think. It's quite possible that you'll be angry with me as soon as you read the first words and you'll decide not to finish reading this letter. Because I'm going to start with the worst: in Tosio's place I'd categorically reject any compromise, any attempt to prolong my life.

Don't you realise that Tosio is happy now? The majority of people get through 60 or 70 years of life without experiencing one moment of real beauty or happiness – just look around you! But he did, he found it right at the end, just when it is most rare and most needed. And it's thanks to you, and consequently you must take the responsibility for it. Don't spoil what you yourself have given him!

Do you know how Chekhov died? He refused to listen to the doctor who wanted to put cold compresses on his chest and asked for a bottle of champagne. He sat up as best he could, propped up on his pillows, and said: 'It's been so long since I drank champagne.' He drank a small glass, smiled, and died.

And Tosio can die like that – with dignity, with a smile, and with a glass in his hand. After all, perhaps he *wants* to die. And you can be happy that at last the thing you've waited for all your life has happened, the thing you've been seeking desperately, obsessively. Don't be like Faust, don't say: 'Last moment! Moment, you are beautiful!' For that same moment would stop being beautiful if it did last. Don't you know that *love dies*? No, you don't and perhaps you hate me for saying it: lovers never believe it. But that's how it is and that's why love so often goes hand in hand with a longing for death. I am no Tristan, but I remember how much I wanted to die when I was with Robert.

'This letter's all about him!' you'll say. 'What about me? How will I survive this?' That question can be answered only partially: I think you'll be very lonely and unhappy, but at the same time enormously proud that you were capable of doing so much and grateful that something so rare has happened to you. You'll finally appreciate your own dignity and worth (…). And, above all, you'll feel fulfilled.

But for the moment don't think about it and live from day to day! Every day, every moment of joy will be another victory for both of you. Spring will come, there'll be walks in the park, vacations maybe, reading together and listening to music; you are still capable of happiness, of having one day which will be worth as much as the whole of your lives up to this moment. You can still joke, make secret allusions which no one else will understand, give each other presents and surprises; you can still have many moments which it wouldn't be right for me to speak of…

And, in addition, a whole lifetime of memories awaits you. And those memories, painful at first but without a trace of bitterness, will, with the passing of time, become sweet. In some mysterious way Tosio will stay with you for ever. Only the dead do that; the living always leave eventually, even if they continue to lie in the same bed.

I love you.

Your Andrzej.

Warsaw, 10.3.74

My dear, Darling Andrzej,

When I received your letter two months ago, I thought it was very beautifully written and moving but only now, after Tosio's death, do I realise how wise it was. When I received it I was still unreconciled: in revolt against Tosio's death. I kept running to doctors, finding out; they kept persuading me to send him to hospital, to let them operate. As became clear later, he was aware of it all; he used to tell a mutual friend of ours: 'I don't want an operation; I don't want to vegetate. A crippled existence like that would rub out the me that I was.'

His birthday was the most dramatic day of all. He was 39.

'Darling', I explained, 'you must go to hospital; that's what your father said.'

'You shouldn't have bothered my father. I won't go to hospital, I'm well. It's my birthday today, let's have a drink, don't deny me anything, and for God's sake don't talk about the hospital! If you really care about my health, then drink to it. And smile…'

'I won't smile. And I don't want a drink…'

And I left. A moment later he brought me a letter. 'Halinka, Darling! No one has ever shown me as much unselfish affection as you have. I know I'm ill and need help. (…) I know that only you can help me. Till now everyone treated me like an object: something that can draw, paint, take pictures, do the shopping. You were the first person to treat me like a human being. That's why I will listen to you, because I trust you. Kiss you, miss you. Tosio.'

That's when I arranged the hospital. The doctors were horrified: he was close to death. He was given 3 litres of blood in the course of one week. A woman doctor started to talk to me about an operation because he was improving each day.

I saw him for the last time on Sunday, 17th February. At midnight he had a haemorrhage. A medical team gathered. They told him the only course of action was to operate. He refused. Then there were further haemorrhages. He lay in intensive care where no one was allowed to visit. On Tuesday, at noon, I received a telegram: 'Antoni Nurzynski died on February 19 at 5 a.m. Hospital.'

Dasia found a large, flat stone and on it she painted Conrad's words: 'A man's true life is lived in the thoughts of other people.' And she took it to Tosio.

Darling, I had to write about this. In the future I'll try to write differently, serenely, even joyfully. Tosio didn't like sad people, and you don't, either.

Kiss you,

H.

Perth, 1.6.74

Halinka, my Darling,

Your letter reached me yesterday – I don't know when you sent it. Reading it a second time I glanced at the obituary and realised how long you've been alone! His photograph showed me a face so charming that even if you'd never written me anything about him, I would still have known what an enchanting man he must have been. But it's good that you did write. Of course you want to talk about Tosio, and you should feel that you can. I tell you what: come to London for a holiday and talk as much as you like about him to me. I'll be home from 15th July to 15th August, I've not accepted any engagements in that period so I can have a chance to do some writing at last. I've started a second string quartet, and I've been messing about with the opera for two years now.

You know that we do understand one another and you are aware of how much I sympathise with you but it would be wonderful indeed if, after those long, empty years, it turned out that the thing you've always sought really does exist. Sometimes you doubted it; after all, hunger is no proof of the existence of bread. But now you know that you were right, that you were waiting for the *truth*. (…)

Darling, don't try to write me any cheerful letters. (…) It's not true that I don't like sad people. I didn't like your bad mood when I felt I was responsible for it. But I like you now because you're not pretending. Write cheerfully when you are cheerful. One couldn't expect it now, and not for a long time yet.

Write to me in London and let me know when you'll be able to come over. I kiss you and Basia with all my heart. How old is Basia?

Your old and, in his own way, faithful

Andrzej.

London, 16.7.74

Funnyface,

As soon as I got back home and read your letter, I wrote to you to persuade you to come over right away! I even imagined I'd sent the letter, but I came across it a moment ago and realise that I must have mislaid it.

It's just as well, really, because what you wrote about my spiritual philanthropy was unspeakable nonsense (where could you hope to find a bigger egoist than me?); there are, nevertheless, two reasons why I can't invite you at this precise moment. To begin with, I'm writing like a man possessed – I don't know how long it will last, but while it does I have to take advantage of the opportunity (in fact, I've no choice in the matter because it does become an obsession), and I'm doing nothing but that. Secondly, which doesn't actually bother me, I'm overwhelmed by debts; though I did make masses of money in Australia I gave it all to a certain starving and brilliant painter. He knows nothing about it because he is proud and would never have agreed to accept the gift; it would have been refused (...) but I opened a bank account for him through a third party so no-one can prove it was me...

But that's the story of a previous obsession of mine. As Staszek once wrote to me: 'Are you working or living; because the two are mutually exclusive? (...)

I don't agree when you write: '... I'd come over if I could be of some use to you.' Darling, you could never be of any use to me in anything, nor can I be of any use to you and that's what's nice, that we like each other *disinterestedly*.

Radu Lupu intends to play my concerto in 1975 in London; perhaps I'll invite you over for the first performance? I'd like to meet Basia, too. (...)

Darling, bye for now, it's a pity we shan't see one another this summer. Maybe we'll manage it next spring?

Your Andrzej.

Warsaw, 16.7.74

Andrzej, Darling, today I received your letter for which I've been waiting so. (...)

Darling, you write: 'What's happened is wonderful.' I don't know how I can make myself feel that it is. Tosio's death has made me aware of what love can be in one's life; and just how empty and senseless our constant preoccupation with unimportant matters and indifferent people becomes. As for Tosio's fate, you're right. I was watching Bergman's *Cries and Whispers* with Basia yesterday, and she said that I was for Tosio what Anna was for Agnes. (...)

Not so long ago I sent a card to – you'll never guess. To the hero of the story of *That poor liar.* When Tosio read it he said: 'This is about me.' In reality the hero's name is Jurek. I left him once in disarray because he drank. (...) In reply to my card, Jurek has sent me a telegram: 'I waited eleven years for a card from you and am arriving on Sunday morning, Jurek.' I fear that I'll soon be like that sorcerer's apprentice who roused the elements and then forgot the spell.

I kiss you, Darling.

Your H.

Warsaw, 17.7.74

I didn't send the letter yesterday, so let's talk some more. Witek also watched the Bergman film and this is what he writes about it: 'Yesterday, I saw an uncanny and absolutely brilliant film, Bergman's *Cries and Whispers*. I don't know whether you understand the term "polymorphism" which the film talks about. Well, "polymorphism" is a multi-dimensional, multi-level, multi-targeted sexuality which mocks definitions and classifications. What this film screams out at us is that there is no standard, no norm, and therefore there is no perversion and there is no illness (after all, this film is about ourselves, about the fact that we are all homosexuals, necrophiliacs, sodomites) (…) People cannot be classed as happy or unhappy, homosexual, heterosexual. At birth we are both the one and the other though in varying proportions. That is my path from positivism to Heraclitus: that everything flows, that truth does not fit any formulae.'

Is that how you saw the film, too? Maybe Witek sees what he himself feels because he's aroused by anything that moves (with the possible exception of the hands on a clock). He grows angry with me when I talk about 'the pathology which the closeness of Agnes's death releases', and claims that 'polymorphism' will make great strides into the life of the rich societies.

Well, let it come if it must.

While I kiss you and kiss you again (taking advantage of your inattention).

Your H.

Warsaw, 15.10.74

Andrzej, maybe you received my letter or maybe you didn't. You've been silent a long time. I wondered if I have disillusioned you in some way. You probably thought I was incapable of real feelings because, in the midst all that sorrow, I wrote to Jurek. But if it hadn't been for that sorrow I would probably never have sent such a card. When someone is hurting so much inside, that's when he needs another human being. Basia says that Jurek is similar to Tosio. Maybe. He, too, is slight, gentle, a bit of a mythomane and misfit; he, too, drank and smoked too much, he, too, is divorced, and, just like Tosio, he's at odds with life.

Even their occupations are similar: Tosio was a cameraman, Jurek is a photographer. I didn't tell you about all this because I've been in hospital. An operation, quite a serious one at that, but all's well now. And now I'm waiting for my next 'operation', of which I'm very much afraid. Imagine if you will – it's marriage. I didn't even want it, I protested, but how can I resist? After all, something I haven't told you, he was once in the national junior boxing team and out of 48 public bouts he lost only 3! And then there is his family history… His great-grandfather was a Ukrainian nobleman called Hieronymus who, in the course of one of his expeditions, abducted a high-born Hungarian girl. He brought her back to his estates, became betrothed, then vanished because, apparently, he grew bored in the girl's company. His brother, the exquisite Kayetan, was also bored, but with him it was because he didn't have the girl's company. So, in time, another betrothal was arranged, that of Kayetan and the Hungarian girl. Hieronymus found out about the planned wedding and arrived during the marriage ceremony at which, in front of everyone, he killed his brother.

He fled, but somehow later they met, the girl and he, married, and produced Jurek's grandad. They settled in the mountains and thereafter the Ukrainian-Hungarian blood mingled with Highland blood, and it is from this explosive combination that Jurek was produced. My family is a little afraid that Jurek will beat me, but at the moment it doesn't look like it: he's nice, gentle, and good.

I am, however, concerned about Basia – she has fallen in love with a schizophrenic. He's a lovely and charming boy, but he is incurably ill. I don't know by what miracle he and Basia understand one another so well. They're constantly talking about angels. There's simply no end to their conversations about angels.

I'm taking advantage of a medical certificate to write a story called *The strange death of Amadeo*. I'll send it to you shortly. Oh, by the way: I've recently had my fortune told by a witch.* She says that everything in my life will be superficial, brief, transitory, except for a friendship with a certain man who lives overseas. (!)

Kiss you, Darling,

Your H.

London, 28.11.1974

Darling,

Ah, how wonderful! Congratulations, I embrace and bless you both (it's best not to get on the wrong side of boxers) In the photograph you and Basia look like a dream. By chance, Stephen Bishop** was at my place today; he saw the snap and immediately fell in love with Basia. Unfortunately, he is completely normal so there is no chance that his love will be requited***. Jurek, too, has a sympathetic physiog, but I simply do not believe his ancestry. If he actually told you all that, then it's proof that he knows exactly what it takes to

---

* Prof. Violetta Koseska, writing horoscopes under her nickname David Harklay
** Stephen Bishop, later Kovacevich, renowned pianist
*** Eleven years later Milan, the son of Basia and Stephen Bishop, was born

seduce you, evidence of which is the result of his efforts! I'm glad you sent the photograph because after that story I wouldn't even have believed in his existence.

Funnyface, what's going on in that scatterbrained head of yours? How could you possibly disillusion me? I've known and also loved your weaknesses for a long time, just as you know mine; as for our friendship, your Witch is absolutely right. In every other respect she's talking rubbish. What, for instance, is it that's supposed to be 'brief and transitory' in your life? Marriage? Basia? What?

Darling, I didn't write because for several months I was in a state of pathological depression – Basia would have fallen in love with me instantly. I have staggered out of it, more or less – less rather than more in that what has staggered out of it is no longer I. There's no cure for it, and that's why I won't write about it for the moment. One day I may tell you, especially as you like men who lose… You can certainly like me. (But then again, Jurek won 45 times…)

You must send me *The strange death of Amadeo*. Just think, I'm also trying to write – not music, but prose, and in English, too. Someone suggested a while ago that I should write a book, an autobiography, and I started messing about with it. To give it some form, and to stop the reader getting bored, I decided to pick and describe just one day from each year in such a way that one will be able to surmise everything that happened between chapters. The hardest is early childhood – all the more so as I'm trying to describe things as I experienced it at the time! I remember little from that childhood, and what I do remember I don't like. Darling, perhaps you'll remind me when exactly the Warsaw Ghetto began? Did we have to wear armbands in the ghetto as well? I seem to remember that we did, but I can't be sure.

Darling, what was wrong with you? What was the operation for? Is everything all right now? You've earned yourself a bit of happiness and I wish it you with all my heart.

Hug you, and fall at your feet KO'd.

Your old,

Andrzej

PS. It is the height of improbability for *Hieronymus* to have a brother called *Kayetan!*

Warsaw, 11.12.74

Andrzej, Darling! I'm rushed senseless because of the wedding. It's to take place on 14th December (the previous one also took place on 14th December – a curious hobby). The Witch did foretell that the wedding would be in February, but somehow that hasn't come true. The most important thing is to have a moment to talk to you before it all happens.

Warsaw, 12.1.75

As you can see, I didn't manage to finish the letter before the wedding; in fact, just to make things even funnier, the wedding didn't take place and all because of that Witch whose predictions have to come true. Well, this is what happened: the wedding was going to take place in Wrocław where a reception was also being prepared. Further wedding receptions were being prepared in Łódź and Warsaw. And then, in Wrocław, some zealous clerk in the registry office discovered that Jurek's place of birth on the birth certificate was different to what it was on his identity card. So, if I married one Jurek born in Lvov and another Jurek born in Tarnopol I would be committing bigamy! Anyway, that's how she explained it to me. There was no way out. Putting on a brave face we played the parts of a newly married couple and managed to get through the wedding receptions in all three towns, gathering all the wedding presents without batting an eye.

(...) The Witch also foretold that Jurek wouldn't get work in January because the person who was arranging it for him would be very ill. And so it came to pass: the friend who was going to give Jurek work broke his leg! Despite that, everything's great because Jurek is constantly coming up with ideas (Marek never had any ideas). Nor did I anticipate that a man of such a restless spirit would be able to cook and clean so magnificently. Life is full of surprises and that is one thing one must always expect to be so.

I must break off now and sit down to Sunday dinner which Jurek has just prepared.

Warsaw, 14.1.75

I'll surely never finish this letter because Jurek keeps kissing my hands and leaves me nothing to write with. So I'll send you what I've written – my book about murders which was published a year ago\*. But on one condition: that the only part of the book you read is the dedication!

What does the word KO'd in your letter mean?

Hug you and kiss you with all my heart,

Your H.

London, 25.1.75

Darling,

Many thanks for your delicious letter! From it I can see that Jurek is an excellent cook because it's a long time since I've seen you in such a good mood. KO (knockout) is a boxing term which means that you lose consciousness after being hit by your opponent. Now you can appreciate how much I love you since I know what I'm threatened by when I hug Jurek's fiancée.

Don't worry about my depression because it's gone. But it started in exactly the same situation as Basia's at the moment, so I understand your uneasiness only too well, and I share it! You remember how Ophelia, thinking (in part quite accurately) that Hamlet had gone mad, cries: 'Oh, what a noble mind is here o'erthrown!' and, to keep him company, goes mad herself? That's what I cried, too and trying to help a completely incurable schizophrenic in Australia I fell into a state which truly bordered on the schizophrenic myself. Everything, not excluding myself, ceased to interest me completely, so I sat in my rocking chair and stared straight ahead. That lasted half a year!

Unfortunately, I have to stop now because tomorrow I'm playing Mozart's Concerto in E flat major (K 271) and Ravel's Concerto for Left Hand, and the day after that I'm leaving for Finland and Sweden, so I have an enormous amount of work to do! I'll be home again in three weeks, so I beg you – write again! You have no idea how much your letters cheer me up.

Many congratulations on your double wedding. I'd like to send you a present, too – what would come in useful? What's your name now?

I hug you, regardless of the consequences,

Your old

Andrzej.

---

\* Halina Janowska: *Zabójstwa i ich sprawcy*, Warsaw, 1974 *(Murders and their perpetrators)*

Melbourne, 1.5.75

Darling, forgive me for not replying for so long. I've been travelling, playing, sweating, laboriously orchestrating the second act of the opera, running errands, talking, and now – as you know – I am also attempting to write a book! Added to that there are lectures, lessons, and so on. Those 'so on', of course, take up most time: a lesson lasts an hour, a lecture – two, and 'so on' takes all night and uses up masses of energy. In addition I'm playing bridge and chess (just for fun I'm taking part in a chess tournament here, though of course I haven't a chance), drinking port and brandy, taking walks and living like the eternal student. I feel so good here that I'm now taking my sleeping pills only twice weekly! At last I belong somewhere: hitherto I have always felt isolated. Though that was my fault: I always tried to be different, to shock, to shine; sometimes I even succeeded. But now, like Tonio Kröger*, I want to be one of 'them' – not to be like other people, to remain being myself – but to exist *in relation* to other people, all of them, not just to some elite. You'll ask me what I have in common with these healthy, young, uncomplicated Australians who drink beer, play football and like women. I don't know, and I'm sure that they don't know, either, but they've accepted me, like me, and make no demands on me. I feel at home here. The most important thing is that the students among whom I'm living like me *for myself*, and not just because I'm a pianist, a Pole, a Jew, a storyteller, or the devil knows what else. What I've discovered is, quite simply, that all people have something in common with one another! For me that is a very important discovery. (…) Write again – I'll be here till June 6th, after that in New Zealand (c/o N.Z.B.C., P.O. Box 98, Wellington), then in Mexico in July, and by the end of August in England again – but probably not in London, because I've decided to sell the apartment and move to the country somewhere so I can concentrate and work better! From July write c/o my agent Terry Harrison.

Kisses (if I'm still allowed to). Give Basia a hug.

Your Andrzej.

Christchurch, 20.6.75

Darling,

Am I still allowed to call you that? Thank God that Jurek isn't jealous of me, otherwise, as a descendant of Kayetan, he would have to run me through with a sword in a synagogue, and it's hard to find me in one. I'm certain that we'll all meet soon and get to like one another – in fact, you ought all to come

---

* The title hero of Thomas Mann's short story

over, not just Basia. I now intend to settle in Western Australia where I had a marvellous time on this occasion. I found myself a new pastime: helping American deserters. Truth to tell, the plural is a bit of an exaggeration because so far I've helped precisely one of them, but it was so much fun and so exciting that I've a great desire to make it a regular undertaking. Imagine, at 12 I'm playing a recital at the university, at 6 – Mozart's Concerto in C minor, and between the first and second engagement I'm dressing a sailor up in my own pants and sweater and burning his uniform (Mr Tchaikowsky, what do you do in your spare time?). I also had to conceal him with some friends, find him a lawyer so he would be allowed to stay in Australia (I don't yet know if Australia will agree to him staying), and buy him a guitar because he likes to play rock and roll on his guitar. I stayed an extra day in Australia to make sure he wasn't found before his ship sailed away, and that evening we organised a feast! All the plotters were present, the ship sailed away, and the sailor sat with us drinking beer, singing and playing, not at all badly, as it happens, on his guitar.

The tour I've got here is crazy: four or five concerts a week, each one in a different place and with a different programme. This is how each day looks: I get up (this is the hardest part), go to the airport, catch a plane, get off, give a press interview and a radio interview, hang up my tails in a hotel, eat, sleep after lunch – if I can manage to, then meditate (you must have heard about meditation), go to try out the piano, put on my tails, and play. Sometimes, after the concert, there is also a reception. The next day it's the same thing. Five of the concerts are with an orchestra, so add to that the rehearsals...

Still, I'll get through somehow, and in three weeks and one day (yes, I'm counting the days!) I'll be on holiday. I'll return to London at the beginning of August, but go on writing to me at the following address: c/o Terence Harrison, 22 Hillgate Street, London W8 7SR. He's my agent and he always knows where I'll be even if I don't know myself! Small wonder, since it's he who arranges my hotels. Write to me again! I hug all three of you with all my heart.

Your Andrzej.

London, 29.8.75

Darling Funnyface,

I don't know if I'm allowed to address you like that now. For a moment I was afraid that Jurek might follow in Hieronymus's (or is it Kayetan's?) footsteps and send me your left hip by registered mail. That would be somewhat pointless since I'm more stimulated by your head than by your hip. Couldn't you send me some of your literary works?

And what about my autobiography? Well, two chapters are more or less ready – 1942 and 1946. As I mentioned, I'm describing one day in each year, starting with '39 (the day of surrender) and ending in 1948 (the breaking of relations with my father in Paris). It's going slowly because I've forgotten a lot – I've spent 30 years trying to forget and now, when I've finally managed to, I'm suddenly supposed to be writing a book about it! But I think I will finish it in time. I'm trying to write it from the contemporary point of view – e.g. the bombing of Warsaw was, for me aged 4, a splendid game, and everything that went on in the ghetto I regarded as perfectly natural. The outrage and the fear are for the reader to feel – I felt none of that. How could I know that everything surrounding me was abnormal if I could remember nothing different?

The person who understood and described this attitude best of all was Kosinski – *The Painted Bird* is, in my opinion, the most shocking of the novels about the Second World War.

Darling, which records should I send you? Write soon and without any false embarrassment. God forbid that you should send me any Penderecki. Better to send Basia and Staś. But when?

Hug you with all my heart, Jurek too; he'll just have to get used to it.

Your old

Andrzej

London, 14.10.75

Darling, crazy, and (fortunately) incurable Genius!

Kafka is nothing! *This* is the way to write. Your *Amadeo* is hilarious and terrifying. I laughed till I burst, and discovered that the phrase 'laugh fit to burst', which I had never comprehended till now, describes a very painful experience. Each one of us is an Amadeo, though the majority of us cope with it somehow. Will you send me some more of your stuff?

It seems that I, too, am incurable because, despite a very thorough lesson last year (which I've only just got out of) I am, don't laugh, in danger once again. You and I both have holes in our hearts, so you'll understand and maybe you won't laugh.

Imagine: 28th October is the date of the world premiere in London of my Piano Concerto. Radu Lupu is playing, Uri Segal is conducting, the Royal Philharmonic is accompanying. The trouble is that they have time for just one rehearsal – on the day before the concert, and the score is incredibly complicated. They'll go through the whole programme just once, on the day of the concert, and that's it. To make things a bit easier for Uri I spent about 100 hours (I didn't count, but it was 2-3 hours a day for a few weeks!) correcting the orchestral score which was, of course, full of errors. (…) But the piece is so difficult that bits and pieces of it can look unplayable! What will I do if, on the day before the concert, the orchestra announces that it can't be played?

Everyone is getting nervous: Radu, who plays the piano part phenomenally, Uri, the orchestra, the impresario, the publisher of the score, and I. But I am nervous for a completely different reason! (…) Imagine that I received two tickets for the world premiere with the following note: 'At the concert I imagine that you'd rather sit with anyone than me! Either way, let me know. I don't feel great, but you're probably feeling worse. Love, John.' I admitted that I'd prefer the seat next to mine to be empty because I'll be tense enough as it is, and I'll have to go on stage to take a bow. (…) Till now I've done well in John's eyes thanks to my negative strategy. The fact that I took the initiative in breaking off in some sense brought us closer. But I don't want a negative strategy, I don't want a strategy at all – I want to live and love spontaneously.

These are the things with which my mind is preoccupied, and everyone's sympathising because they think I'm getting nervous about the world premiere! Perhaps you'll have time to drop me a few words. From Sunday on I'll be in London again.

For the moment, bye, my most sincere congratulations on your story! I hug you, Basia, and Jurek, not in that order, but simultaneously. Maybe I'll send you a fragment of my autobiography soon…

Your A.

Warsaw, 3.11.75

Andrzej, dear Darling one,

I kept my fingers crossed on the 28th, but I didn't pluck up the courage to telephone, or telegraph, fearing that your post-concert date was still in progress and not wanting to interfere with it. Maybe your imagination is a bit too intense, or a bit single-tracked? (Basia says: 'The trouble with your generation is that the only things that matter to you are sex and money') Write soon and tell me how it went! Anyway, we both kiss you most tenderly on this (auspicious) occasion and congratulate you with all our hearts. In fact, Basia is longing to see you sometime; she claims that it's her 'last wish' (to see Naples and die).

I've been writing recently, but only verse and they're not at all good, so I'll spare you that. Generally speaking I've plenty of ideas for stories, but I can't get disentangled from everyday life, which is strangling me.

I envy you your solitude. I often have a longing to run away to the end of the world. Durrell writes that the best use one can find for a husband is to exploit him as a literary theme. It's a good idea but an unrealistic one while the marriage exists because husbands take up time and disturb the silence which is beautiful.

I kiss you. I need you.

Your

H.

Nedlands, 27.3.76

Darling,(…) I can't remember when I last wrote to you, so I'll give you some of the latest news. Thanks to Radu Lupu's brilliant performance, the Piano Concerto was astoundingly successful* and this so encouraged me that I completed the Second String Quartet in record time. Then I took a holiday so I could make a fair copy and write out the parts, and on my return was struck down with flu and bronchitis. This was exceptionally inconvenient since I'm supposed to be playing all 23 Mozart concertos, of which I know less than half! I'm learning them as best I can between rehearsals and performances. I'm enclosing the programme…

I've moved out of London and I'm looking at a run-down but pleasant little house outside Oxford (30 The Park, Cumnor, Berkshire), where I intend to move when I get back. But to be on the safe side send your reply here (Currie Hall, University of W. Australia, Nedlands, W.A. 6009 Australia), where I'll be staying till the end of May. After that I'm playing in Cape Town where at last they're allowing people of all races to go to the same concerts; in June I return to England.

How is Jurek? How's his hand? Is it anything to do with the boxing? Write to me, Funnyface, I'm a bit anxious about you.

Hugs to you, and to Basia and Jurek, too.

Your Andrzej.

Cumnor, 22.6.76

Halinka, my Darling,

On my return to England I found your penultimate letter and only now do I realise just how hard your life is. I so want to help you, even if it's a little! I'll most certainly invite Basia over. Though you write nothing about her problems, only about Jurek's illness, I can tell from the tone of your letter that she is going through a difficult time, too, and that must be a great burden to you because you are responsible for both him and her! I appreciate that you can't get away anywhere yourself: Jurek would go mad if you left him alone now and would crack up completely. Write in more detail about the whole of your present

---

* This is now catalogued as Tchaikowsky's second piano concerto but the composer himself did not think much of his earlier one (and he had written an even earlier one, since lost). Music critic Joan Chissell wrote in *The Times* (29 October 1975) that in the present time it was rare for well-known pianist also to be an accomplished composer '[So] Last night's premiere of the piano concerto No 1… by the eminent Polish-born pianist André Tchaikowsky, was an event.' Her lengthy review praised composer and soloist: 'Piano and orchestra are as closely integrated in a disciplined, purposeful argument as in the concertos of Brahms. (…) If nearer in spirit to composers of the Berg-Bartók era than the avant-garde, Tchaikowsky still speaks urgently enough in this work to make his idiom sound personal.' In his diary André expressed his surprise at 'the rave review' since this critic had apparently 'hardly ever found a good word for me as a pianist!'

situation. It must be very serious indeed if it has forced our Halinka into realism…

I, on the other hand, am so well-off it makes me ashamed. From the moment of my return to England I've been living in the country. The house is quiet, large (after the London apartment it seems to be palatial), the neighbours are nice but keep their distance, I can play as much and whenever I want to because my playing doesn't bother anyone. After work I go for walks, the area is beautiful and Oxford is scarcely 5 kilometres away. I practise three hours a day, compose a bit (…). I am sleeping much better than before and, most importantly, without drugs.

You wouldn't recognise me: I've put on weight, grown a beard and lost the rest of the hair on my head; apparently I look like Lenin. I think I've probably changed mentally, too: I'm calmer. In Australia I met Wanda Wiłkomirska, who is delightful and plays like an angel; she promised to get in touch with you so she'll describe me to you.

Write to me as soon as possible, even if it's just a few words. Write straight away telling me how I can help you and with what.

I hug you with all my heart,

Your Andrzej.


Cumnor, 18.7.76

Darling Funnyface,

I hope you've received my telegram and will reply to it immediately! My bank has been informed and is now waiting only for the precise details of where the money is to be despatched.

Judging from the photographs you sent, Basia has every chance of seducing me, and, from purely egotistical motives, I wish her every success in that venture! But I don't understand what her 'year-long solid preparations' consist of? Am I supposed to be preparing something, too? And how? (…) Seriously though I wouldn't want to disillusion a truly beautiful and delightful girl… (You, too, are beautiful and delightful: on one of the photos I couldn't be sure which one was you and which one was she).

I have only a poor quality cassette of the Concerto on which the brass and percussion instruments are the most clearly audible! It was recorded by Ann at the world premiere in the face of enormous difficulties because it's illegal to do it and Ann had to keep the recorder hidden in her handbag – she couldn't even take the microphone out. Maybe it will be possible to play it back onto a tape – if it is, then I'll send you a copy some time. Now I'm writing the first act of *The Merchant of Venice* (the second is finished).

My life and my work are coming along wonderfully. I feel so well and so calm that I'm almost scared.

I'll try to find Basia some work next year if she decides that seducing an elderly gent is insufficiently hard work for her! Will they teach her that in the convent? It must be a very progressive convent. I kiss you with all my heart, as always; Basia gets a kiss on account.

Your old

Andrzej.

Warsaw, 28.7.76

Darling Andrzej,

Many thanks for wanting to help us. Your remark about the progressive convent made me laugh. Do you know how Basia got there? Well, school lessons were boring her and she used to spend the time either with the hippies in the Old Town, or in a record shop close to the school. She used to go there, put on the earphones and the assistant grew accustomed to the fact that this young lady didn't buy records, just listened. Then Basia signed an agreement that if her grades were poor she would go to a convent school. So she went. If you're interested in the atmosphere of a convent school, then listen to a fragment of her letter:

'Mummy, sweetest! The retreat is finished. The first day there were masses said from dawn. Between times, so-called concentration period. The girls sat at a green table with lighted candles and discussed subjects to do with the Holy Book. I suggested, as a topic for discussion, "Coping with the reality of living in communist Poland" by offering up a quote from Jacek Gula's poem "A rose in a motionless orgasm, my youth a severed hand" but my proposal met with no enthusiasm. The world here is all medieval prints. During the "concentrations" songs are sung about miraculous conversions. My friend with the face of Beethoven looks at me meaningfully. She says that atheists can't be happy. During meals Sister Mary reads mystic romances about women who became nuns. A girl called Ziuta. Sister Mary read Ziuta's advice on how to spend time usefully while watching a bad film. That is, in time to the words flowing from the screen one should pray for the director, the actors, and the audience that's being bored. (…)

'I look out of the window. I see a strange metamorphosis. Warm air spills out into the yard and returns. As if an impressionist picture had come alive. A mass of crazy little worms…'

And so on. At the end Basia swims out of reality 'amidst rhythmic gentle splashes'. That's her favourite pastime. But all's well that ends well, and thanks to the patient kindness of the Sisters she returned after 4 months pleased, happy, because virtually all her grades were excellent.

I'm finishing now, and kissing you,

Your H.

POSTCARD OF ABINGDON LOCK, RIVER THAMES, LONDON

4.8.76

My Darling, Everything's all right!

There are no dollars here, so I'm sending you 100 pounds (170 dollars, more or less). Look out for them when you get back, maybe they're already there. Let me know if there are any difficulties.

Would you like me to send you both a new photograph of myself? It's just that I fear Basia might call the visit off…

Meantime, I hug you both, it's safer that way.

Your Andrzej.


Warsaw, 5.8.76

Sweet, Darling Andrzej,

Many thanks for the letter, the postcard, and the cash. Not only have you freed me from my debts, but you have also made me feel rich for the first time in my life! Jurek also thanks you because now that he is the husband of a rich wife he will be able to devote himself to the pursuit of his artistic passions. He and a certain young cameraman are shooting a political film about vampires in a blood-donor clinic. There the vampires can feed themselves without using their fangs – they take it straight from the bottles. They dance with joy when they see a platoon of soldiers marching in to give blood. The film ends with a humanitarian slogan: 'BECOME A BLOOD DONOR'. Perhaps you can tell me why this film is supposed to be political? It must be about your lot, 'the capitalist bloodsuckers'.

The young cameraman has worshipped Basia for the last year but she stubbornly maintains that she has never kissed him ('Mummy, maybe you kiss men you don't love, but…'). The cameraman's father likes Basia a lot, and because he's about to move into his new villa he offered them his old 6-roomed apartment. Basia, however, says that the six rooms would be useful only inasmuch as they would give her somewhere to run to to get away from the young cameraman.

And what about me? At present, following Durrell's instructions (about the use to which men can be put), I am writing a work called 'A chronicle of marital happenings'. Basia tells me that Bergman has already written something along those lines and says I should read it or I might end up writing something identical… (…)

The notes are purely for self-therapy: the angelically kind and good Jurek is constantly driving me crazy – with his childishness and his lack of a sense of reality. Reality serves only to let him create false impressions of it. The consequences of that are frequently tragic and nearly always costly. In moments of extreme depression I repeat, just to calm myself, a charming fragment from *The Stormy Life of Lasik Roitschwantz*: a neighbour complains to Lasik Roitschwantz that he bought a cow which doesn't give milk. 'What is there to be angry about?' says Lasik. 'If that cow doesn't give milk then it's surely not because she doesn't want to give milk. It's because she can't give milk. Has that cow got any milk to give?'

Basia won't let me speak ill of Jurek. 'Please do not shout at my favourite man!' She also likes to dress him up in her own things. Jurek dresses up willingly and looks like a transvestite who begs outside the church (he, too, is wasted away and has a grey beard).

But enough confessions. Tell me, do you know and like the work of Carson McCullers? I'm reading her work for the second time, and for the second time I am deeply moved. (…)

I kiss you, Darling, and once again thank you for everything.

Your H.

London, 26.8.76

Darling Funnyface,

I'm glad you received my letter and my card, but has the cash arrived yet? (…) You have nothing to thank me for, I'm just glad that for once in my life I've been useful to you! (…)

Apropos Carson McCullers, I know and admire *The Member of the Wedding*, and on your recommendation I shall now buy some other novels of hers. What would you advise particularly? I know nothing about her life – yesterday I looked for some biography of her but found nothing. Why was her life 'uncanny'? You write that there is no woman in literature who can write like her and who understood life so well. Do you know *Wuthering Heights* by Emily Brontë? In my view, that is the most wonderful English novel ever; Conrad is nowhere compared with that…

I am at present reading only German, or rather Schweizerdeutsch, because I've started with Frisch and Dürrenmatt. Maybe I'll finally get to learn that dreadful language! Sollen wir vielleicht unseren Briefwechsel auf Deutsch weiterführen?* I close in confusion, afraid that you'll take me seriously.

I hug you and kiss you,

Your Andrzej.

PS. I forgot to mention I was completely flabbergasted by Basia's reaction. Don't tell her, naturally, but the reason I sent her the photograph was to

---

* Maybe we should continue our correspondence in German?

*discourage* her and so that the three of us (with you) could have a good laugh at the suggested seduction. Now it seems that I am beautiful! Somehow nobody here has noticed that. Still, blood is thicker than water: knowing the perseverance she's inherited from you, I accept Basia's sentence and resolve meekly. She'll get what she wants: either she will do it herself or she will produce a baby who will, at the early age of five, for inescapable genetic reasons fall head over heels in love with me and will be the prop of my lascivious old age.

I hug you and kiss you masses of times, share them with Basia…

Your old, as well as 'mature, virile, extraordinary'

Andrzej.

Warsaw, 5.11.76

Darling Andrzej,

We both laughed at the futuristic visions you described in your letter, but he who laughs last… We've nothing to laugh about, truth to tell. Lili examined Jurek (God, just as she once examined Tosio) and said: 'There's something nasty in the right lung, I'll have to wait for the X-rays.' And, according to her, the X-rays showed 'a tumourous mass in the right lung which requires precise examination.' Jurek went into hospital yesterday with suspected God-knows-what. Meanwhile I've managed to contract pneumonia and Basia is commuting between hospital and home in the role of a sister of mercy.

As for Jurek's illness, I have the worst possible forebodings: he has lost 20 kilos in weight, he's getting thinner all the time even though he has an excellent appetite. Just one thing about Basia: she wrote you a letter which, in its entirety, read as follows: 'My dear and wonderful Andrzej – Basia.' I told her the letter was too short. (…) So she got down to writing you another letter but it transpired that she has lost your photograph and searching for it is taking up all the time she has left spare from caring for her bedridden family.

So now you know everything and all that remains for me to do is to kiss you.

Your H.

Cumnor, 16.11.76

Oh, Funnyface, I'm so worried about you!

Drop me a few more words to let me know you're better. It makes me sad that I can't help you, merely, at best, entertain you, and so I've decided to send you two chapters of that wretched autobiography of mine after all. It'll be a photocopy of the manuscript, so you can keep it, but don't show it to anyone else yet because, as you'll realise immediately, I touch on some embarrassing subjects.

All this secrecy will probably amuse you because if I ever finish it and publish it, then any fool will be able to read it! Yes, but then it will be a *book*; reading a manuscript is like eavesdropping on neighbours who are arguing on the other side of the wall.

In January I'm leaving for another long tour (Hong Kong, Bangkok, Singapore, New Zealand, and, for geographically incomprehensible reasons, Venezuela), so I'll probably start scribbling something in aeroplanes; in March I'll be taking a vacation which I intend to spend quietly somewhere in New Zealand, so I'll have time to write.

Since I've moved here my rate of composition has accelerated. Lately I've managed to combine it with practising because I can get up earlier, play for about three hours, and write in the evenings. I've written half of the first act since June. Now, however, I really will have to stop for nearly a month because I'm giving seven concerts in the course of three weeks: Ravel's Concerto for the Left Hand, Beethoven's C major and Mozart's E flat major K 271 (perhaps you remember me learning that in Warsaw?) and four recitals with two different programmes. I'll be in England till the end of November, then I have a quick trip to Denmark and Belgium, and I return home December 10th.

Every two or three days I take the bus into Oxford, which enchants me and at the same time amuses me. Let me give you an example.

I'm standing in a pub and I'm reading the posters: LOVE AND HATE with the Dionysiacs. 8.15 tonight, Harper Room, Jesus College.

I look at my watch – 8.10. I know Jesus College, it's virtually opposite the pub. What can it be? The word 'Dionysiacs' suggests wine and orgies; thank God I had a bath before I came out. For a moment I feel slightly apprehensive: what if this turns out to be some pop group? Well, that won't matter, I'll simply slip out and still catch the 8.35 bus home. And they can't bar me because if it was for students only they wouldn't have put up the poster! Reassured and courageous, I walk across to Jesus College, find the Harper room, take a seat.

I look around: young, pleasant faces, with no electric guitars or microphones, the majority of guests (or is it members?) holding books in their hands – I've obviously struck lucky. A quarter of an hour later a fellow with a beard strides in: first of all he apologises for being late, then he apologises for opening proceedings in English. I stare at him: is he a lunatic? But he looks normal enough. It soon transpires that I've come to a discussion about love and hate in ancient Greece – in Greek! The poster forbore to mention that detail.

What can I do? I can't leave because the chair I'm sitting on is in the corner of the room diametrically opposite the door, so I'd have to push my way through a crowd of students who, following my entrance, have made themselves comfortable all over the floor. For no good reason I desperately need a pee – it must be the nerves. But the worst of it is that this is an open discussion so at any moment someone might ask me, in Greek, what I think of love and hate in ancient Greece. In reply I'll have to gesticulate a great deal to prove to them that, despite linguistic difficulties, I'd have felt quite at ease in Plato's company…

From time to time somebody apparently makes a joke because everyone laughs; I laugh, too. I find it harder not to laugh when they are serious… Somehow, I managed to sit through to the end of the discussion and then I was enrolled as a member of the society. For just one pound I shall receive essays in Greek for a whole year. That's quite a bargain: how much would Socrates have had to pay for the English press?

They've finished the photocopying so I'll end now and send you everything together. Give my regards to Jurek, and I hug you and Basia without the least restraint.

Your Andrzej.

Colombo, 6.1.77

Darling Funnyface,

Well, at last I have some time to write a few words. I'm on my way to Colombo where, on Sunday, I'll be playing for the Samaritans. The Samaritans are always in need of cash because they have to pay for the rent, the telephone bills, advertising (people often commit suicide because they don't know that there is someone in their town to whom they can always turn), the facilities to offer their guests tea or some tranquillisers, postage and telegrams etc. And this is where I can come in useful because from time to time I give a recital for their benefit (the next one will be in England in April) which brings them some money and, at the same time, publicity. The guy who set it up is called Chad Varah and he's one of my best friends; I could write you a separate letter all about him.

What next? Hong Kong, Bangkok, Singapore (unless this last is cancelled because the impresario there has disappeared and has apparently been seen recently selling matches in England) and, as virtually every year, New Zealand. I'll be staying a whole month there, from 24th January to the end of February, so I hope you'll write to me there.

First of all, tell me how Jurek is. It's idiotic that they're not letting him work. When he has had a rest, and is feeling better, then I'm sure they'll let him work again especially as medical theories are constantly changing! In Mexico, sore throats are treated with tomato compresses applied to the toes.

Secondly, how are you feeling? While Jurek is ill, you have to be well otherwise who'll look after him and Basia? It is very important to want to be well. My granny, with whom I have recently become reconciled and with whom I heartily sympathise (I would even like to write the next chapter of my autobiography from her point of view), had a heart attack in 1938. The doctors told her to take some drops, to rest, to stop worrying about things because any exertion or anxiety might instantly bring on a new, and much more serious, attack. Then, as you know, came the war; I don't have to tell you how granny had time to rest then. But the next attack didn't come till 1947, that is to say, not before she could spare the time to have it.

Thirdly, Basia. I'd like to know who is going to seduce me, and is it essential for her to have passed her exams to do it? (…) I won't send her a photograph of myself just now because I don't want her to get agitated during her exams; but I am sending you all a tape of one of my concerts which the BBC broadcast live and of which Stephen made a cassette. In the first half of the concert I played Rakhmaninov's Rhapsody, in the second Ravel's Concerto for the Left Hand.

Funnyface, I'm inordinately curious about your unexpected reaction to the fragments of autobiography I sent you. Why, specifically, is what I wrote 'abnormal'? Do you mean the events were abnormal, or is it my reaction to them? I certainly agree with the former. Darling, I'm sorry that I made you cry, but since that is what you felt, *share it with me*. Anyway, it's thanks to your encouragement alone that I shall be trying to do some work on it again during this trip…

Seriously, do write. I have few close friends (apart from you, precisely three, and I've lately been having serious difficulties with one of them); I rarely feel lonely because I've constantly got my nose stuck in a book or a score, but you cannot imagine what an important event it is every time I get a letter from you, how much I look forward to it. Whenever I am overwhelmed with joy at the sight of your handwriting on an envelope I sometimes even suspect that, subconsciously, I might have been lonely after all… But don't worry about me because I am playing, composing, orchestrating, writing a journal and letters, messing about with my autobiography from time to time; I read a lot, I'm learning German strenuously, so with all of that, I don't have time to be bored

I hug all three of you very warmly,

Your

Andrzej.

Christchurch, 13.2.77

Darling Funnyface,

Are you absolutely certain that after your surgery* you really were clinically dead and it wasn't simply a nightmare hallucination brought on, very logically, by a lack of oxygen? I have a friend who studied this matter very thoroughly but after 16 interviews assured me (he is, in fact, writing a thesis about it) that after-death experiences are, without exception, unusually pleasant: people levitate, swim, feel an enormous liberation from feelings of guilt and all complexes and feel enormous resentment towards the doctors and nurses who have saved them. Maybe all it means is that they went straight to heaven, whereas you… Don't be angry.

Talking about the autobiography: the fact is I did get that prize for the poem (I can still remember how live, healthy mothers sobbed at the public reading of that poem), but the whole of the conversation with mother is invented. Twenty years later, under psychoanalysis, I came to realise that I resented my mother's death greatly because she *could* have saved herself: granny had prepared false papers, a hiding place etc., but she didn't do it because of my stepfather Albert: she didn't have the heart to leave him in the ghetto.

So because I now know what I thought in 1946 about my mother *subconsciously*, I have used it as a counterpoint to that hideous and vulgar poem for which, to this day, I cannot forgive myself! Otherwise I would be ashamed even to write about this episode. (…)

Send your reply to the following address: Avon Motorlodge, Christchurch, New Zealand, where I shall be from February 25th to March 10th. From April Fools' Day I shall be at home but write back *immediately* and then – write again!

I hug you most warmly,

Your Andrzej.

Los Angeles, 24.3.77

Funnyface, what's happening? You've written just enough to terrify me, but considerably too little for me to be able to make any kind of reply. Do try and write, and I'll do the best I can to cheer you up. After all, you're not alone in the world…

I'll be home again in a week's time. I'm ready to do everything possible to make things easier for you somehow, but you must help me in that yourself

---

* Halina had written to André about her operation in December reporting that she had experienced clinical death followed by intense anxiety and inability to eat

just a little! Write one sentence a day for a week: in seven sentences one can say something, then write the address as an extra and send it to me. Surely you can do that much for me?

I hug you most warmly, Jurek and Basia as well,

Your Andrzej.

Warsaw, 3.3.77

Most Darling Andrzej: don't worry about me any more. I was, in fact, in a terrible state. I simply went crazy after those few hours of recovering from surgery. When I have my fearful attacks, I'm ready to jump out of the window. But I won't jump; I'll live a little longer. I'll see you again.

I kiss you very much,

Your H.

PS. I've written seven sentences, just as you wanted.

Cumnor, 8.4.77

Darling Funnyface, *at last!* I really was worried about you. You have no idea how much I admire the fact that in these circumstances you've pulled yourself together – personally, I'd never have been able to do it (added to which you've cleared your debts, with no help!). I am proud of you, your courage and energy: is it something one can learn?

I'm sending Jurek a card. If he writes back, I'll willingly correspond with him further.

(…) In New Zealand, they recorded two of my concerts, the last Mozart and the Beethoven C major. But as far as I remember (I haven't listened to the tapes yet) they weren't very good. In the Mozart the orchestra was poor (they were very tired because it was their last concert); in the Beethoven, sitting in the front row was a lunatic who kept making terrifying faces throughout and who, immediately after my first entrance, stood up and came over to the piano. This so frightened me that I stopped playing completely for half a bar or so! But if it would amuse you, I could send you those recordings, too.

I've neglected my autobiography somewhat, in part because I started to write five chapters simultaneously of which I have not finished even one (of course), but mainly because I have lately been so divinely happy that I wanted to live and enjoy the present day and not mess about in the misty past... Something has happened which I had been dreaming about for many years and which I had abandoned hope for even in my dreams. I feel ashamed to write to you about it at this precise moment! But this happiness has stayed with me and I can always tell you about it. If it should interest you I could make a photocopy of four pages from my diary (which I have been writing for a few years) and from that one fragment you'll learn everything…

Life has suddenly become easier: work, relationships with people, even getting to sleep… (…)

Darling, keep writing about everything, about your own health, about Basia, about Jurek; be in constant contact with me. Congratulations that, despite everything, you are so bravely and wonderfully keeping together!

I hug you with all my heart,

Your Andrzej.

Warsaw, 27.4.77

Darling Andrzej, both your letters have finally wandered their way here (one has been wandering about for thee weeks, and the other for four). They are so lovely, just as your letters always are.

Basia is going across to you at the beginning of July. She is taking with her the historical 100 pounds which you sent to us that time, so her stay shouldn't ruin you. I can tell you that you can buy 15 thousand kilograms of bread for £100 here, so over a period of 10 months one could, for that money, consume 50 kilograms of bread each day! If you keep bestowing scholarships to Switzerland and keep inviting young ladies for holidays to England, you may end up bankrupt, in which case you can come over to me at a moment's notice and I'll guarantee you food to the tune of 15 kg of bread daily; in addition – and this will please you even more – I will move out of my apartment and let you stay here so you can compose in peace.

Darling, I read the 1942 chapter of your autobiography with Staś: he laughed, I cried, so perhaps it was intended to be a Chaplinesque piece? The chapter is written from a double perspective: the way you experienced it at the time, and how you see it now, from a distance. From the first point of view, everything is justified because you are describing a child's feelings, which are direct, literal, tragic, comic; but looking at it from a distance what is needed is just one line, even if it's a humorous one, explaining how hard-pressed St. Monica was when she gave you shelter. If this chapter appeared in print in its present form it would create international ructions, much as Kosinski's book did in its time. St. Monica, whose one human trait is her pregnancies, would develop into an unfortunate international symbol. And I doubt if that would be just.

Besides which you let your imagination run away with you, and that detracts from the realism of certain otherwise splendid and very dramatic scenes. E.g. in the argument between granny and Monica, the sentence which granny utters: 'Monica, just think how you'll look when the Germans hang you upside down' (when they discover she has been concealing a Jewish child) is quite impossible. That's you, seeing in your imagination a woman you already hated hanging with her skirt round her head and showing her dirty knickers, but your granny could not have seen that then, fighting as she was to save your life and using threats inspired in her by a desperate fear (…).

I have no time for anything at the moment. My doctor's certificate following the ghastly neurosis has expired, but the disease lingers on and I have to skip work to go for therapy. I'm still taking psychotropic drugs. I work seven hours a day, then visit Jurek in hospital, then return home where I am now living with a mother-in-law who is perpetually in tears. Finally, it's bed where I constantly dream about death.

Jurek guesses nothing. He is enormously brave. He reads a lot, talks, laughs, cracks jokes.

I'll send you the Bulgakov and Kubin's *The Other Side* soon – I don't like sick literature at the moment because I am sick inside myself and I am holding on by my finger-nails.

For me, the most wonderful medicines of all are your letters. I'm not writing that just to play the flirt: yesterday, when I came back from work, I had dreadful pins and needles in my hands (which always presages an anxiety attack in me), but when I read your letter everything cleared up without any pills – something which has not been happening lately.

I kiss you, my good doctor, and thank you for everything.

Your H.

Cumnor, 6.5.77

Darling Funnyface,

Forgive me, but I simply can't reply to your letter at present! I've been rushed off my feet this last week, I haven't even managed to get to a piano for three days, and tomorrow I leave for Amsterdam for two days. I'll reply to your exceptionally wise letter when I return, but meanwhile I just wanted to reassure you that you can send Basia to me without worrying. Don't be concerned about cash because Stefan Askenase has lent me more than £1000 till the end of September which is enough to pay the taxes and the most pressing debts (or, in Poland, to buy 150,000 kg of bread). The one thing I'm not sure of is where to place Basia. How good is her English? Would she prefer to spend more time in London or in Oxford? I suspect hers is the kind of intelligence which, like ours, is not suited to practical matters. That's the one thing that disturbs me because, to be frank, I won't have time to look after her. I'll invite her to dinner or lunch once or twice, I'll show her round Oxford, I'll introduce her to a couple of people I myself like, but then I'll get down to composing and I fear she'll be bored silly then. What do you advise me to do? After all, I can't abandon the child in some hotel. Yet I will have to abandon her, I'll be able to see her only from time to time…

You write with amazing perspicacity about the autobiography – I'll write to you on that subject in a few days. Meanwhile you should know just one thing – you're right! With one exception: granny was never ashamed or afraid of anything or anyone. Those two emotions were simply alien to her. During the war granny used to have rows not just with the people who were concealing me, but with the Germans! On my return from Amsterdam I'll give you a few examples which I can't even use in the book because no one would believe them.

For the moment I hug you with all my heart, Basia too, and poor Jurek (if it weren't for Jurek I'd invite both you and Basia together, but I appreciate that you can't leave him at this time!).

I love you, and sympathise,

Your Andrzej.

Cumnor, 9.5.77

Funnyface, I've found Basia a place! I've rented a room for her from July with my neighbours the Allisons. They're very nice people, they won't instruct her or bother her. She'll eat at my place – I'll give her a key and she'll eat what and when she wants, sometimes with me, sometimes without. She'll have those famous £100 for pin money (one does not live by bread alone, regardless of its quantity). (…)

And now, coming back to my autobiography, a few examples of granny's courage:

1) One of my numerous aunts had exceptionally Semitic features and a Volksdeutsch arrested her in the street. Granny went to the prison (I don't know which one) and made a savage row: 'But she is my cousin! I've known her since she was a child. Have you got the effrontery to suggest that there are Jewish women in our family?' I wouldn't believe it either if my aunt hadn't told me this herself.

2) During the Uprising of 1944, our house was taken over by the insurgents, and then by the Germans. They led us out into the yard, ordered us to stand facing the wall with our hands in the air, and pushed us along using riflebutts in our backs (I'm not sure if it was the butts because I didn't look round). We all thought this was the end: someone started to pray. Then granny said, in a calm, dispassionate voice: 'Don't be afraid, Darling, it's only a moment.'

3) A few days later, I fell ill in the camp near Pruszków. Granny went to the officer and said, in German: 'My child must have immediate medical attention. That's what you're here for – to take care of it. What are you waiting for? Do you want me to complain to the kommandant?' – and they drove me to the hospital immediately!

Besides which, granny loved having rows, regardless of the situation, for purely theatrical reasons. If she truly can't tell Monica what she'll look like in the Mussolini position, then the whole chapter will have to be changed because a sentence like '… especially as unwanted children are your speciality' would, in this situation, be even more insulting.

Granny's entire attitude relied on not allowing the danger to penetrate her consciousness, even though she had already lost both children in this time! But she truly didn't let it penetrate, just like me – I didn't miss my mother in the whole of this time, she didn't even enter my mind.

Now, however, I have abandoned irony and I am writing the year 1947 from granny's point of view – basing it on what she did not say because she was always hysterical about trivial matters, but when she talked about her own real tragedy she did it in such a banal way, it was as if she had read it in some cheap novel. You have no idea how sorry I am for her today. The fact that they killed her children isn't even the worst: the crux of the matter is that she didn't die herself. And what did she live for? Nobody wanted her, I least of all. But she did live, unwanted, sick, chronically exhausted, without hope, without a moment's rest.

You probably feel just like that now yourself, do you? Funnyface, I would so like to calm you down, cheer you up, hug you… At least everyone likes you because you are enchanting, intelligent, full of originality, imagination, sense of humour, but granny didn't have so much as one of these qualities: she was fat, ugly, stupid, vulgar, hysterical, shameless – and brave… infinitely brave. Maybe I'll succeed in describing that. I'll send you the chapter when I've finished it.

Darling, if you haven't sent Bulgakov's *The Master and Margarita* yet, then don't because I have it in an English translation! This must be the most brilliant Russian novel since Dostoevsky. If you know of any greater praise than that, tell me.

Be an angel, write back immediately. With every letter you become closer to me. Is it you who are changing, or I?

I hug you tightly, tightly.

Your Andrzej.

PS. Give Basia a hug from me, too, and Jurek; I don't have the heart to wish him good health.

Warsaw, 1.6.77

Darling Andrzej, yesterday, your very first music teacher, Miss Emma Altberg, sent me some compositions you wrote as a child and dedicated to her. They look so terrifying that I'm not sure if Richter himself would be capable of performing them. Basia will take the manuscript over to you and it will make you laugh, you'll see. Miss Altberg is ill, asks after you frequently, and, when she hears of your triumphs, is extremely pleased.

How are things with you? Have you got down to composing yet?

To pay you back for those chapters about your childhood, I'm sending you a fragment of my own childhood memories; it's a cutting from a weekly which published this essay (it was a competition called *My first love* – I got a distinction, which I tell you with pride). Everything you'll read in it is true with the exception of one tiny detail: the episode where the old woman's finger was shot off through the wall as she was knitting happened not to my father but to a drunken cousin of mine. (…)

Finally, as for Basia's arrival, I beg you don't put yourself out for her, don't feel responsible for anything, nor tied down. Don't judge by appearances and think she is shy, helpless and needs care. Basia is more capable and independent that the pair of us put together.

I sign off now and kiss you most warmly,

Your H.

Cumnor, 15.6.77

Darling Funnyface,

I haven't actually got time to write but I want to thank you quickly for your nice letter and the charming humoresque! I don't know how one laughs fit to burst, but I must have been close to bursting because the neighbours came over to find out what was making me laugh so loudly. I asked if any of them knitted. None of them did. 'That's good', I said, 'because it's a very dangerous pastime.' They looked at one another with terror and left in silence. (…)

Darling, please send me Miss Emma's address. I think of her now with great gratitude which in those days I couldn't even feel, let alone show! What sort of illness does she have? For God's sake, how old is she? I mean, she was already grey when she was teaching me the C major scale, or at least she became grey towards the end of the lesson. In fact, to this day I can't play scales, so poor Miss Emma went grey in vain…

I solemnly promise you that I won't worry one bit about Basia. I do, however, often worry about you… But you must ask Basia not to look after me, either, then we shall surely have a great time together.

When are you going to write your autobiography?
I hug you all with all my heart.
Your old

Andrzej.

Cumnor 3.6.77

Darling Funnyface,

Enormous thanks both for the letter and for the books! I'm truly moved by the fact that in your present situation you still manage to make the effort to write to me. I am equally grateful to you for the astonishingly objective description of Basia: you don't advertise her good points, which hardly ever happens amongst mothers (not to mention amongst Jewish mamas). Thanks to you I feel that I now know Basia and I agree with you that I have nothing to fear.

But there could well be one complication. Basia is not the only maiden who is coming to see me in July. I'll describe her rival briefly.

Do you by any chance remember the French pianist, Monique Duphil, who stayed with me in Warsaw in 1955? Her fiancé, the talented violinist Maurice Hasson, was with her then. Shortly after that visit she married him, which proved not to be a good idea. She emigrated to Venezuela with him and gave birth to two daughters, Ondine and Ariadne. Then they divorced, he married again and is now living in London. Monique and her daughters stayed in Venezuela.

Towards the end of March, on my way back from New Zealand, I gave a recital in Caracas and spent a few days in their house. I liked the whole family: her, her second husband (I'm not sure he is her husband, but he loves her and looks after her), and both daughters. But most of all I liked Ondine, for two reasons: first, she reminds me of John, from whom I had to part recently; secondly, she adores French literature, a passion she can't share with anyone in Caracas! (I experience the same deprivation in England.) When she learned that this Polish pianist with a British passport knows, by heart, all her favourite poems, the tragedies of Racine etc., Ondine nearly went out of her mind: seeing me off at the airport, she wanted to accompany me to England and stayed in Caracas only because she didn't have her passport with her!

A few days ago she phoned me from Caracas and told me her father had invited her for a holiday and had paid her for the flight; so she would come over in July if I were in England then! Pleasantly surprised, I said of course I will be.

Now you can see what lies in store. (…) I consider that Basia ought to know about this in advance; I hope that despite this she will come, but I also hope that she won't sulk, won't be jealous, and won't make reproaches. (…) I'd like to get to know her, I'll probably like her, but one can't guarantee that in advance! And I already like Ondine. Now show Basia this letter.

I hope you won't be angry, both of you. You must both know in advance that at the first scene of jealousy or any other reproaches I'll immediately break off relations with Basia (which would be easy for me in that there is nothing to break off at the moment!).

Forgive the brutal tone of this letter; I prefer to be brutal now rather than later, and the very last thing I want is to lay a trap for your daughter (it's only now that I realise that our misunderstandings in London in '69 were my fault because I was pulling the wool over your eyes). Knowing myself a little better now I even suspect that I like Ondine because, hitherto, she hasn't frightened me! And if she tries to frighten me then maybe I'll throw her out of my house, and then I'll be crying in Basia's arms. And what can one do with such a fool?

I started writing this letter in a jolting train out of London, continued to write it in a convulsive bus and I fear that after all that epilepsy it is now illegible!

Write back if only to prove that that's not so.

As for Jurek, what I fear most is the moment when he realises what is wrong with him. I don't know if it's going to be worse for him or for you, because one can't even begin to imagine such things. If you didn't have to be with him, I'd simply force you to come over just to give yourself a rest…

I hug you with all my heart,

Your Andrzej.

Kąty Wrocławskie, 15.6.77

Darling Andrzej, I'm with Jurek at his house near Wrocław. I don't know what's happening in your world, but we are spending our time here pleasantly, cheerfully: we take walks, we talk, we read, we make love – we are living for the present. The ghastliest moments are those when, cuddling up to him, I suddenly imagine him dressed in black, pale, lying motionless in an open coffin.

Have you heard of Halina Poświatowska? Lutosławski wrote music to some of her poems. She suffered from heart trouble, died very young; she lost her husband – like her, he had heart disease. I'll copy out two of her poems for you:

*I Remember*

If you die
I won't put on the lilac dress
won't buy coloured wreaths
with the whispered wind in their ribbons
none of that
nothing

the hearse will come – it will
the hearse will leave – it will
I'll stand in the window – I'll watch
I'll wave my hand
flutter my handkerchief
say goodbye
in that window alone

and in the summer
in lunatic May
I'll lie down on the grass
on its warmth
and with my hands I'll touch your hair
and with my lips I'll touch the bees' fur
its stinging beauty
like your smile
like dusk

then it will be silvery – golden
maybe golden and only red
because that dusk
that wind
which stubbornly whispers to the grass
love – love
will not let me rise and go
just like that
to a cursedly empty house

*A Poem for Me*

Hala Halinka
don't be afraid
you have such lovely lips
and such eyes you know –
you'll shut your lovely lips tight
you'll close your lovely eyes
and fold your hand into a tiny fist
Hala Halinka
you had a dress with polka dots
you did
you liked to ring your coral beads
you did

and the town that comes at night
you loved – yes
look – it's not so distant after all
they call it – heaven
look – it's quite near
they call it – night
and you – will return to that town
you'll blossom with this name
on those lips
Hala Halinka
it's time to go now
so come.

And I'll copy out one more poem for you:

There's a whole earth of solitude
and only one nugget of your smile

There's a whole sea of solitude
your tenderness in it like a forlorn bird

There's a whole heaven of solitude
and only one angel in it
with wings as weightless as your words

Kiss you. H.

Warsaw, 26.6.77

Darling Andrzej, I've just returned from Jurek's. He's feeling better because they've drained a litre of water from his pleura and he's breathing a bit now. As a consequence he's planning to spend a vacation in Golden Sands and to make a film about the boy scouts during the Warsaw Uprising. You write that the worst moment will be when he realises… Well, I'm convinced he's known about it for a long time. But the farce that we are playing out for him is something he somehow needs to enter into too… the same double awareness that each of us healthy people has. After all, we know that we'll die but – privately – we also know that it's 'always someone else who dies', not we.

At the end of his book *The Last Journey*, Andrzej Banach includes a letter from his dead wife, Ela Banach. The letter is so shattering that I quickly gave the book to someone as a present because every time I looked at it I cried like an idiot. He, too, played out a farce in front of her and she helped him do it. In the posthumous letter she explains why it was better to maintain this mutual deception.

After each hour-long attack of coughing Jurek thanks me for everything and says: 'I know there's nothing that can be done to help me.' When he is feeling better he works on the screenplay of a film he is writing about the children in the Uprising. It was just the same with Tosio. He said goodbye to me in exactly the same way, but when he felt better he talked about a screenplay dealing with our house which is 'an ant hill' teeming with thousands of people: an abundance of drunkenness, misfortune, suicide, and even homicide. As you can see, the only thing that changes is the subject of the films that will never be made.

I've just read your letter about Ondine and Basia. My immediate reaction was to reply curtly: 'Don't worry yourself about Basia, it wouldn't cross her mind to fall in love with you and to compete with the beautiful Ondine. Basia will cope very well on her own.' On reflection, however, I came to the conclusion that the question is much more serious because it's to do with your own inner conflict, which I've written about before. You suffer from the Tonio Kröger complex. The fact that Tonio couldn't be loved by the fair-haired, blue-eyed Ingeborg, for whom at root he felt a touch of contempt, made him feel sad and helpless. He couldn't be 'ordinary' and felt humiliated by that. He understood that this 'handicap' was the price he had to pay for his art, he was a great writer, but he couldn't console himself with that. You, too, long for that 'ordinariness' and you want to be 'the same as the others', but it's my profoundest conviction that you'll never even try to become that. You prefer to think like Tigger in *Winnie-the-Pooh*: 'Tiggers can fly, only they don't want to.' And the love of women confirms you in your conviction. You don't even know how much you need their idolatry, which you are such a genius at provoking. I don't know if all the women are as grateful for your 'mental seduction' as I am, because I consider that what there is between us is the best thing that has happened in my life. I don't know how things will turn out with Ondine and Basia, or rather I do know, but I won't tell you because what would be the point?

If Basia becomes an irksome guest she'll leave immediately and go to London which is where her 25-year-old cousin Anat lives (Anat married when she was eighteen, divorced when she was nineteen – and when she was twenty she received a state prize for a book about her unsuccessful marriage!).

Kiss you, Darling,

Your H.

Cumnor, 28.6.77

Darling Funnyface,

Both letters from Wrocław arrived today. I'm very moved, but at the same time horrified, by Jurek's optimism. He's a poor child who doesn't know anything about things! He won't be able to visit me this year; he'll write his next letter by himself; he wants to make the film within a year! Only now am I beginning to comprehend the horror with which you must listen to these dreams, nodding all the time. And you have to lie constantly, lie out of love, which is surely a contradiction in terms! I don't know who I sympathise with most – though probably Jurek because, after all, what's waiting for him is the very worst thing possible, but I certainly admire you more and more.

Poświatowska's poems seem to me to be absolutely marvellous – the second one especially moved me close to tears. I wouldn't dare to translate them – in my view poetry simply cannot be translated because its rhythm and sound is no less important than its meaning – nor to write music to them because why spoil such masterpieces? But do send me a small volume of Poświatowska's work, or give Basia a copy to bring with her.

Funnyface, if it's not too expensive I'd very much like to ask you for another present. Is it possible to obtain a pocket score of Szymanowski's *Stabat Mater* in Poland? I think it's probably his masterpiece. I'm asking you for it partly because I know that you'll be showering me with presents for the whole of your life so at least I'll be making the choice easier for you.

I'm sending you this fragment of the memoir but it must stay between the two of us. If there's something you don't understand don't ask anyone, I'll clarify it for you.

I'll write to Jurek now, give Basia a hug from me; I cuddle you and kiss your tear-decked eyes…

Your Andrzej.


POSTCARD: MAORI WAR DANCE (HAKA), NEW ZEALAND

Oxford, 5.7.77

Funnyface, many thanks for your fascinating letter, I'll maybe reply to it even today, but for the time being I'm sending you my telephone number: Cumnor 3730. Is anyone going to meet Basia at the airport? If not, then maybe I'll manage to get out and collect her, but I must have the day and the flight number (as usual, of course, I'm not promising anything). I'm very pleased she's coming, and I am extremely devoted to your letters!

Love you, Andrzej.

Cumnor, 5.7.77

Darling Funnyface, I sent you a postcard a moment ago because it really will get to you more quickly, and now I'm replying, albeit briefly, to your letter. It stunned me and moved me, all the more since I was afraid I had upset you both and that Basia would take offence and not come; there were times when I wondered whether you might not, by any chance, be jealous… It seems I didn't know you and didn't give you enough credit, while you know me eerily well, and give me too much credit.

Darling, in my thoughts I've been comparing myself with Tonio Kröger for 20 years. With him, and not with, for example, Aschenbach*. It's nothing to do with love, or at least not love alone, it's to do with something a great deal more universal and fundamental. I have quite simply never felt that I belong to anything, not just because others treat me like a curiosity (though that doesn't help), but most of all because I have never felt at home anywhere – neither among Poles, nor among Jews, nor among homosexuals. The more people wanted to join me to some group, the less I felt I had in common with them – everything isolated me somehow. And the constant admiration which, in my folly, I myself demanded meant that, in the end, I was human only for myself, but for others I was a giraffe or something of that sort.

And you understood all that! Recently this feeling has abandoned me. I have somehow found my place in the world. That's exactly what I've described in that short fragment of the journal I sent you – did you receive it?

Kiss you with tender gratitude.

Give Basia and Jurek a hug.

Your Andrzej.

Cumnor, 19.7.77

Darling Funnyface, I thank you with all my heart for the letter, the truly funny souvenirs, the cascade of fascinating presents, and most of all, of course, for Basia. She has just arrived this moment (it's 10.20 in the evening) and is taking a bath. While she was reading two letters from her cousin, I quickly read yours to me. Before this interlude Basia stared at me with eyes popping out of her head for a good five minutes; suddenly the thought that this might be her method of trying to seduce me made me suffer a sudden attack of laughter! I've opened a bottle of red wine, we'll be drinking your health in a moment. I'm worried about your disc… But then it is possible that this is how your organism is forcing you to take an essential rest. Other people use their holidays to go on

---

* The hero of Thomas Mann's *Death in Venice*

vacation, you go to Jurek's clinic where you constantly force yourself to make the pointless effort of lying to him, made all the more pointless by the fact that he is perfectly aware of everything! Maybe I should wish you just an iota of healthy egoism? I have too much of it, you not enough. In any case, until your disc is straightened out you must take care of yourself, for your own sake, for Basia's, even for Jurek's. And maybe a little for my sake, too?

Don't worry about me or about Basia – I'm a one-man school of independence. I won't take any notice of her at all and we'll both do very well out of it. Besides, I'll regularly tell you about everything in my letters.

I hug you with all my heart,

Your Andrzej.


Cumnor, 4.8.77

Darling Funnyface,

Thank you for your card, I'll send it on to Basia now, because she's already in London. You were right to say she is efficient, she's found a course, a job and a room in a student hostel at 205 Earl's Court Road. She arranged all that herself. To my frank question as to how she was fixed for money she replied equally frankly that she was 20 pounds short which I'll send her in the next few days.

I can't tell you about her because I didn't manage to make any contact with her. She has left one suitcase here so I'll probably see her again, but it's not certain. Despite your pleas I didn't manage to be nice to her at all because she ignored me completely: she didn't react to what I said, what I did, what I am, where I am, because Oxford didn't interest her, either, and she replied to my questions with remarks like: 'What am I supposed to say?' But since I forgive you for sending her to me, forgive me for getting rid of her after one week – it's obviously been of benefit to her.

So write to us separately – in any case, I nearly always reply to your letters on the same day, just like today!

Hug you and kiss you,

Your Andrzej.


Cumnor, 16.8.77

My Darling Funnyface,

(...) Don't worry in the least about Basia – she phoned from London yesterday; she's in a good mood because she's met some 'weird' people (in her lexicon it is, I suspect, the highest compliment and the very fact that she's talking about something must be evidence of extreme enthusiasm). She's working as a waitress in an American restaurant, she's extended her visa for another two months, and she's refused my loan of 20 pounds because, she claims, she was extremely well paid at her previous, Turkish, restaurant. She's found time to work in a laundry – you must admit that, for a fortnight, this is some record.

For me, on the other hand, work is crawling along. I determined to finish Act One of the opera before the start of the season, and I'm playing my first concert on September 8th! As usual, before I became determined things were going much more quickly. But I must try to finish it otherwise the last two scenes will be going round and round in my head and I'll play like a lunatic crawling round the rooftops – that's happened to me more than once. For instance, now I'm practising for 2-3 hours each morning, but I'm so distracted that I don't know what I'm doing in that time. My only chance is to finish the act quickly, rest, practise intensively – even for a short time, but with a clear head I swear that whatever happens this will be my only opera!

I hug you and Jurek with all my heart.

Andrzej.

PS. Ondine is also already in London.

Warsaw, 25.8.77

My dearest Andrzej, I've just returned from Łódź where I discovered that I was suffering from myocarditis. But don't worry about me because I'm in a wonderful frame of mind!

My good mood stems from the fact that I've received letters from you and from Basia. You were right – it's turned out best for her that you and she parted company. Basia's letter is 20 pages long, so I'll quote only a few fragments for you: '…When I arrived I was so exhausted that I was incapable of making any kind of good impression on anyone. I wanted everyone to leave me alone, and I was very aloof with everyone. This clearly irritated Andrzej which made me withdraw even more ("the more it snows the more it goes the more it goes on snowing"*) and the situation became unbearable. Andrzej wanted me to be companionable and chatty, but it's hard to be what one isn't. Now, our relationship is very good, Andrzej offers me his help and is very pleasant.'

And further on: 'I met Stephen Bishop, and I liked him very much. We went to a pub, I told him all about my umbrella**. I went to his concert. He is great.'

Later, Basia writes this about her boss in the Turkish restaurant: 'At first glance he was an angel glistening with altruistic goodness. He even promised to

---

* From *The House at Pooh Corner* by A A Milne
** A large, black, broken-down umbrella which went everywhere with Basia as a symbol of non-conformity

find me somewhere to live and changed my hours so I could go to classes. Then came a meeting, during which Mr Manager received me wearing only his Y-fronts in a sunny room where the only piece of furniture was a bed. When he realised that he wouldn't overcome my resistance, he said: "No matter, if it's not this one, it'll be someone else, am I right?" I replied that I had great faith in his abilities. He retained his style because, despite my refusal, he continued to make promises. This idyll might have gone on for quite some time if it hadn't been for an unexpected accident. In the restaurant I met a very pleasant Iranian couple; they kept asking me questions and one evening they insisted on giving me a lift home, and that's what they did. The next day my manager made a real Turkish scene of jealousy. I ignored this "scene", or cut it off with shafts of brilliant – in Turkish terms – wit. Mr Manager simmered. The cup overflowed when he slipped on a tea towel and heard my mordant cackle. Following the tea towel the manager paid me off and told me that he has "too big staff". I was rather sorry, because I'd grown to like them all very much. They liked me, too. Every time I went into the kitchen they sang merry Turkish songs while I, wearing my green dress with golden patterns, danced in the kitchen spattered with the blood of wild animals. They called me "habibi" which in Egyptian means "Darling".

'That job was like a surreal dream. After all, imagine a fat Turk with three chins smiling at me lecherously as he rolls out minced meat into the shape of a penis. A guy who, the first time I set eyes on him, pinched my bottom. I felt like a fallen baroness in a third-rate Mexican film.'

Then Basia met a black Jamaican, a follower of Krishna, who, with the help of his Persian friend, found her a job in a Chinese laundry. 'The job was wonderful, I could read books and day-dream.' At the same time some Italian found her a job in a restaurant where she receives tips and where a professional pride has been born ('I'm a real waitress here whereas there I used to do all the dirty jobs'), not to mention class rebellion ('I slaved away, smiled, and everything went into the pockets of Mr Manager and his cronies').

The black Jamaican, Jethro, is 'completely crazy' but he takes Basia to places in London which send her into the greatest raptures. Jethro is studying Indian philosophy and Basia takes part in masses where the 'priests in gold glasses and pastel robes look as if they've escaped from a concentration camp (because they're vegetarians)'. After the masses they serve vegetarian food. They consider that the wave of sex in the West is the epitome of corruption and they propagate chastity: 'Jethro, an enemy of sex, is trying to convert me though he doesn't know that those Turks converted me long ago. Jethro claims he's the son of a millionaire and immediately after we'd spent a night together – on the stairs of a hotel – he proposed to me and told me we would rent an apartment with a huge bed in the middle and we will do nothing.'

Many pages of Basia's letter are descriptions of her impressions of visits, sightseeing, social meetings etc.

So you can see how much good you've done her, firstly by asking her over, and secondly by asking her to leave. She is happy and thrilled by this holiday.

Darling, I'm not writing anything about Jurek – there is no reason for you to sympathise with me. What have I done to deserve that? Nevertheless, if you do write anything uncensored on the subject of his illness, address it to my place of work.

Kiss you. H.

Cumnor, 31.8.77

Funnyface, once again you've written a wise and charming letter! Added to which, this time it took only a week to get here… You ask how I am and you couldn't have chosen a better day to do it. This morning I finished Act One of the opera! Maybe it won't seem to you to be such an important event because, after all, I had to finish it some time, but what's important is that the season is about to start, my first performance is tomorrow week (Ravel's Concerto for Left Hand), so I promised myself that I would lay the opera aside at the end of August, regardless of whether the act was ready or not, to concentrate exclusively on playing from September 1st. Now imagine how I would have felt if the act hadn't been ready. Like an addict deprived of his morphine day by day! But I would have laid it aside, otherwise the obsession would have destroyed all the concerts. And now look at the date of this letter once again.

I haven't the strength to write any more. I haven't slept for a week even though I've been drinking too much and taking all sorts of pills because I thought I should get some sleep in order to write the next morning! Nothing worked and now – just for a change I'm not swallowing anything – I feel drunk and I'm going straight to bed. I don't know if I've written something good or just shit. I only know that it exists. For the time being that's enough for me and tomorrow I'll be sitting at the piano again and learning the Ravel and the Chopin E minor.

Forgive me this scrawl, I can't do anything any more and my eyes are hurting me.

Hug you and kiss you.

Your Andrzej.

Cumnor, 3.10.77

Darling Funnyface, once again I don't have time to reply to you! And I've got so much to tell you. I've already noticed this when I'm writing my journal: the more things happen that are worth noting, the less time there is, and energy, to note them down. On Friday there's the first performance of *Ariel*, the song cycle I was writing in the days of Robert (and even, I believe, in the time of your stay in London). I'm enclosing the programme from which you'll notice that, for the first time in my life, I shall be playing the celesta! The vocalist, Margaret Cable, you know from my record of *Seven Shakespeare Sonnets*. (…)

Funnyface, I'm not renouncing anything; if one loves one's work one is consumed by it and misses nothing. It stops being work and becomes love! You'll be convinced of this one day. And that's what I recommend to you, because people go mad, die, or simply leave, so fall in love with something which nobody can take away from you.

By the way, your idea of an autobiography consisting exclusively of school reports, curricula vitae, application forms, medical reports etc. is phenomenal. That's precisely what you should write, think about it.

Well, kiss you, I must close in a rush.

Andrzej.

ALEXANDRA COURT HOTEL, LIVERPOOL

3.11.77

Darling Funnyface, Forgive me for not having time to reply! But I wanted to thank you at least for the birthday greetings and the photograph and to beg you to keep sending me your letters (not presents). I'll be home again in three days.

I received a long and frank letter from Basia in which she confessed that the reason she avoids people is because all her previous attempts to create any sort of relationship were a fiasco. I wrote back that her letter alone was an attempt at creating a relationship and a proof of trust for which I was grateful (it's a bit like someone trying to demonstrate, by sending a correctly written letter, that he is illiterate).

Bye, Funnyface, I must split! This week is very hard: my birthday was as miserable as Eeyore's.

Kisses,

Your Andrzej.

PS. Regards to Jurek.

Cumnor, 1.12.77

Darling Funnyface, what's happening? If you think of me as a friend then never believe that you 'will bore me' – that's quite impossible, and a card like that is much more disturbing than a long letter. I've just written to Basia. Once again I've received a long, pleasant and entertaining letter from her. I'm trying to persuade her to finish her sentences, but she doesn't always feel like it. In a previous letter she wrote: 'On the one hand I dream about you, but on the other…' I wrote back: 'But what on the other?' and received the following explanation: 'The writer of the sentence ON THE ONE HAND I DREAM ABOUT YOU, BUT ON THE OTHER wanted to express thereby.' Oh, well, that's one way of doing it.

As for her supposed illusions, I don't intend either to banish or maintain them!

Darling, haven't you realised yet that it's impossible to base one's life on illusions over an extended period? You are truly incorrigible: how long will Jurek's illusions last? (…) The only thing we have in life is the *truth*, which we must get to know and, as far as possible, overcome. It's *not possible* to evade it. As long as you fight against it, it will overcome you. So simply shake hands with it. 'Thy will be done' is the wisest sentence I know, it doesn't try to change anything with the exception of one's attitude (I am not a Christian, after all). Besides, by the nature of things, that is one prayer that is always answered…

I kiss you with all my heart,

Your Andrzej.

Warsaw, 14.12.77

Darling Andrzej, do you by any chance happen to know what Basia is up to? She hasn't written to me for five weeks, and she probably writes to you since she 'dreams about you on the one hand…'

Darling, I didn't quite understand what you had in mind when you wrote about the truth. After all, I know what the truth is and I am reconciled to it – but I can't wait for Jurek's death, I can at most expect his death. That is an enormous difference in attitude. That's why I must treat Jurek like a living person and everything between us – like an accelerated version of normal life, like in a film – within a period of two hours the heroes meet, fall in love, then one of them dies. That is the exhausting and boring truth and it requires an enormous effort. What's most paradoxical is that our marriage has never worked better. Now I'm simply not trying to change anything, not fighting against anything and that's why Jurek has stopped being afraid of me, has stopped lying and suspecting me of God knows what. (…) It's not important how long you are with someone, what is important is how you are with someone. That's why I'm not thinking about the day we'll part; does that mean that I'm living with illusions?

Forgive me for writing so little these days. I don't want to put you in an awkward position with these letters – wondering what you should write back to me. I'm pacing round in circles in my hopelessness, what right have I to invite anyone to pace round with me? It's embarrassing. Sick animals hide themselves in various corners, holes and nooks – why should I have less tact than some miserable bear?

Kiss you with all my might and thank you for your warmth.

Your H.

Cumnor, 24.12.77

Darling Funnyface, at last! You have no idea how much your letters mean to me. I have an ambivalent attitude to people: on the one hand I avoid them, I'm constantly afraid that someone will expect something from me or will even try to claim some rights over me, will count on my gratitude or loyalty etc., yet on the other hand I often miss them, particularly those rare people whose friendship I don't especially need to 'earn'. Now you are far dearer and closer to me than you were in the past when we had to entertain one another endlessly or fascinate one another.

As to the truth, you no longer live with illusions but you're constantly helping others to live with them. It's nice that you feel sorry for them, but there is in that pity surely a certain element of contempt, too; how can you be sure that they are all incapable of the effort which you can make?

The day after your letter came, Basia phoned. She's written long letters to both of us, but so far she hasn't sent them. (…) In reply to the question: 'Are you happy?', her answer was: 'How should I know?'…

On January 23rd, in London, there is the first performance of my Second String Quartet, of which I will, of course, have a tape made so you'll hear it sometime! I feel that it's quite a good piece.

Hug you with all my heart and send best wishes to Jurek.

Your Andrzej.

Cumnor, 17.1.78

Darling Funnyface,

Thank you with all my heart for both cards – thank Jurek, too, of course! It's hard for me to collect my thoughts to reply because from the time I found out, from you, that I am overtired I've accepted that you're right and I can't be bothered to do anything except what is most essential. Today, for example, I returned from Sheffield where I assisted at rehearsals of my Second Quartet, whose first performance is taking place in London on Monday. It was as well I went because I changed a couple more details, especially at the end; I didn't really give them any good advice because the Lindsay String Quartet is an ensemble which understands everything perfectly and have only to learn these few passages. The nicest thing about it was that they prefer the new quartet to the first, though they liked the first as well! I'm curious what the general reaction to it will be, though I won't be crushed if no one shares the performers' opinion.

I had another long conversation with Basia (…).

I carry on writing the autobiography whenever I can (i.e. on trains and in planes), and over the last two months I've orchestrated some 30 pages of the opera – half a page a day is very little, but some of the more polyphonic sheets take three hours each.

Are you still surprised that in Oxford I can't allow myself to fall in love?

Anywhere else I can go mad, suffer, spend other people's money and my own emotions, but I must have one place on earth where the work does march on. So forgive me for not writing to you about it now; after a 6-month quarantine I've just achieved a comparative equilibrium which a letter like that could well destroy once more…

Darling, bye for now because if I don't stop then I'll be writing all night and tomorrow I'll do nothing again. What happens with my performances is that the more they matter to me, the worse it goes – best would be not to give a shit and play just for fun, but somehow I'm incapable of that. Surely, eventually something will come of all that practising, won't it? Meanwhile, I have at least got the soothing knowledge that I'm doing the best I can.

Hug you with all my heart and send best wishes to Jurek.

Your Andrzej.

Cumnor, 21.3.78

Darling Funnyface, I've just returned from the jungle and found your letter and card. In the card you ask about Basia, and in the letter you reproach me for knowing more about her than you do! It's amusing because there were also two letters for her waiting here, but there was no word from her. I was just wondering which institution to phone or rather which one to start from when the telephone rang and it was her. The strangest thing is that she is still at the same address. I don't know any more than that because we were cut off.

Now I have to confess to something dreadful. Just imagine: I read your letter to Basia! And it wasn't by mistake, it was on purpose. And this is how it happened: for ten days I'd been getting bored in Curaçao where I knew no one. Two days before my departure I received mail from home containing, among others, your letters to me and to Basia. Since I didn't know her address I decided to send it back to you but suddenly I realised that that would make you sad and anxious, so I threw the letter into the waste-paper basket. An hour later it occurred to me that it was a pity to waste a letter which now nobody would read. I'd almost taken it out of the basket when I suddenly thought that one can't do that, it's shameful, it is, after all, almost like theft. And at this moment the temptation became truly irresistible. Understand that I have never stolen anything yet and I rarely do anything shameful, yet I've worshipped Dostoevsky for a quarter of a century and would willingly rape an under-age girl if I could be sure in advance that she really would hang herself…

But what's worse is that I don't even have any pangs of conscience about it. If there had only been some secrets in the letter, but there was nothing! The whole letter was about telling fortunes from cards. I laughed about it for half the night, laughed dreadfully loudly, and I only need to think about it to start laughing again. Now I have her address so I won't play any more games like that, but don't say that you've lost your respect for me because that would make me laugh even more. I never knew that shameful crimes could be so entertaining.

Basia promised that she would write to me again. 'Only do it grammatically,' I demanded, because I often don't understand her letters. 'Why dramatically?' 'Not dramatically, but gra…' and just then we were cut off. I'm looking forward to her letter even more now in the hope that she will try to write it dramatically.

Lately I've been playing reasonably well and I'm in a good frame of mind. After the success of the Second Quartet they're persuading me vigorously to write a piano trio, but as you know, I compose only during the summer so I would have to set the eternal opera aside again! On the other hand, the trio would be performed straight away while it's very hard to stage an opera, not to mention the costs. But what can I do now that I have this opera in my blood? If

I do have a desire to write anything else then it's a concerto for clarinet and strings – maybe because no one's asked me for it…

Funnyface, I know things are hard and sad for you but I'm writing as if I didn't know because what can one say in this situation?

Hug you and kiss you,

Your Andrzej.

PS. Could you send me the Polish version of President Carter's speech in Warsaw?

Warsaw, 31.3.78

Oh, Andrzej my dear, how I laughed! But immediately afterwards I thought that you'll regard me as an out-and-out idiot because of the predictions. You see, there is an area of my life which you know absolutely nothing about. I don't know if I can do it, but I'm very fond of telling fortunes, especially under the influence of alcohol. When I was last in the sanatorium, I told one of the men there he would meet with an accident and the very next day he slipped in the swimming pool and broke his leg. From that moment on any rest I might have had in the sanatorium came to an end, because every day I was approached by complete strangers – the healthy, the sick, some of them on crutches – who begged me to tell their fortunes, offering me mind-boggling sums of money to do it. I left the sanatorium early and extremely tired. (…) As for that adventure of yours with my letter to Basia, something similar happened to me with her diaries. She left two volumes of them when she left for England. It's true that sometimes she did say she had no secrets from me, but I didn't have her permission to read the diaries. The temptation, however, was strong and I cracked. Doing it I felt as awkward as you did when you opened my letter. And, like you, I laughed afterwards because I had understood next to nothing of the diaries! Her style is too modern for me, a stream of thoughts and connections without full stops or commas… Has the spirit of the times become so schizophrenic and sown such confusion in the minds of young people?

Have you by any chance read Arrabal's *The Stone of Madness*? Compared with that, Kafka's obsessions are mere child's play, and de la Serna writing: 'She learnt to make waistcoats on the typewriter and in this way she could use her time at the office usefully' – is a down-to-earth realist!

Jurek is staying at his mother's, in her little house. She fought stubbornly for it, and she was right. He's comfortable there – a huge room, a garden, two elderly ladies who run around preparing recherché meals for him. Whereas here, unfortunately, I return from work as late as five o'clock and, since we have no telephone, all the time I'm at work I worry that he might have fainted, or had a haemorrhage, that he's hungry etc. I'm ashamed to admit I'm in a good mood. I'm simply cheered by everything: spring, the fact I've bought a dress, that I've been to the cinema to see a splendid but ineffective film called *Room with a View on the Sea* (I've completely stopped thinking about Jurek's impending death; a letter comes from him every day from which I deduce that he is alive and everything is in order). That's what I've become like. The film begins with a boy standing on a ledge of a tower-block and warning that if anyone tries to get near him, he will jump. The action starts; it involves two psychiatrists, a police commander with a whole staff of workers, a public prosecutor, a priest, the boy's girlfriend, and his entire family. The boy couldn't be seen clearly, they made some blurred photographs and attempts at identification turn out to be a complete fiasco: the girlfriend and the entire family turn out to be that of a completely different boy, but each one of them had 'something on their conscience' and they all apologised to him abjectly in the room from which he couldn't be seen because he was standing away from the window and wouldn't let anyone approach. The rescue lasted 13 hours, and in fact there was no real action, just everyone distracting him with conversation. The boy was saved by this old psychiatrist (wonderfully played by Holoubek) who didn't dissuade him from committing suicide, quite the reverse, but explained that suicide is also a choice and makes sense if it is the result of a real choice and not false pride or fear. He spoke long and beautifully, with the voice of a wise old Jew. And what he said was aimed not only at that boy, but at each one of us.

Darling, I can't keep bothering you every day like this, so I kiss you tenderly and everything.

Your H.

London-Oslo, 7.4.78

Sweetest Funnyface,

Your letter arrived today so I'm replying to it in the departure lounge at London Airport, and I'll send the reply from Oslo, where I'll be landing soon. I'll be staying there five days recording for Norwegian television Mozart's Concerto in C major K 246 (an early, modest, beautiful – and completely unknown piece), and Bach and Brahms for the radio.

Darling, I also received a letter from Basia, fragmentary and incomprehensible, but very pleasant. She enclosed photographs of her friends Ryszard and Kasia who really is a little similar to you. Ryszard on the other hand is unlike anything, and the paintings which you can see on the photograph remind me of freshly vomited jelly which proves once again how little I know about painting. Basia has invited me to her place and I'm sure I'll make it there some time (…).

I'm still concerned that you keep assuming that people are incapable of living without delusions and, out of the goodness of your heart, you yourself keep offering them these delusions. It's a bit like someone distributing morphine out of pity, because it's awfully difficult to cure someone of mythomania and everyone over whom you have some influence becomes addicted to dreams and, as a consequence, tells you you are right. You've brought Basia, for example, to the point where, after a week's unfortunate acquaintance with me during which I didn't even hear her voice, she regards me as someone really close. I have nothing against Basia but I can't be friends with her just for genetic reasons and I don't yet feel any connection with her. (…) And I wouldn't want to hurt her. (That's precisely how Stavrogin in *Demons* hurts people: all he needs is to show himself somewhere and his indifference drives a hundred people to distraction. Though it's true to say that Stavrogin is handsome). (…) You're visualising my attitude to Basia on the basis of my long, intimate, affectionate friendship with you. Darling, you are mistaken, she is too different from you. It's certainly true that she has an imagination, but it's a different kind of imagination, more painterly, less verbal, and it cannot create a bridge between her and me.

You've forgiven me so much already, so forgive me this letter, too.

Hugs and kisses.

Your Andrzej.

Cumnor, 16.4.78

My bewitching Monkey, Many thanks for the gorgeous letter! I'm so pleased that, despite everything, your mood's improved. Meanwhile, I've given you a severe ticking-off about Basia, for which I apologise from the bottom of my heart.

As to your fortune-telling talent, I'd pay you enormous sums of money not to tell my fortune. Not because I don't believe in it, but quite the reverse – because it scares me. How do you know that you are simply telling fortunes and not, perhaps, casting spells? Maybe that man in the sanatorium wouldn't have broken his leg if you hadn't foretold it. You can't, after all, prove a lack of a causal relationship – in Africa, people dutifully die to prove the witch-doctor right. And you still call it a laugh!

I'll look in on Basia in May, when I'll be a little freer.

I like the idea of *Room with a View on the Sea* very much. Give me the director's name because it could be shown here under a different title. I'll do what I can to see the film.

Have you seen the American film *Duel*? In it all you can see throughout is a car and a truck, and the thing hinges on the fact that the driver of the truck, for unknown reasons, wants to kill the guy in the car. The best thing about it is that you can't see the murderer either: his hand appears, and once during a stop at a petrol station, his shoes do. Nothing is known about him and his victim doesn't know him. It's an absolutely first-rate film.

Did I write to tell you that the Second Quartet has come out really well?

Hug you and kiss you,

Your Andrzej.


Warsaw, 19.4.78


Darling Andrzej, thanks for the letter. As for the question of mythomania, I won't give up that easily. You compare mythomania with drug addiction, and I simply can't agree: drug addiction makes us weaker, whereas mythomania, despite appearances, makes us stronger. You have a good example of that with Jurek. If not for mythomania he'd have stopped living long ago. You'll ask if it's so great to live as he does – to vegetate. It's all relative: within his own capabilities he has certain triumphs and joys. Two months ago he got together a photographic exhibition (*People at Work*) at his local arts centre, he writes a few poems, he is cheered by my weekly visits (just as you are by a successful concert), we exchange presents like a courting couple (I've just received Yesyenin's poems with a moving dedication: 'To my beloved Wife, as bewitching and touching as Yesyenin's poems, Jurek').

As for Basia, she isn't, and never has been, a mythomane. Her sense of reality has always shocked me. It's the facts of her life that are extraordinary, not the way she imagines them. I don't know if I've ever described this funny incident in her life, one of many such, but it's very typical, so listen.

There was a jazz concert at Congress Hall – a group of Armstrong's pupils and colleagues were appearing. People paid mind-boggling sums for tickets, bribed the ushers, slipped through the police cordon (there to ensure there were no breaches of public order). And in this situation Basia, with no ticket and no money, sets out to the concert with her friend Hania. She is holding a yellowy-red, autumnal leaf she picked up in the street. She comes up to the usher and, smiling radiantly, hands him the leaf. The usher cannot believe his eyes, but he, too, smiles and lets Basia through; but he stops Hania. Then Basia says, in a gracious tone full of dignity: 'The lady is with me.' And the usher lets Hania through, too. Is that mythomania?

If Basia regards you as someone who is close to her, then it's not as a result of my mythomanic suggestions, but because you are, quite simply, nice to her. Besides which, you also have an exaggerated sense of responsibility. Don't you know that repulsing someone can be a very healthy jolt for them?

When people suffer a little then at least they know they're alive. My God, how empty my life would be if it weren't for all the things I've suffered through you! I'm not joking at all, on the contrary – I'm hugely grateful to you. I think that you, too, remember people who made you suffer more frequently, more tenderly and more touchingly than those who didn't. So don't lay claim to imagined faults unless, of course, you enjoy it.

You're wrong when you claim that I turn people into mythomanes, it's rather that mythomanes seek out my friendship because I don't brutally yank them back into reality the way others do. Do you remember that mentally ill tailor? He believed himself to be the King of Poland and asked me to be his wife and help him rule. I didn't explain to him that he wasn't the King of Poland, firstly – because he wouldn't have believed me anyway, secondly – because his faith in his own power made him happy. I did not, however, promise to marry him, explaining that, unfortunately, I already had a husband. A delusion or mythomania is the same as creating a different reality, in the same way as art is the creating of a different reality. Surely what is important is what a person experiences, not judging to what extent it's borne out by 'reality'.

But I'll stop now and leave you in peace, Darling.

Heartfelt kisses,

Your H.

Cumnor, 28.4.78

Funnyface, once again you've written me a bewitching letter and once again I don't agree with any of it! But I'll preserve it, and I'll transcribe the story of Basia and the autumn leaf into my diary which I've been writing sporadically for a long time. In the past such things happened only in the Green Goose cabaret*. If they are actually happening now, then it's true that Basia 'creates a different reality'. Whatever the truth of it, I laughed fortissimo.

Since objective experiences don't interest you greatly, I'll give you just one reason for my dislike of mythomania. At some time or other these delusions must come to an end. Maybe Jurek is still deceiving himself, but for how much longer? And death will be that much more cruel for him since he is not prepared for it.

Furthermore, I cannot, as you can, think 'touchingly and movingly' about people who have made me suffer. To this very day I hate the people who hurt me – you can see that clearly in the fragments of autobiography I've sent you. Unlike you, I can't forgive humiliations and that's why I myself try not to humiliate people (in the past I used to do it constantly and with delight).

As you can see, I've become subjective again! Let's go on, then. I can't bear to lie, the deceit of others is a matter of indifference to me, but my own

---

* The Green Goose cabaret are short performance pieces of a humorous and often absurd nature by the poet Konstanty Ildefons Gałczyński.

makes me nauseous. And that's why I avoid situations where one has to be either deceitful or brutal! (Generally it ends up with me falling into both traps, because I start with polite deceit and then I lose patience and I attack the object of my politeness brutally as if it were his fault). As for my sense of responsibility, I don't feel in the least responsible for anybody's delusions on condition that I did nothing to provoke them! Unfortunately, out of cowardice, I often do provoke them because I hate being brutal. But I always reproach myself for it and in addition I can't forgive the people I've deceived: it always seems to me that they forced me into doing it.

And your comparison of mythomania with art is insolent nonsense. It's true that art creates a new reality: after all, Chopin's preludes exist to this day regardless of how he was feeling when he wrote them! And you know, maybe that's precisely why mythomania is so unnecessary to me: because I play, I write quartets, and in addition I lie shamelessly in the autobiography to which you have been introduced, so I don't need to imagine that I'm the king of Poland or even a tailor.

I started this letter in the train from Birmingham, where I was playing a recital. That was yesterday evening, and today I have a free day (no practice), so I'll just try to rewrite the last part of that chapter.

I like days like this awfully, when there's nothing happening and I can get up in the afternoon without feeling guilty, sit in the bath for an hour, go for a walk… But it often ends with my sitting down to some work because lack of constraint is the best encouragement.

Hug you and kiss you,

Your Andrzej.

Cumnor, 2.6.78

Silly, but enchanting Funnyface,

I haven't a clue what makes me like you, but I know I do like you more and more! (…)

Your poor, demented child did not come to my recital (even though I did invite her); she appeared instead at Stephen's and announced that she was getting married – this time not to an umbrella. Do you know anything about this project? You should come over for the wedding, stay with me and teach me to tell fortunes from cards. Now is a very pleasant time for me because I won't play again this season (except for one recital in Finland at the end of June), but I haven't started composing yet, so I've decided to give myself a four-week holiday here, at home. This is my only chance because when I start writing again I won't be able to stop! When I'm on holiday I am not a recluse, because generally speaking I like people (some of them, anyway), though it's rare for me to show it.

In the next day or two I'll send you a copy of the immeasurably long chapter written from granny's point of view! It will enable me to describe, among other things, my parents' betrothal, wedding, and divorce – I myself found out about it all very late. Oxford is full of enchanting students till the middle of June. I wander along the river and watch them rowing. The 17th is the day my holiday ends, a date I've set myself, so that's when I'll get down to some work.

I hug you with all my heart, as always,

Your old

Andrzej.

Warsaw, 9.6.78

Dearest Andrzej,

Your letter made me very happy. At the moment I'm terribly shaken up internally, because I've had too much sad and cheerful news all at once: Jurek is closer to death than ever before – the disease has spread to his liver, kidneys, and bones; if it goes to the brain – he'll never be conscious of the fact that he's dying. At the moment he is planning to spend a holiday with me in the Bieszczady Mountains, he asked me to write to an aunt to book a room. Added to this Basia phones me every few minutes (four calls, and one conversation with me). My future son-in-law is a young engineer, fair haired. I don't know any more than that.

If this wedding does take place then I'll probably go over to London this year to get to know my dear son-in-law. At the moment, though, it's impossible.

If Basia invites you to the wedding – I beg you, go! Perform the last rites for me!

Hug you endlessly,

Your H.

Cumnor, 16.6.78

Sweetest Funnyface,

I've just received a 60-page letter from Basia (I can just see how jealous you are of me again). So this wedding really is happening, and in the middle of next month already! Do what you can to come over, and stay for a holiday with me after the event. What do you say to that? Will you be able to obtain a passport and a visa? Could I help you in any of that? If you're short of cash, I'll send you some. Will Jurek agree to your leaving him behind?

Hug you, my Darling,

Your Andrzej.

Warsaw, 14.6.78

Sweetest Andrzej,

Basia's surprise wedding is now definitely on. The newly-weds are planning to honeymoon in Greece. Unfortunately, I can't get across to the wedding, because Jurek's state of health is very poor. Perhaps you could take my place?

Generally, though, I've long been meaning to write you a world-view letter. I wanted to explain why I'm almost a total stranger to the feeling of humiliation which torments you so. But I can't explain it as well as Laura Huxley does in *You Are Not the Target*. One of the things that emerge from the book is that if someone wants to humiliate us, then it's not we who are the 'target'. This poor person is only trying to resolve some difficulty of his own and the more he tries to humiliate us, the more he ought to inspire our pity. Someone who does the humiliating only seems to be stronger. After all, whom did the world proclaim as God? Christ – humiliated, beaten and crucified!

Besides this, Mrs Huxley teaches people to have a good attitude to their own selves; if you genuinely like yourself, you'll be pleasant to others, too. You won't take it out on them in revenge for the fact you don't like yourself. Notice that the people who inspire our greatest distaste are those next to whom we like ourselves least. And mythomania? That's simply one of many self-defence mechanisms. To me it's more likeable than, for instance, aggression, and more amusing than infantile regression. You're right: works of art or of civilisation are not mythomania, but you must accept that they must be preceded by imagination, experience, ideas, dreams. 'The very substance of the soul is the shadow of a dream' – says someone in *Hamlet*.

But enough pontificating, I'll finish now.

I forgot to tell you that Basia's wedding is on July 14th. On the anniversary of the capture of the Bastille, Basia will lose her freedom!

I beg you, send them a few flowers from me, I can't do it from Poland. We'll send the family letters and telegrams from here, but for the rest you are our only hope!

Kiss you most gratefully,

Your H.

POSTCARD: BODLEIAN LIBRARY, OXFORD. LETTER WRITTEN
BY KING GEORGE V AS A CHILD TO SIR HENRY ACLAND

Cumnor, 23.6.78

Darling Funnyface, I'll reply to your letter this evening or tomorrow, meanwhile I give you Basia's address. (…) Judging from the 60-page letter, your future son-in-law is very pleasant, but most important he loves Basia (she 'likes him very much and sometimes loves him'). Of course I'll go to the wedding, I've already promised her that.

Kiss you with all my heart,

Your Andrzej.

Jyväskylä, 25.6.78

Demented and enchanting Monkey,

Over the last few hours I've been in Jyväskylä, a small Finnish town where there is a festival in progress. Actually it's only about to start because my recital the day after tomorrow marks the opening of the fun and games (for me, too, because it's the last recital of the season). But they've arranged things perversely: they've got Dmitri Bashkirov here who is, apparently, a brilliant pianist (as well as a charming fellow, we've just had dinner together), and they invited me to play and him to teach. I'm a much better teacher than I am a performer because I nearly always want to talk and I rarely want to practise, so maybe I should persuade Dmitri to swap. Added to which, he'll be listening to the mess I make of the Chopin Ballades!

I'm awfully glad you're coming to England. For me, the best time would be in September because I'll no longer be composing then and so shall be relatively sociable! Added to which, it just so happens I'm playing my own concerto on October 1 and 2 in Ireland so if you could get all the way there you would become acquainted with a piece you've heard a lot about and would probably find interesting…

Write to me when you've read the chapter about granny. You're the only one of my readers so far who knew her, so I'm positively weak with curiosity.

I wish Jurek a speedy spread to the brain because that would be the best thing for him. As for you, I hug you, caress you, and kiss you, and await you.

Your Andrzej.

Warsaw, 29.6.78

Darling Andrzej, this is the third sheet I've put into the typewriter. First time I wrote 'daring', then 'Andrex'. My brain's all mixed up because of all these experiences. I'm leaving any moment now, summoned by a telegram from Jurek's mother: he can no longer write to me because he's just a scrap of a human being, nothing but suffering. I'm very glad you were, I'm sorry, you will be at Basia's wedding. I'm showing clear signs of mental instability. Today there was a notice in the lift: 'Will exchange my M2 size apartment for larger'. I read it as 'barge'. Another announcement I saw as promising a: 'Large reward to the finder of Emily, my lame frog' (Emily was, of course, a dog). Some guy at my institute was giving a lecture on 'The Constitution of the Polish People's Republic', which surprised me because I heard it as: 'The Prostitution of the Polish People's Republic'. As you can see, we must meet again before my brain succumbs to a total eclipse.

As if this wasn't enough, there's so much work at the institute that I haven't the strength to live. Write, and that will save me!

Your H.

Cumnor, 1.7.78

My Darling Funnyface,

I hope that, despite everything, you will come, if not for the wedding, then in September. You simply must come, even if Basia changes her mind (which doesn't seem likely at the moment). Thank you for telling me the date of the wedding; I hope Basia will let me know where it's happening. If she invites me, I'll go there as your representative.

I can see from your 'world-view' letter that we shall have some fascinating discussions! Of course I agree that one has to love oneself because one can only share things which one already possesses! Besides, I'm literally devoted to myself, I'd follow myself to the end of the world and have done more than once.

For the moment I hug you with all my heart and I'll write again soon.

Your Andrzej.

Cumnor, 12.7.78

Darling Funnyface, I can't go to the wedding because I don't know where it's taking place! Your child, exhausted by that *lettre-fleuve*, has clearly forgotten to invite me to it. So I've sent her a basket of lilies to the last address she gave me.

You simply must come over, but not in the winter because England is virtually invisible then: it's cold, gloomy, no snow – just rain, mist and damp.

Besides, there are no students here at Christmas, and what is Oxford without students? A mute keyboard. If you don't manage to come in the autumn, then I suggest the spring, I'll be free from the end of May.

I've been very stimulated lately because I've found a subject for my next opera (even though I'll be writing the first for another three years!). It's a shattering play called *Total Eclipse*, about the inner crisis that forced the 19-year-old Rimbaud to abandon his writing for ever. Its author, Christopher Hampton, gave me permission to do it the day before yesterday. But don't tell anyone about it because it's a hellishly difficult subject and it's likely that nothing will come of it!

For the moment I hug you with all my heart, as always,

Your old Andrzej.

PS. In the light of your present hallucinations, I wonder what you've read in this letter.

Warsaw, 11.7.78

Darling, I've dropped into Warsaw for a day and I'm leaving again. My anxiety neurosis has returned in all its glory. My nights there have been dreadful. Jurek keeps waking me to make sure I'm still there. And when he wakes me, I think he's dying and it's all making me go mad. It's never ending.

Forgive the delay in writing back, but at the moment I'm like a psychiatric patient of my boss's who, when asked what ailed him, replied: 'Nothing really, I just feel rendered impossible.'

As a result of your enchanting letters I fell asleep yesterday without any pills.

Thank you. Kiss you.

Your H.

Cumnor, 19.7.78

My Darling Funnyface,

Heartfelt thanks for the card and the book; you spoil me awfully! Unfortunately, I don't know when I'll read your present, because I'm now on holiday which means I'm dreadfully overworked. I'll tell you what I'm doing in my next letter. But that's not what you're after. I know very well that you've been waiting for this letter with more impatience than for any other. And indeed, it was well worth waiting for. Put the letter to one side, unbutton your blouse, sit down calmly, and take a couple of deep breaths. Have you done that? Well, now read on.

Yes, you've guessed, the wedding did not take place. Basia broke off her engagement to Mick. This is the exact order of events as seen from where I was standing:

At 9 o'clock last Wednesday morning I received your letter in which you asked me to attend Basia's wedding and to send her some flowers.

At 10 I ordered the flowers by telephone.

At 11 I wrote you a letter informing you that I had sent the flowers and a telegram.

At 11.30 I sent this letter.

At 12 a letter came from Basia, from a different address, informing me of the broken engagement. I phoned the flower shop but it was too late; the flowers, white lilies, were delivered to the abandoned fiancé from whom she had just moved out. This made me laugh so much that I couldn't do anything for the rest of the day (I know, I'm a heartless monster).

Well, I went to London to visit Basia. She's living modestly but calmly with nice people; that's as much as I managed to ascertain because I didn't find her in. When I returned there was another letter from her waiting for me, and in the evening she phoned ('I've come to my senses, he was just nonsense').

And now I'll copy out her last letter which arrived this morning. Here are some fragments: 'My future husband, David, is the most charming person you could possibly imagine. You'll fall in love with him just as I have (no conflict here). To cap it all, he is an artiste. He dances and sings on stage dressed as a woman. What gowns he has! And what hats with feathers and sequins – it's amazingly camp.'

As you can see, despite everything life marches on!

I await your letter with joyful impatience.

Hug you with all my heart,

Your Andrzej.

Cumnor, 21.7.78

Darling Funnyface,

Many thanks for your letters which both came yesterday. I'm very glad you liked the chapter about granny; the comparison with Hłasko would have flattered me even if it had been unfavourable! But it's true that when I was writing Mala's letter I consciously tried to find another style, so I'm very pleased that it's obvious… The fragment about my parents' wedding is written in a very old-fashioned style, a bit like Henry James; I was trying to submerge the reader in a distant past when an unsuccessful marriage was regarded as a catastrophe because, after all, nothing worse could happen… I wrote that chapter slowly and carefully over a long period, so your reaction makes me blush with pride and joy.

But that's not what I meant to write about at all. Once again I've shown you how egocentric I am! I'm writing to ask you not to give up your application for a passport even though Basia isn't getting married. Firstly because she'll still get engaged a hundred times, and secondly because you'll positively need a holiday after the worst thing finally happens. So come here, cry your eyes out and rest.

Hug you with all my heart,

Your Andrzej.

Cumnor, 1.8.78

My Darling Funnyface,

And are you still surprised that Basia's letters please me so much? I'm enclosing her latest. Naturally, I'm getting ready assiduously for the wedding; I even know who'll be wearing the bridal gown there (with sequins)! But that last sentence of hers makes me rather suspicious that she's made it all up.

Still, that's all right, let the child have her fun. The bit about the nun is her reply to my suggestion that she start a new order based on the vow of nudity (God sees everything anyway, so there's no need to adorn oneself for Him).
I have a feeling that Basia and I will, eventually, become good friends.

Hug you with all my heart,

Your Andrzej.

Cumnor, 4.8.78

Silly but bewitching Funnyface,

Yesterday I went to Basia's wedding! And as a witness to boot; I had to show my passport and sign the register. Afterwards I took them all out to lunch. (…) It gave me an opportunity to inspect them all closely. Basia has truly developed enormously – she is beautiful, charming, much less shy but still incurably innocent. Her innocence shows itself in her gratitude to people who exploit and maybe even rob her. As a consequence, she probably feels needed (and that's always nice). (…)

After the wedding Basia decided to take a holiday at some ecumenical Christian retreat freshly founded by some Korean who claims to be the Messiah. Life is very simple: every member of the church is an Abel, and the rest of us are all Cains. Rysio explained it all to me.

But Basia looks splendid and is happy.

Hug you,

Your Andrzej.

Warsaw, 31.7.78

My Darling, fondest Andrzej,

I haven't written for a long time. Jurek is dead. I got there the day he died. He was conscious, and glad. During the night, he lost consciousness (…).

Darling, don't give me any sympathy because of Jurek's death. Everyone's doing that very sincerely, with tears in their eyes – they even announce their sympathy in the newspapers. This embarrasses me greatly because one can only sympathise with Jurek, and he doesn't need it now. He wasn't at fault in any of this, the poor boy who couldn't cope with life. And yet I am angry with him, very angry that he has died. I know it sounds absurd, but that's how I feel. There was so much love in him, so much sensitivity… Read a poem he wrote shortly before his death.

*My Time*

Someone once said to me
You can you're able to you like
to organise fill exploit
your time.
But my time is strange and independent
without surface horizon
or hours.
My time now has only a bed
a paper a book and emptiness.
My time has become
one-dimensional objectless.
I read I think
I write I think
I'd like not to be alone
to read to talk
to listen to tell
to converse.
Why am I still alive
in this lifeless time?
I live because I love
I long so I live.
I live because I believe
that tomorrow
I'll see you again.
*[Kąty Wrocławskie, June 1978]*

Continued                                                                1.8.78

I haven't sent the letter yet. Darling, I don't know if there's any sense in my coming over now. I'm shattered and sad. Yesterday, I sobbed all day because of… Tosio's death. I pulled out some old souvenirs and found some poems which I've never shown anyone.

   We used to call Tosio the 'Black Cat', he and Basia used to pose for portraits. Tosio used to paint various kinds of flowers, too. When I came home late he used to change the flowers for cog-wheels – they were 'cog flowers'. He used to make artificial flowers out of chocolate boxes, they were 'pop-art' flowers. The last picture he painted was *Seven sad and strange flowers*. And the last poem is about how I led him to the hospital ward through a cold garden and how, returning later – when they'd told me he was dead – I talked to myself.

   I'm enclosing the poems. I kiss you.

                                                                      Your H.


*Games with the Black Cat*

Tosio!
Basia!

Basia likes the Black Cat
The Black Cat rushes to Basia
Flies in like a cloud
And sits
And Basia proud
Next to him
Paints the Cat's portrait
– Steinberg's line –

The Cat is not angry
and in good faith
sits patiently
though on the paper
it's an old man missing an eye…
'Where's the other eye?'
he asks hesitantly
'count them
there's one eye too few'
To which she replies
(as if giving a lesson)
'Art demands selection'

*Tosio's Flowers*

There are 'cogwheel' flowers
painted in anger
pop-art flowers
ruffled with knives
'seven chief flowers'
forked sorrowful
like poor little maidens
which from hand to hand
become more and more strange
slender naive
delicate sickly
pale-coloured
trembling and plucked
degenerate
more and more unhappy
tearful and sensitive
in bronzes and clouds
on lost pathways
they stand listening
to the approaching playing
of silence which brings with it death

*The Hospital Garden*

Slowly we followed the avenue
you had no strength
it was cold
it was sad
You begged
'let's go back home'
I said
'Darling be sensible
they'll cure you'
Slowly I walk down the avenue
for the very last time
it's cold
it's sad
I beg
'let's go back home'
A man in a greatcoat

on crutches
turns to me
'were you speaking to me?'

Cumnor, 8.8.78

Darling Funnyface,
You ask me not to sympathise with you. No fear of that. I sympathised with you earlier (…). I believe you should certainly try to get here in September because it's precisely now that you most need a holiday. Your sorrow won't irritate me; I'll drag you into my own interests and affairs, and that should help you. Besides, there are many other reasons for you to come over (…). One of them is – Basia. Although nothing drastic has happened, everyone's exploiting her and she kisses their hands with gratitude.
Jurek's poem is very moving indeed. While we're on the subject of poems, do you remember the epitaph that was doing the rounds a quarter of a century ago amongst Polish musicians?
'God's latest miracle from on high
He's finally let Tchaikovsky die'.
That's how I think of Jurek now.

Hug you and kiss you.

Your Andrzej.

PS. Only for God's sake don't get married to anyone this year! It doesn't do you any good, nor them, despite the best intentions from both sides.

Warsaw, 30.8.78

Andrzej, my Darling, thanks for your letters. You're helping me more than anyone in the world! And fate, instead of rewarding you, is taking its revenge: Basia has renounced her whole family – her husband, her father, her mother, and stays in contact only with you. (…)
I'm not worried by Basia wasting money because she's known how to earn it since childhood (recently she sent me 200 pounds telling me to buy myself some dresses; can you imagine? For that sum of money I can buy at least 130 dresses here!).
Before my trip I'm teaching myself English intensively using Szkutnik's *Thinking in English*. Reading it improves neither my English nor my mood. Here are the titles of the various chapters: Separation, Nostalgia, Why not

Together?, Goodbye, Wait for Me, Be Cruel if You Must, Loneliness, To Lie or to Hurt?, We Ought to Part, I Have no Courage to Live, Silent Death, etc… There are 139 of these chapters, and the most cheerful ones are about a heart operation that the hero has to undergo. There is one chapter which is truly jolly! The hero sees a blind man with a white stick and acknowledges that he's better off because he doesn't have to walk around with a white stick, though he could do if he wanted to.

It'll be interesting to see if knowing these texts will come in useful during my stay in England. And so I'll come over in October because I have a business trip to Prague at the end of September.

Once again, thanks for everything.

With joyful kisses.

Your H.

Cumnor, 31.8.78

My Darling Funnyface,

I enclose Basia's wedding photos, but as they're the only ones in existence you must look after them till you bring them back here! The gentleman with the rose in his teeth is your son-in-law, and the bald man dressed up as a black cow with red spots is me, so there's your proof that I really was at the wedding. Your Basia becomes dearer to me with every letter; it's got to the stage that I actually understand what she writes! I'm just going into town to make a copy of the trio which I finished after two months of mental wanking. I don't know if it works, but rather suspect that it doesn't, but the relief is making my head spin. Because of the trio I've let things slip so badly, I can't even play *Twinkle, twinkle little Star* (which I haven't been asked to play). But on the other hand I'm still pleased with the piano concerto, so I'd really like you to hear it sometime. Unfortunately, I don't know it yet and the conductor in Ireland is said never to know anything, so don't be too upset that you won't get there in time. If you haven't got the cash I'll gladly pay for the journey, only you must explain how these things are arranged…

Bye for now – it won't be long!

Your Andrzej.

PS. Do you by any chance know what it is that lesbians do? Isn't it like a violinist leaving his bow behind and playing an entire concerto pizzicato?

Cumnor, 12.9.78

Enchanting Funnyface,

Thanks to you, today was like Christmas: two cards and a letter! Many, many thanks. Basia is going crazy with joy at the thought of seeing you! By the way, I spent many hours with her because she's unexpectedly become lively and talkative. She talked about Sam, a sociologist from Florida. He's working on the demolition of a house for which he is not only being paid but also having his accommodation provided free. The only thing that puzzles me is that this accommodation is in the attic of the house which Sam is demolishing. He and Basia both regard it as perfectly natural; Basia was very surprised when I advised her to meet Sam at her place, not his.

Now surely you can see how much you're needed?

Hug you and kiss you a million times, which should be enough for 6 weeks.

Your Andrzej.

PS. The very worst thing is that whatever I play in Ireland everyone will think that I wrote it. Normally I pray that my mistakes will pass unnoticed – this time my prayers will be answered.

CARD: BODLEIAN LIBRARY, OXFORD. CATS. FROM A BESTIARY EXECUTED
IN ENGLAND IN THE SECOND QUARTER OF THE 13TH CENTURY.

Cumnor, 7.10.78

Darling Funnyface,

(…) For the scores thanks with all my heart, but confine yourself to the Szymanowski or give me a present of *Crime and Punishment* or *The Idiot* (thanks to you I already have the rest of Dostoevsky).

Kiss you with Karamazovesque elation and impatience.

A.

# *Part Four*
# **1978 – 1982**

Warsaw, 18.11.78

Darling, I keep wondering what I can write after our strangely tragic encounter. Really, though, it's all very simple. You were always the most important person in my life. But now I simply have to say: 'This love must be killed.' For years now I've thought of us as friends, and believe that that is more important than anything. But such was this last meeting (and the previous one, in '69) that I've ceased to understand. Why can we behave like best buddies at the beginning, but when parting's near we're like fighting lovers?

In friendship, people are usually frank, and they don't humiliate one another, and they don't make each other cry. Our relationship undergoes violent change over a short period. We swing from warmth to enmity, humiliations, tears, pity, dislike, tempestuous conversations – apparently sincere, but in fact leaving us dissatisfied. I sometimes think: 'Maybe I'm insincere with him, maybe I'm insincere with myself, maybe lurking at the root of my attitude towards him is a completely insane lust?'

But, Darling, you know only too well that it's not sexual difficulty or inadequacy that's most humiliating – it's sexual rejection. So why do you constantly provoke me? So as to have the satisfaction of humiliating me? That last night in Cumnor you gave me a thorough psychological 'going over', it was as if you wanted me to tell you then what I'm writing to you now. You shouted at me, you accused me of cowardice, frigidity, insincerity, lack of spontaneity. What were you really after? What did you want to provoke? Confessions, declarations, tears?

I'm angry with myself for having written this letter, but despite that I shall send it.

Kiss you,

Your H.

Cumnor, 23.11.78

Halinka,

Your letter awoke feelings of amazement and respect. But I find it very hard to reply to it. It arrived this morning and, at first, I decided to wait at least three days so I could mull it over. But this whole thing is torturing me so much I'm going to try to reply – as best I can – right now. Understand that though I don't love you, have never loved you, and will never love you, I like you so much I find it hard to turn my back on you. But our relationship always seems to be at cross purposes: you sense love in it, I sense friendship, and the result is we end up with neither the one nor the other. Friendship, after all, is not 'love minus sex.' The difference is that lovers are essential to each other. This difference isn't revealed in our correspondence because then it's only a partial relationship (we can't see each other's eyes, hear each other's voices), and therefore bound to be ambiguous.

But when we're together, I start feeling uneasy. To begin with all I notice is that I can't get down to anything, and I don't know why; after all, you encourage me to write, practise, etc. But I perceive a painful nostalgia in you because you are feeling nostalgic about me while you are with me! To me, you seem sad, helpless, somehow thrown onto my mercy and I feel I have to neglect either you, or myself. I apportion you some of my time but with growing reluctance, but I soon lose patience and right away show you as much. You sense it almost sooner than I do myself and you say quickly: 'Right, I won't get in your way any more,' as you leave the room, or: 'Don't take any notice of me.' This provokes enormous guilt complexes in me, and I become even less friendly because I resent your having shamed me! The more guilty I feel, the more boorish I become because I'm ashamed of my lack of hospitality. In short: a vicious circle. (…)

Your love for me inspires pity, embarrassment, and a sense of guilt. I know you don't demand anything from me, but this is a question of needs, not demands – needs which I can't, won't and don't want to satisfy. (…) It is the only hurdle between us; without it, you would be my ideal friend. To begin with, we have so much in common, we have a shared past and similar interests, and you also have virtually all the qualities I prize most – intelligence, goodness, sensitivity, a sense of humour, and above all, an exceptional imagination. And, on top of all that, you know me so well! That's why I'm appealing to you: can't you 'cure' yourself of me? I know that, in the past, you haven't managed it, but maybe you could now? You must understand it's hard to be at ease with someone you are constantly denying something to. After all, in such a situation we both lose…

You once wrote about Basia that: 'Unlike me, she is proud and independent.' The pride matters less, but try to acquire her independence. Then I, too, will feel free and I won't be afraid to call you 'Funnyface' or to invite you here again. In any case, I beseech you – be honest! Just as you were in this last letter, which impressed me because of its honesty. *Don't feign* pride, or independence, or even friendship. Write what you feel, without wondering how I'll receive it: what use is a relationship where one has to lie?

You showed great courage in that letter: it will be easier from now on. Only a short while ago, in Cumnor, I told you I despised you, yet see how you've made me respect you now! There's no self-abasement in your letter; it's as if you were telling me that you've got diabetes. I've suffered, too, and I may still suffer in just the same way in the future – something that divides us yet bring us, together, too.

Well done, Halinka. Write more.

Does this letter make any sense?

Your Andrzej.

Warsaw, 21.11.78

Andrzej dear, though I haven't received a reply to my first letter, I'm writing you another because I've lots to tell you and our 'revels now are ended'…

Everybody likes the Quartet and I don't know if that's good or bad. Majka* was enchanted by it, saying: 'It's interesting music and at every moment he knows exactly what he wants' (and how can sweet Majka possibly know what you want?). Basia concluded that your music generally 'moves and touches her, because it's so… punk like' (see what you've come to?).

I've just sent you *Crime and Punishment*, but find it hard to part with Kępinski's *Fear*.

On reflection I've come to the conclusion that you create such heat during our meetings not because I'm exceptional but because you hunger for stimulation, you simply must have something happening around you, whatever the cost. Real mutual relationships don't give you such electric situations. That's why, subconsciously, you aim for a situation where one person will dominate the other, or make them exceptional, or humiliate them. After all, what is humiliation? People can humiliate themselves if, through cowardice, they commit some dirty trick, but they can only be humiliated by someone else in this way if they *feel* they've been humiliated. The intention to humiliate simply isn't enough. That's why people who are friends can't feel humiliated by anything that's said because they'll either admit that the friend's criticism is just and accept it, or that it's unjust and they defend themselves. If, however, the criticism is merely a *pretext* for expressing negative emotions, then it's hard to speak of friendship since the person criticised becomes merely the object of mental vandalism: I'm destroying someone, therefore I am strong. Added to which we have projection: if you suppress your own aggression, you ascribe aggression to others and start to fear that they want to oppress and humiliate you. That, too, is a vicious circle.

Yes, I do mean you because if you truly believed in yourself and felt good about your own personality, then you wouldn't see the world through the distorted mirror of wounds inflicted and humiliations experienced. That view of yourself

---

* Maria Jurasz, a friend of Halinka's, a pianist, member of the Warsaw Chamber Opera

hinders you in everything: your relationships with people, love, even your playing. The one thing it doesn't hinder you in is your creativity. And I think it's only in your creativity that you're a mature and independent human being. In all other situations you manipulate yourself and you manipulate others. This game sickens you and you feel it's an unnecessary waste of time, but because you are fundamentally unsure of yourself, you seek out people who love you, admire you, accept you, because without them it's hard for you to live. And this – even short-term – dependence often brings out a dislike of, even enmity towards, them.

Once again I've turned myself into Owl.*

Kiss you with all my heart,

Your H.

Cumnor, 4.12.78

Halinka,

I've just received your second letter and I agree with almost everything you say, but not entirely. I became aware of this 'dependence' many years ago, and resolved then to free myself of it. And (though I know in advance that you won't believe me) I give you my word that, to a large extent, I've managed it. But it's easier to achieve independence in newly-formed relationships than in those weighed down by emotional habits and Pavlov (now *I* am Owl)! With you, I react like Eliza in *Pygmalion*: when she meets her father she automatically reverts to the accent she has just learnt not to use, and that's why our meetings are such a disappointment to me. You write that it's hard to have a mutual, or equal, relationship with me. Naturally, while you're still in love with me, it's not only hard, it's downright impossible. Partners are together out of free choice and on an equal footing. I have equal relationships with Stephen, with Eve, Terry** and twenty other people about whom you don't even know.

I want to be on an equal footing with you, too. So write and tell me what bugs you, not what you think I'll like! You wrote that second letter because you were afraid I might resent the first, but the only thing I resent is your fear and desire to be liked, even though I've frequently ingratiated myself, too, and always hated myself for doing it. I resent the thought that if I asked you to eat my shit, you'd obediently do it so I wouldn't resent your refusal.

As for humiliation, the reason I'm so sensitive to it is that I felt nothing else throughout my childhood and youth; neither, I suspect, did you but, unlike me, you not only don't avoid humiliations, you seek them out because we all

---

* Allusion to Owl from *Winnie-the-Pooh*
** Stephen Bishop/Kovacevich, pianist; Terry Harrison, Andrej Tchaikowsky's agent; Eve Harrison, art historian and wife of Terry, Andrzej's close friend

feel safer in situations we know from experience. But since it is, after all, a touchy subject you pretend to yourself that this docile tolerance gives you some sort of moral advantage (as you can see I too can play at Freud).

I'm pleased you like the Quartet – I, too, was pleasantly surprised by it. Of course you're right when you say I consider playing the piano a waste of time! I personally know 150 people who play the piano incomparably better than I do, but very few who, in my opinion, write better than I do (e.g. Lutosławski). And my whole life has sunk to this messing about on the keyboard! Talking of which, I'll shortly send you a cassette of my Piano Concerto in my own rendition at a concert in Dublin.

Many thanks for *Crime and Punishment*! Dostoevsky was obsessed by – humiliation, too. I'm not surprised – epilepsy itself must have got him accustomed to it. May I show your letters to Basia? The relationship between a mother and daughter is one of the many which I can't even begin to imagine!…

Bye for now, Your Andrzej.

PS. I'm sending you my best wishes and asking you to keep writing!

Warsaw, 4.12.78

Darling, your reply to my last letter hasn't reached me yet, so this is a reply to your previous one.

I keep getting the impression we're not being totally honest with one another, though when we speak or write we believe we are.

What's certain is that in some way we both really need each other, but I'm afraid to say how in case it would lead to us stopping to need one another. Are you encouraging me to say it? Very well then, I'll tell you what I need you for. I'm sure you remember Thomas Mann's novella *Disillusionment*. It's the confessions of a man who is disillusioned with life because he never experienced real happiness or real suffering.

Only words inspired in him the intimation of experiences which he was never capable of experiencing in reality. He dreamt of 'a liberated life in which reality dissolved in great feelings without the tormenting effects of disillusionment'. And that is the problem of my own life. I'm really only pleased by what is imagined or potential, possible only on condition that it's not turned into unequivocal reality which I cannot or which I'm afraid to feel.

That's precisely why I need you so much: what there is between us is no threat to reality, it's theatre, words, fiction. I'm talking about my insane feelings towards you; you alone in the whole world believe I am capable of such feelings, you alone treat me seriously even though, apart from words, I have never given you any proof of my feelings. Because you, too, need only words.

When you wrote from New York saying you needed me, wanted to have children, wanted to 'have someone to live for', I was more terrified than joyful. And what happened? As a result of that terror, I married Marek after knowing him only a few weeks. If I'd been your wife, I'm sure I'd have betrayed you because of my anxiety and I'm sure I'd have run away from you, just as I've run away from everyone else. But it would have had nothing at all to do with you, because my fear is irrational and completely independent.

Now you know what I need you for. When you believe in my feelings towards you, I too believe in them and I weep over your lack of reciprocation just as Balzac wept over the death of Eugenie Grandet. You don't love me and so my faith in my insane love is not threatened by any touch of reality. So I can feel safe, happy and my mind is easy about our relationship.

And what do you need me for?

You like me in exactly the same literary way I love you. You can, better than anyone else, stoke up the very feelings, provoke the very declarations of love which you then reject. When I am close, you do it brutally because, like me, you're afraid the game will grow too serious; when I'm far away – the perspective changes, you become kind and tolerant. You'll never admit it because your subconscious is as unexplored as the ocean and only occasionally does a little fish emerge – a frail speck of self-knowledge. I thought the first six days in Cumnor were marvellous. You were the kind of friend one simply doesn't come across! I believed that things were just exactly as they should be between us at last: I adored the dinners together, listening to music, I was talkative, full of laughter, happy. We spent the days in Oxford either together, or separately (after all, I was attending a course in meditation). You went to London; we were at home together only in the evenings. So when the hell did you have the chance to sense that 'painful nostalgia' of mine which made it impossible for you to work? This romantic notion was obviously born only after you'd read my first letter. After all, in Cumnor you accused me of being reserved, of emotional frigidity, you even expressed your contempt for me because of it! You know yourself that if I'd flirted with all the men I've met as much as I flirted with you, I'd have stayed a virgin to this day.

And I didn't let myself be provoked even when you accused me of frigidity and of inner emptiness, even when you talked half the night about sincerity and truth, even when you obstinately kept recalling our night together those twenty odd years ago which you thought would lead to the birth of a Gaspard, or Daniel.

You know better than I do what you were doing. You were probably unloading some inner tension. But where did that come from? After all, you should have been happy that the person who had been interfering with your work for eight whole days was leaving at last.

I wrote my first, slightly emotional, letter with premeditation, though, in my own way, sincerely. I wanted to understand what you really expect from me, and what you're afraid of. And I came to understand that what you expect are words, just words, balancing on the cusp of your expectations and your fears. You are, however, very much afraid of some 'emotional outbursts' from me, and this fear is without substance because, even if I loved you I don't know how much, I still couldn't feel any desire for the simple reason that fear is the most infectious of emotions, and it snuffs out all desire.

If you still like me after this letter, then good. It's three o'clock already and I haven't any strength left. So it's goodnight, Darling.

Your H.

Cumnor, 16.12.78

Halinka,

I've received three letters from you since you left. The first, as I wrote you, aroused my admiration and respect because you finally laid your cards on the table. But now I see that was only the first deck. Each time you've dug out of your extensive innards interesting details which, unfortunately, no longer interest me. The fact that these curios are mutually contradictory does nothing to stop you (…).

Halinka, I don't know why you need to commit this gradual hara-kiri, but I have no desire to watch it. And I absolutely do not agree to your cutting into my innards. Even if you really did know anything about such matters (and I'm not sure you do), you could never be objective where I'm concerned: in your subconscious you'll always find the very thing that you need for your own ends. This kind of analysis may actually prove harmful to the doctor, and it will never cure the patient.

The reproaches you make are easy because by their very nature they're impossible to answer. For instance, you accuse me of a lack of self-knowledge. Well, surely none of us is capable of judging, let alone proving, how far we know ourselves, so there's no room for discussion here. After all, everything is equally possible in our subconscious: perhaps I'm in love with you, or with Mickey Mouse, or perhaps my deepest desire is to become the Dalai Lama.

Fortunately, there's a very simple way of discovering which one of us is right. Quite simply, let's stop writing to each other. If, as you claim, I really do need you for something, even if it is for those provocations, rejections, and sadistic psycho-games, then sooner or later I'll start to miss you (particularly as no-one else loves me in such a 'literary' way), and finally, with tears in my eyes, I'll beg you for a letter. This will give you the satisfaction of confirming your diagnosis, and it will give me the 'self-knowledge' which, in your opinion, I so woefully lack.

Goodbye and good luck.

Your Andrzej.

Warsaw, 21.1.79

Dear Andrzej, I don't expect any letters from you because my predictions have come true with a vengeance. After what I wrote to you not only do we have 'less need' of each other, we've become totally unnecessary to each other, and, like you, I consider that the severing of contacts is unavoidable. That's why I'm taking advantage of this last opportunity to thank you for being so helpful to me at various difficult stages of my life, and for the various kindnesses I received from you and which I can't forget and for which I must thank you.

I also feel a need to clarify certain matters you touch on in your last letter. There is no contradiction in my relationship with you. You were the one who talked about the literary character of my feelings for you in Cumnor ('admit that, more than anything, I work on your imagination'). As for 'desire', I could equally well write the same thing about Jean-Louis Barrault. I went to see the melodrama *Children of Paradise** three times and I sometimes thought that at the root of my attitude towards this gentleman was a completely insane desire, because he attracted me more than any other man! Nevertheless, if fate decreed that I meet him the prospect would arouse terror not desire. Those are two different questions and not at all difficult to comprehend.

But your attitude towards me is nothing but a series of contradictions: and that's precisely what makes understanding and friendship impossible. When I sincerely tell you something pleasant, you accuse me of arse-licking and wanting to eat your shit. When I sincerely tell you something unpleasant – you accuse me of 'digging around in your soul without permission'. When I write about desire – it inspires 'pity and embarrassment' in you; when I write that fear extinguishes all desire – you're hurt. You find it hard to give up my friendship, but I'm not permitted to write about myself because it doesn't interest you, nor about you, because 'you don't agree to have me cut into your innards'. When I behave like a buddy – you accuse me of emotional coolness; when I talk of my emotions – you tell me to cure myself of them. I'm incapable of meeting your contradictory expectations because no one would be capable of meeting them. This game has become unpleasant, tiring, and that's why it has to end. But believe me, the fault is not mine.

I wish you well,

Your H.

---

* Marcel Carné's 1945 film *Les Enfants du Paradis*

Cumnor, 2.2.79

Dear Halinka,

I find it sad to say goodbye to you. But I can see that breaking off with me is something you need now: you have to free yourself from me at last. Your letter alone is evidence of this – it's full of the dignity and independence which I always undermined in you, and which I then accused you of lacking! Now I can see that the accusation was unjust, but I admit with shame and sorrow that you couldn't prove it to me any other way.

But don't burden yourself with any more anger against me. Enjoy the freedom you've acquired so painfully and experience the happiness you've had so little of with someone who will love you and understand you.

Of course 'the fault is not yours'. I treated you like a ruthless brute, but it was myself I hated, not you! Since your visit I've reproached myself more and more and taken it out on you in my letters. I'm not at all surprised you've had enough. But in turn you must believe that I'll always think of you with warmth because hardly anyone has given me what you have. And if you ever want to strike up a new, completely different relationship, unencumbered by old resentments, it would give me quite exceptional joy.

Be well and happy,

Your Andrzej.

Cumnor, 3.2.79

Dear Halinka,

You'll probably be surprised to receive two letters from me (which might arrive together) when you no longer wish to have even one. I know you may tear them up unread or return them without opening the envelopes. But yesterday's reply, written and sent off immediately after receiving your farewell letter, seems to me so superficial and inadequate that I must try one more time.

I've read your letter many times since yesterday and I give you my word that I've rarely been as impressed by anything before. At the same time, I was surprised by my own increasing joy. Perhaps you'll think: 'He's happy because he's rid himself of me.' But the opposite is true – I feel that I haven't lost you, but found a friend in you, regardless of whether we see each other again, or whether or not you write back. (…)

In the past, what I had in you wasn't a friend but a slave. In our relationship you always lost any sense of your own worth and your own rights; what I felt or thought was always more important than your own experiences, and – in your own eyes, too. Finally I had to injure your pride to assure myself that it actually existed. And I also wanted to give you final proof that you are stronger than you thought, that you don't need some unattainable, hopelessly desired idol. It wasn't you I wanted to destroy nor our friendship; I was destroying only the altar where you've been burning candles this last quarter of a century. Or rather, I wanted you to destroy it yourself, to rebel and challenge me, just as you have done now with such extraordinary dignity. You've been asking for a long time what I wanted from you; now you know, because it's happened.

But you know yourself what brutal work it was. And since I am, by nature, an artist not a butcher, I was disgusted by it and by myself. Someone else might well have been able to do it all differently and without all the violence and outbursts; I couldn't. The fact that you wanted to keep in contact with me 'at any price' seemed unworthy of you – I had to find the price you wouldn't pay.

And whom did I humiliate? Myself. After all, aimless, hysterical scenes humiliate only their perpetrators. But for the first time in my life humiliation doesn't bother me – it doesn't matter who's 'on top' nor who is right. What I mean is I've liked you all my life, I like you now and will like you, I respect and admire you more than ever, and I'm at your disposal for ever. I daren't ask for a reply. But I hope that now you'll understand why I tormented you and that I didn't do it just for fun.

I doubt if you'll let me embrace you, but I assure you nothing else would prevent me doing so.

Your devoted

Andrzej.


POSTCARD: BIENNALE OF POSTERS, A CARD WITH SCATTERED LETTERS
Warsaw, 18.2.79

Dear Andrzej, If I'd heard on the BBC that Queen Elizabeth II had left Philip to live with you I would have been less surprised than I was by your last letters. It's hard to reply straight off because it would have to be done in a more orderly way than in this picture.

Hug you with all my heart.

Your H.

CARD: HOUSE WHERE CHOPIN WAS BORN

Warsaw, 20.2.79

Look at the picture. Just like Cumnor. Pat is just carrying the washing in. But this isn't your house, it's Chopin's. I'm finding it difficult to write a letter. The world is full of sadness and I'm sad, too. Your last letters have helped me understand my idiotic attitude to life. Not just towards you.

Your H.

Warsaw, 26.2.79

Dear Andrzej, I can't understand why I'm finding it so hugely difficult to write to you. There is considerably more in your recent letters than even you suspect. They're a *total* negation of my attitude to life and people. The blow is accurate and painful. You've uncovered my lack of authenticity, that my individuality is predicated on a lack of individuality, that I'm constantly playing a role – out of guilt, out of a conviction that 'accepting *someone else's* assessment' is the safest approach to life. I've lied to myself so much playing this role that I'd give a lot just to discover what I really do feel. I'm like the actor with whom the queen of England once fell in love. He appeared clandestinely in her room at night. She said: 'Be Caesar', and the night was wonderful. Next time she said: 'Be Antony', and their love transcended all boundaries, so the next night she begged him: 'Be yourself'. But nothing happened. In despair she asked him: 'What is the matter? You were a magnificent Caesar, a matchless Antony…' And he replied sadly: 'Because I was acting, Your Royal Highness'.

Yes, I'm capable of acting. And nobody notices. But you suddenly noticed and it terrified me. So no new role, no pretence of joy, simply 'being oneself' and showing others one's own barrenness, one's emotional incapacity? It will be awfully difficult for me to talk to you now; I even find this letter hard to get down. I predict that it will be difficult for you, too. I do so because what has happened between us is completely different from anything before. I'm completely lost in it all. Yesterday, Piotr's son, three-year-old Paweł, was here. We were playing hide-and-seek. He got bored, sat in the armchair and finished the game with the statement: 'I hid and I hid and now I'm all found out.' I'm found out, too, but the game is over. Is that good or bad?

Your H.

Telegram in English, Cumnor, 7.3.79

The game is over but life is only just beginning have courage love Andre.

Cumnor, 8.3.79

Darling Halinka,

Well, at last! I congratulate you with all my heart. I didn't help you at all, though I'd very much like to claim the credit; you helped yourself because you are honest and brave. I had no idea that the very thing which interfered with our relationship applied to your relationships with other people, too. You were always asking: 'What do you expect from me?', when all I expected was that you should stop asking that question. Others helped you play your game by giving answers which let you take a suitable role ('I want you to be a wife – a lover – a mother – a sister etc.'), and you always obliged. But I wanted to be friends with the Halinka who's existed since birth 'in herself', even if she isn't aware of the fact (America existed before Columbus, too).

Except that are you in mourning: Jurek has died, Basia has grown up, and I'm making demands which are beyond your strength. But your birth pains are the best proof that real life is only just beginning – as I telegraphed you yesterday. (…) And I beg you, don't let yourself be exploited again because any moment now somebody will appear and demand that you be what he is dreaming of, and you, God forbid, will agree.

To begin with, I'm inviting you to come here for a holiday in June. I know I spoiled your last holiday, but now we know why, and part of our troubles stems from the fact that we see each other too rarely and that's why we're afraid of these meetings. If I gave only one recital a year, can you imagine how nervous I'd be?

Besides which, I love the Halinka who exists independent of the demands of others (even my own) and I'd like to see her at last.

Hug you,

Your Andrzej.

Cumnor, 9.4.79

Darling, if you're afraid to do something then do it straight away, otherwise the fear will last all through your life! That happens to be a maxim of mine and it's probably why I play in public: the more afraid I am, the greater the relief later (regardless of the quality of the concert). The only exception to this is suicide, naturally, because there's no hurry with that – it's the one thing that will never run away. And you can be sure I'll never run away from you (do you remember the witch's prediction?); our real relationship has only just begun.

As for Basia, I don't know. I've only just returned from a three-week journey round Scandinavia and there was a letter from Basia waiting for me. In it, she informs me she wants to become a nun. I'll throw her a word telling her to phone or come down.

Lately I've been playing, almost exclusively, Mozart concertos. I can't do them like Barenboim, of course, but I didn't do them too badly.

You simply must come! Hugs and kisses. Your Andrzej.

Warsaw, 23.4.79

Andrzej dear, do you know what the consequences of your psychotherapy on me have been? You'll laugh and you won't believe it, but – because of you – an agreement on cooperation between two institutes has been dissolved, someone is adopting an orphan, and I haven't got married unhappily for a third time, quite the opposite, in fact – I've been awarded the Distinguished Service Cross and published a story!

So, first the director of our institute asked me to write a review on his behalf of an article written by the director of another institute. I thought: 'If you want a review, a review is what you'll get!' The result was that the other director took offence at our director and an agreement between the two institutes has been cancelled.

I had a girl friend who took up half my waking life with her stupid chattering. One day I simply threw her out – she went into a depression and decided to adopt a little orphan.

I didn't want to go out with a certain gentleman who had considerably more money than charm and was intending to marry (not necessarily me), so who knows what might have come of it.

Wanting to convince you that you're wrong about my literary talent, I sent an article to the weekly *Szpilki*. I was deprived of the opportunity to say I told you so because the article was published immediately!

I had a row at work so they gave me the Distinguished Service Cross.

Darling, will you really still like me in this changed shape? That is the question…

I'm planning to visit Basia at the beginning of June so I hope we'll see each other then. How's your work going? What's happening to the opera? What's happening to you?

All the best.

Your H.

Cumnor, 4.5.79

Darling Halinka,

Bravo! Wonderful! What pleases me most is that you'll be here in June. I also inform you that the 'changed shape' is your only and true shape, which I, unlike you, have always known and liked and which I always fought you for so savagely.

I received and have kept your March letter because from the time of our estrangement every letter of yours is an event; when you come here we'll read the whole chronicle together.

Hug you with all my heart and joy.

Your Andrzej.

Warsaw, 6.5.79

Darling, a brief note, because I've got so much work. So this is what we're resolving: we shall be honest with one another, we won't get in each other's way. You will be neither too gentle (because afterwards you don't like me), nor too brutal (because then you don't like yourself). I promise you complete openness, I'll even tell you frankly: I want to write a story that's been going round in my head and I want to do it at your place because you provoke my imagination, and I hope I won't provoke your irritation. I'm sinking in a morass of the routine, the mundane, normality, and I need your climate to write something again. A schizophrenic wrote this in his journal (read Kipphardt's *Märtz*): 'What does normal mean? A normal person spends his whole life not doing what he wants to do. That's how much pleasure duty gives him. The more he succeeds in not being himself, the more they pay him. Then a normal person retires. Then he has time for himself. But unfortunately he has forgotten himself.'

That's how I'm experiencing my 'normality', more acutely than ever before, because it hurts me and humiliates me. I dream about writing like one dreams about a great love affair.

I'm really pleased that we're going to see each other.

Hugs and kisses.

Your H.

CARD TO ANDRZEJ. FROM THE SERIES THE CIRCUS:
THE LION AND THE CLOWN

Warsaw, 20.5.79

'I think, myself, it is pride which makes friendship most difficult. To submit, to bow down to the other is not easy, but it must be done if one is to really understand the being of the other. (...) Yet, it is terribly solemn – frightening, even.' – From *The Katherine Mansfield Notebooks*.

Cumnor, 23.6.79

Darling,
Your circus card arrived today, after a month! I saw Edward yesterday. (...) Everything's been cleared up, at last. Imagine, all that depression for nothing. And, what's more, it all had to happen in the five days of your stay... It's only today that I realise how exhausted I've been by this completely unnecessary crisis. I've tried to practise, but I simply can't concentrate, and there's certainly no question of my being able to compose! Eve is coming over this evening, I hope she'll manage to unwind me somehow...

Next week I'll get down to some proper work. (...) As soon as I get something down on paper my mood will improve and so will my desire for life. And how are you? How long were you in London? When are you spending those two weeks with your mother?

Hug you with all my heart

Your Andrzej.

Warsaw, 11.7.79

Andrzej, Darling, it was nice of you to write. I've been torn out of my recent apathy by the enchanting poetess Elżbieta*.

I showed her some of my stuff and she said (because she knows about poetry) the poems are poor but (because she knows less about prose) the stories are very good. She told me to make a fresh copy of the stories and take them to some publishing house in Kraków (because she's from Kraków). It cheered me up, but not for long. I'm sipping brandy so as not to fall into sorrow again.

Our last meeting was very brief and very nothing. We were both lousily depressed and nothing more to each other than sombre witnesses to our own failures. I've been thinking about you a lot. I was very much influenced by

---

\* Elżbieta Zechenter-Spławińska, poet, writer, author of the musical *Orphea* with music by M. Sart

Canetti's article on Kafka's *The Letters to Felice*. You must read it; I found it even more interesting than the letters themselves.

I was in London for a week. Basia introduced me to a certain aged, cracked; but highly intelligent Englishman of Ukrainian descent. He impressed me with his enormous erudition, not to mention the seven languages he spoke in my presence for five hours. When I discovered that this gentleman intended to accompany me to the end of my sightseeing in London, I took the first plane out and flew away the next day.

Kiss you. H.

Cumnor, 20.7.79

Darling Halinka,

(…) You saw me in one of my periods of depression which happen, on average, every eighteen months. While they last everyone gets on my nerves but my friends have learned to ignore that, they know it's nothing personal. You found it harder because you were away from your home, your work, your language, your friends – and you were completely dependent on me, and I found that hard to take. Especially since, though you came here to write, nothing came of it because of my gloomy company. I assure you, though, that I didn't want to torment you (generally speaking I torment only myself). It's a fact that you did get on my nerves even though you tried to spend as much time as possible in your room; I was irritated by your sadness, your apathy, your lack of initiative. Your mute face was a constant accusation. You appeared not to reproach me for anything, yet I knew how bad it was for you and I knew it was my fault…

But now I have a plea: let's forgive one another (in my view, there isn't even anything to forgive, it's like an unsuccessful concert) and let's write to each other like old, understanding friends. I agree completely with your poetess. You know very well that I've always considered you a born writer, but you find it as hard to believe in your own talent as I do to believe that someone might like me! Remember what I told you about writing in Cumnor: there's no risk because if something doesn't work, you simply don't show it to anyone! (that's what Hans Keller told me about composition). (…) Prove to yourself that you don't value yourself enough, because no one else can convince you of it.

Despite everything, I do hope you'll come here again, if only to visit Basia. But for the moment don't point out my faults any more – you say yourself that I 'explain everything to my own disadvantage'. Write instead telling me why you still like me, that will help me like myself…

Hug you tightly and with all my heart,

Your old Andrzej.

PS. I now have a new record player which sounds wonderful! And I've also read several good books, particularly an excellent biography of Joe Orton who wrote three astoundingly insolent comedies and was then murdered with a hammer by his male lover (these are the things I read most willingly).

It's just that my eyes hurt with all this reading so I try to do as little as possible – that, to me, is the greatest act of heroism!

Warsaw, 17.8.79

Darling Andrzej,

You're right, I do respond to you in an exaggerated way but not because I'm – as you put it – 'like the moon', nor because of any singularity in my attitude towards you. It's more to do with the fact that you have an exceptional influence on people, an exceptionally powerful 'radiance'. Your emotions are so strong they simply infect people. That's why you have the gift of making people happy and unhappy. As for 'tormenting', you said yourself it applies only to those you love, not so much to your friends. In the first case your aggression stems from an imagined fear that you really can't be loved, in the second case you tremble for fear of being oppressed by someone's expectations or demands. Michael could serve as an example of the first delusion, as a result of which he ran away to another continent; and for want of a better I could serve as an example of the second because for 25 years I've tried to interfere as little as possible, yet whenever I appear even briefly, you see it as a visit from Dracula.

You write that your complexes relate to only a few subjects but I don't know how I can help you since success depends on believing in success. A colleague of mine who weighs 240 pounds believes she is worthy of love and her hugely handsome husband loves her passionately.

In conclusion, let me recommend two charming books by Kurt Vonnegut, Jr: *God Bless You, Mr Rosewater* and *Breakfast of Champions*. There are ideas like this in it: an advert for straw hats! 'For prices like this, you can run them through your horse and put them on your roses.' Incidentally, I'm a fan of Kilgore Trout's philosophy of life.

To finish I'll quote you a poem by the poet Elżbieta (Zechenter-Spławińska):

> Your name
> opens all locks
> on castles in Spain
> metamorphoses all metaphors
> into the literal
> arranges other names
> into dictionaries

of foreign words
Your name
is a tautonym that can stretch
as far as love reaches.*

Kiss you.

Your H.

Cumnor, 21.8.79

Darling Funnyface,

I've just finished the epilogue! I've written it down in my journal and you're the first to know about it. Celebrate with me because I've worked damned hard and over the last three weeks I haven't even practised because I could no longer hear what I was doing! I hope I'll learn it before October, but it's going to be a nightmare job. Barenboim once advised me to spend two hours every morning on practice and two hours every evening on composition: then I would have time for everything and everything will work out by itself. For him, maybe, but not for me – I really can only achieve things in a state of obsession. In fact, as you know, I prefer extreme states – passionate love, passionate hatred, exaltation or depression, and every few weeks unavoidable exhaustion when I can't even get up.

On Sunday Staś was here with Basia (…). Staś, who is very nice and entertaining, handed over Erhardt's beautiful book about Stravinsky from you, for which I thank you with all my heart. I haven't started reading it yet, but I noticed that the dust jacket claims that Stravinsky was of Polish origin – 'Elephants and the Polish Question'.

Basia intends to set up a Club of Polish Wives of English Homosexuals! (…) Be good to me and write again otherwise I'll think you're angry with me. And that isn't so, is it?

Hug you,

Your Andrzej.

PS. I'd really like to show you the ending of *The Merchant* – I like it so much I can't stop marvelling at it…

---

* Untitled poem from *Ósma Góra (The Eighth Hill)*, Wydawnictwo Literackie, Kraków 1979.

Łódź, 19.8.79

Darling Andrzej,

I don't know whether you replied or not because I'm with my mother in Łódź. I feel as if I'm in a psychiatric hospital here. Despite terrible dementia, mother is being re-educated splendidly. I've discovered a simple method: I write letters to her, then she spends hours reading them which gives me some peace and quiet. The funniest thing, though, is that mummy helps me with the style of the letters. I write them next to her, reading aloud as I write, and mummy corrects them. For instance I want to write: 'They'll bring you your pension on the 18th', but mother corrects it thus: 'On the eighteenth the postman will deliver the amount due for my pension.' Mother asks: 'Does Jurek visit you?' In the letter I write: 'Jurek died. We don't see each other.' Mother amends it to: 'We don't see each other *because* Jurek died', and then asks in a dreamy voice: 'Does Jurek still love you?' And so on.

Darling, if you have time read Grotowski's *Towards a Poor Theatre*. I skimmed through an article about it. Don't be put off by the word 'theatre' because the whole of Grotowski's revolution is based on a war against traditional theatre; he is creating a theatre which aims at discovering the truth about human beings, the truth about yourself. I know that this interests you. (…)

Do you know Lutosławski's Cello Concerto? Jabłoński played it recently on television. I was enormously taken by both the concerto and by Jabłoński. I have a new record player – your concerto sounds like a dream on it!

Kiss you.

Your H.

Cumnor, 28.8.79

Darling, I was very pleased by your letter (the one about my 'radiance'). I feel we've come to understand one another again. I'd like to write you a 30-page letter but now, once again, I'm trying to combine practice with the orchestration of the epilogue so I can't afford such luxuries! If you were here we would surely talk the whole night through, with mutual pleasure. But if you were here, I wouldn't have received your letter! Because you know, when you're with me you only ever behave naturally when you're angry with me. On the last day of your stay you decided there was nothing to be lost and you told me all the things that are wrong with me, and I started to radiate. (…)

I know better than anyone about the intensity of my moods, but what can one do? They exhaust me, too. When I finished the epilogue I laughed and prayed with joy, but the next day I spent the whole day in bed because I couldn't do anything. Just think how much I suffered because of Edward, and now he's phoning, writing, and I feel sure of his commitment for the first time. All that depression while you were here turned out to be unfounded! But can anyone unlearn these things? As for my erotic complexes, let *me* give you *my* sexological lecture (at the same time asking you for yours). The difference between the sexes is that a man *looks* while a woman *listens*; men have to like the look of you, while women have to be interested in you. In this respect homosexuals are no different: you have to seduce them with beauty. I could conquer any woman: I'd be tragic with one, playful with another, enigmatic with a third (except that if I loved women I'd be shy, awkward with them and nothing would come of that, either). The thing is that with women different experiences intertwine with each other, while men have their own separate 'compartments'. An ugly man who manages to fascinate you will, eventually, be sexually attractive to you. Whereas a man will say: 'Yes, he's interesting', but then will pick up a very ordinary but young and handsome boy. He'll often even give up a boy to talk to you, which is undoubtedly laudable but then man does not live by bread alone.

And what am I? Fat, bald (which you're going to cure me of), but worst of all aware of these facts. Here we're in agreement. If I could only think for one moment that I was attractive! But I can't, so what's to be done? You could help me a lot here. (…)

Next time you come over (because I hope that despite everything there will be a next time), I'll rent you a room right away and you'll be independent. And what's the betting that, right away, I'll start persuading you to move in with me? I feel things so strongly it doesn't matter what I felt the last time, even if those feelings were completely different.

I'll remember the Vonnegut, and I recommend Camus' *The Fall* which I'm reading a second time. In fact I'll give you the titles of the books I've borrowed from the library for this week: *The Fall, A Case of Poisons, Night of the Long Knives, Crimes of Passion*, and *Satanic Mass.*

I've read the first two already. No wonder I'm in a splendid mood! Added to which, the weather is phenomenal…

Hug you,

Your Andrzej.

Cumnor, 13.9.79

Darling, thank you so much for the books! Also, Basia was here just now and we even bought a card to write to you together, but we forgot to do it before she left… Forgive us! It was awfully nice: on Monday we fell asleep listening to records, and on Tuesday Basia lay in the garden and read my autobiography, and then we went boating. We've been having wonderful weather lately, and

I'm out in the garden again. I've given myself a day's holiday because over the last 6 days I've been dutifully working on the *Kreisleriana,* Sonata in B flat minor and the orchestration of the epilogue which I quite immodestly like.

I'm enormously curious about your stories. I assure you it's not just Elżbieta who believes in you.

Hug you with all my heart,

Your Andrzej.

Warsaw, 20.9.79

Dearest Darling, having spent 16 days getting here all your letters have somehow managed to arrive. I use up so much time enjoying your letters I don't have time to write back. I'm meeting Anna Linke in an hour (she translated, among others, Kubin's *The Other Side* and, brilliantly, Thomas Mann's *The Holy Sinner*), so I have to hurry. You know what she says? That if one isn't aggressive one shouldn't set about making art (so you can set about it, I can't). She laughs at me for reading the Latin American writers because, according to her, they're 'hysterical cowherds'.

Your sexological lecture leads to astounding conclusions: if all homosexuals loved only younger and prettier partners the population of homosexuals would consist entirely of delightful, wonderful toy boys, but it isn't so. After all, you're the man who picks up 'an ordinary, but handsome boy'.

The fact you don't do it is a result of two erroneous convictions: that you're not attractive and that male-to-male love is different from any other. So how is the poet with the face of a gladiator and just seven hairs on his head such a success? You're under the illusion you're fat – you're not; you're under the illusion you're ugly – you're not. And if you want to have more hair than you've got, use Bánfi lotion (but remember that hair will grow in every place touched by the lotion!).

I'm talking superficially about your problems but I'm coming to the heart of the matter: what interferes with your erotic successes is mental, not physical. If you're an exceptional individual you should be consistently expansive and courageous in every walk of life. You can't be a genius in one field and a shy pussy cat in another because that's incomprehensible and frightens the other party. Maybe you've got moral scruples? One of my acquaintances seduced a 14-year-old girl and then told her: 'Unfortunately I can't marry you because I love my wife.' You'd say: 'Because I love my art.' And you'd feel like a heel. (…)

I think, however, that, despite appearances, it would be easier for you to arrange your private life with some student girl who was madly in love with you – as many exceptional people have done. You'll say I can't imagine the problems of homosexuality – maybe not; but then neither could Freud. I still see your homosexuality as a neurotic fixation which needs unfixing. So you can understand what I mean by fixation, I'm sending you a charming little book called *Seduced* by Jeremi Przybora. There's nothing at the root of it except fear, especially with someone as super-male as you. I read some advice for anxious and fearful men recently: they should read aloud the first lines of *Pan Tadeusz** at the same time, etc. Jerzy Kosiński used to study atlases opened over his partner's head. I suggest you should study scores.

But really, you should read Masters. He claims that men just don't have a clue what to do with a woman; he sincerely advises women to look after themselves or their girl friends. In other words, most men *imagine* they're men.

I'm stopping now. Or maybe not yet. Yes, I am.

Hug you with all my heart,

Your H.

Cumnor, 29.9.79

Darling, Thank you for the card. Staś wrote at the same time. It doesn't surprise me that you're missing me: it sounds very conceited but after all what binds us together is identity, not fleeting moods. A bad-tempered and moody Andrzej is still Andrzej, and that's enough for you to like him regardless of whether he deserves your friendship or not.

When you realise it's mutual you'll stop worrying about my specific reactions and everything will become lighter and easier. Write anything you want to boldly. Bye for now because the season is starting next week!

Hug you with all my heart,

Your Andrzej.

Warsaw, 27.9.79

Darling, I've just received your letter about the orchestration of the epilogue and Basia's visit etc., and a letter from Basia who recalls her visit to you with delight. The reader's review of my miserable stories has arrived from the publisher. The man who wrote it must have thought I'm a teenager because he writes, among other things, this: 'It has to be emphasised that the author is capable of telling a given story. With distance, even with a discreet wink, using psychological and narrative surprises as well as implication and interruptions. One cannot then deny that the author has literary as well as narrative talent, but

---

* Poland's national epic poem by Adam Mickiewicz

she must be aware that formal skill, of which she has given undoubted evidence, is not everything. The themes she chooses are banal, the portraits she sketches do not go beyond a very conventional psychological framework. *What is striking is the lack of any social and psychological insight'* (my emphasis).

The reviewer doesn't dismiss the possibility of publishing a volume of my stories, but he most decisively dislikes those that have already been given prizes and published. According to him 'They are unsuitable for publication', but he would like to see some new pieces. I would willingly write them if it weren't for the fact that first I'd have to develop intellectually which I probably won't have time to do.

I'm ending on this sad note because I'm in a terrible hurry.

Hug you.

Your H.

POSTCARD: BODLEIAN LIBRARY, OXFORD.
P.B. SHELLEY, ODE TO THE WEST WIND, ORIGINAL DRAFT

Cumnor, 3.10.79

Darling,

Many thanks for Jeremi Przybora's *Seduced*; so far I've only read the jacket, but the title has already amused me. On Saturday I'm giving my first recital with *Kreisleriana* and the Sonata in B flat minor so I'll be able to tell you about it then.

When will you send me something of your own?

Kiss you,

Your A.

Cumnor, 9.10.79

'Esteemed Sir!

Thank you with all my heart for your generous review, and particularly for the remarks from which I deduce I should continue with my education. The wisdom of this advice struck me so forcefully that in my youthful enthusiasm I anticipated it by over a dozen years so I'm grateful to you, Sir, for my PhD in sociology, my two academic books and my five literary prizes. Since, however, my education has proved insufficient, I would be grateful if you could provide me, as a model and for encouragement, with a list of your own qualifications.'

Type this out and send it to your Beckmesser, and you'll feel better straight away! I recall to this day a New York review of 1957 where I was advised to take up farming: 'As long as there are jobs vacant in agriculture, this wellmcaning young man should never be allowed to sit down at a piano; this atrocious misunderstanding should be spared both to him and to us.'

I've already played my first recital of the season, of which the Chopin Sonata in B flat minor came out best; *Kreisleriana* was worse (somehow I'm just not convinced by it), but worst of all was the Prelude in C sharp minor which we all played in '55 at the contest. I thought it was easy, but I should remember there are no easy works. I started with Beethoven's Sonata op. 90 and I stuck the *Barcarolle* in there somewhere – both went well.

My friend Jaś Pęski (the gentleman who took to painting some 4 years ago) has made two simply extraordinary portraits of Rimbaud from photographs, underlining at his exhibition that they're not for sale, despite which they were particularly praised in the reviews. Now he's given them to me as a present! I'm flabbergasted – you know that Rimbaud is my guardian demon. I'm now trying to persuade Jaś to paint the Grand Inquisitor from *The Brothers Karamazov*.

Well, it's time to go back to work! The scherzo from the B flat minor sonata, then the daily page of orchestration. The epilogue is transparent so it's a pleasure to orchestrate, but it takes up so much time! Verdi wrote *Aida* in two weeks and it's been in the repertoire for over a century – with me it's going to be exactly the opposite.

Kiss you,

Your Andrzej.

Cumnor, 18.10.79

My Darling Funnyface,

As usual I woke up feeling miserable and over coffee I half-heartedly opened *Seduced*. Your letter 'about me' fell out, the one I thought hadn't arrived! The letter sent me into a transport of passionate gratitude. Oh, how is it that you know me so perfectly and at the same time like me so much? Granny always said: 'The people who like you are the people who don't know you', and I believed her. But she did try to marry me off to you so maybe she realised that you would end up being that exception. You know me inside out; I agree with every word you write about me. It'll come as no surprise, though, if I tell you that you don't know as much about homosexuality. I'd *like* to agree with you here because you write so optimistically and so positively that it makes me want to live, not simply write and work. Unfortunately, however, it's not that simple. My conviction that 'male-to-male love is different from any other' seems to me even more objectively based than my conviction that 'I'm not attractive'. Because it's only half the homosexual population that consists of your delightful toy boys, the other half consists of gentlemen who might have been delightful once but you wouldn't say that of them now. And everyone's in love with the toy boys because the elder gents can't love one another but the toy boys can. Eventually the toy boys sleep with each other and the gentlemen write string quartets and write pitiful letters to their intelligent lady friends. Besides, I'm after love, not adventures. Adventures are much easier, one can even pay for them if not with cash, for instance, then by appealing to snobbery and playing the role of a famous pianist. That's how I explain the successes of the poet you write about: he is less demanding of himself. I want to sleep with someone I can love and respect, and I also want to be loved. That's probably too much to ask for.

Yes, I am difficult (…) Funnyface, I can't bear to tell lies, especially in bed! I don't want an exchange of hypocrisies of the kind: 'You want to boast about me, I want to sleep with you, but remember we must sigh romantically as we do it'.

As for the 'enamoured girl', that was my great hope for many years. I even thought of Ondine, we did have a chance because we have a lot in common, we're both crazy about music, about French poetry, and Ondine is enchanting, full of passionate enthusiasms and she liked me a lot, but I lacked faith in that love and in myself… (…) So it finished up with us listening to records, and the next day Stephen arrived and… Ondine went off to London.

Maybe instead of looking after those derailed girls like you're supposed to you could rehabilitate me? Funnyface, when you next come don't doubt my devotion to you! If, God forbid, I'm in a state of depression again treat it like the flu – either wait calmly until it's over, or cure me of it. You would find it easier to do than you think.

Hug you with all my heart.

Your Andrzej.

Warsaw, 13.10.79

Andrzej dear,

(…) I've developed a complex that everything I write is confused and incomprehensible to others. A reviewer in Kraków started his review with a summary of what my stories were about. I was astonished because they're about something completely different! Then again Jagusia sees more in them than I do; she claims, for instance, that one of them illustrates Karen Horney's hypothesis that a neurotic's love for his partner is the same as that of the blind man for his white stick; moreover – according to Jagusia – a story that makes everyone laugh is deadly sad and shows the weakness of men in the contemporary world as they resort to alcoholism, ham acting, mythomania or – at best – ink slinging. Yes, instead of arousing reflection, my stories arouse laughter, even in the unfortunate reviewer. When my hero hangs himself, they roll about laughing, too. Explain it to me, because I don't understand.

I had a very unfortunate experience a few days ago. It was a conversation, which went on for many hours, with a female colleague who'd invited me round for a drink. This colleague is a clinical psychologist and knows about people. I like her, admire her, and considered her to be almost a friend until she told me that being with me wasn't the most pleasant experience. And why? Because I inspire fear by suppressing my aggression. This makes me unnatural; I inspire uneasiness and irritation. Then she asked: 'Has nobody ever told you this before?'

I remembered my conversations with you. 'Yes, but only one other person.'

'Quite, because it's not easy to notice… You're always pleasant and sweet.'

'But I'm truly not hiding anything! I simply don't feel any aggression.'

'You're lying. Tell me what you really think of me?'

'I think you're intelligent, honest, a good colleague, erudite…'

'Don't suck up to me! Tell me what you *really* think.'

I didn't think anything bad about her so I started to wonder what I could make up to satisfy her. But I couldn't think of anything. So she cried out contemptuously:

'You're even afraid of thinking badly of people, it's like a disease!'

In no time at all we were both hopelessly drunk. I didn't want to drink any more, but she shouted: 'Why don't you want to drink? Do you always have to be in control? Save face, humiliate others? Do you have to put on that damned, sleek mask on your face? You disgusting little innocent! You crippled human being!'

I left her place at 3 o'clock in the morning. She told me I was a wolf in sheep's clothing. And that's how I felt. I wasn't afraid to walk back on my own. What can a wolf fear at night in a town where people walk unarmed? Suddenly, I started to think about you. Maybe you fear love like I fear aggression? Maybe you, who are so soft and gentle, put on a wolf's skin for protection? You said yourself that you wound those you love… I also thought: if it's true we're such masters of disguise then we'll never understand one another.

Hug you with all, all of my heart.

Your H.

Cumnor, 22.10.79

Darling,

I should in fact be writing you two letters, one about your stories, the other about the argument with your colleague. I'll write about the stories when I've read them myself, though I know professional critics don't always put themselves to the trouble. For the time being I'll just remind you that when Kafka read the recently completed *The Trial* to his friends, not only did they fall off their chairs laughing, but he himself laughed so much he had to stop reading.

Our century's most characteristic trait is probably that we're likely to laugh most when the subject is cruellest because we've run out of tears. (Example: Beckett, Ionesco, Bulgakov, Kafka's *Metamorphosis*) It's also possible that your stories end on a note of irony – lacking confidence you deny yourself the right to *make* the reader react seriously. I don't know if I'm right – I don't know the stories.

Now on to the next subject. I'll tell you the worst straight away: nobody can understand your colleague and everything she said better than I do!

When I read your wonderful letter recently, the one which fell out of *Seduced* (the one which you later thought was stupid), I wanted to have you with me for a lively conversation that would last all night. But I also knew that you would never talk to me the same way you write to me.

St. John wrote that perfect love overcomes fear, but your fear is at an unreachable level of perfection which means your love must hide itself away, as they say, which is precisely what it does.

You think your presence gets on my nerves. No, Darling: it's your half-presence. You were fully present only on the last day when you were angry with me and you talked to me with no inhibitions. But it wasn't your anger I felt: for the first time in a week I felt some contact.

And remember I always feel this contact just when you think you've 'overstepped the mark': in the letters where you break off with me, in our farewell conversation and in the sexological lecture which you later claimed had been stupid.

You think you were cheerful and lively right from the start. But just as I didn't sense your anger, I didn't notice your liveliness. To me you seemed quite simply polite. You entertained me politely with your conversation like a poor relation who knows her place…

Darling, don't think I want to reproach you with anything. You'd have more to reproach me with! But that's not what this is about: I just want to get to the heart of the matter, to shed some light once and for all on this constant misapprehension between you and people with my kind of temperament who are made uneasy by emptiness or passivity.

After a few days with you I felt that 'nothing was happening'. Seeing my irritation, you thought to yourself: 'I'm getting on his nerves', but what was really getting on my nerves was your lack of confidence. Who wants to live with a hen-pecked Cinderella? The more you tiptoed round the place and spoke in childish endearments: 'Don't worry, Darling Pussy cat, you go on playing and I'll just go for a little walk', the more you tried to belittle yourself, the more disillusioned I became because I had expected that positive and bold attitude I knew from the letters. But that's not the worst. The worst is I can't stand myself in your presence. Understand that when one person loses his patience while the other continues to behave faultlessly, the moral superiority of the other is unusually demeaning for the first person. And that's where your special form of aggression is to be found, the aggression your colleague was probably talking about. It always ended with me being the executioner and you being the helpless sacrifice, and we were both equally conscious of your innocence. Darling, that could well have given you a kind of satisfaction, but together we could have surely found greater pleasures.

Funnyface, don't be angry with me for these remarks. You wrote yourself that you were 'wounded', so I just wanted to show you how others see it. I, too, am 'wounded', but the wounds will heal if I have the courage to remove the bandages. In this we can help each other. (...)

Hug you with all my heart,

Your Andrzej.

Warsaw, 1.11.79

Darling, yesterday I received your kind but surely sad letter – the reply to mine which fell out of *Seduced*.

Love and stage performances are precisely the same: if you think obsessively that you've got an audience which you maniacally want to impress, that you must on no account make any mistakes, that you have to succeed – then you'll play dreadfully. But if you forget about all that, and start to take pleasure in playing something beautiful, in the wonderful opportunity to make someone happy with your music – then you'll play like a true artist. Waldorff was so right when he said about Zimerman: 'He was the only competitor in the contest who was glad he could play the piano for a bit and be heard by others.' You'll say he had faith that he could make others happy with his music, and you don't have faith – at least not in emotions and love. Believe me, the fault lies in your lack of confidence in yourself and in your pride. If I am to nurture you then I must dig that pride out of you like weeds out of the earth. I've already given you the example of Christ: it's hard to find someone else who allowed himself to be so bloodily humiliated. And yet out of it all he became God!

You felt humiliated by the Ondine affair, but you didn't for a minute consider that she might have felt a hundred times more humiliated. That's the only reason she said: 'You don't interest me. I feel ill-at-ease with you.' And that's why she went to London. But in your blindness you're in no fit state even to notice the other person because you're obsessively thinking about your pride and about not wanting it to be wounded. It's a paradox but when in love one thinks only of the other person, about what they feel, what they desire, and what they fear, then one's own happiness rains down as if from heaven. This superficially banal wisdom is not something I thought up, but God Himself did when he set down that the second biological law would be more powerfully active amongst living creatures than the first law. In a moment you'll say that I'm boring you to death with these abstract meditations which have nothing to do with your problems. But they have! Because the source of your problems is your personality and no miracle will take place until you change. Your fear will continue to paralyse and repulse people you want to love and want to be loved by.

Darling, I've been very affected by the role of mentor which I've been accorded. For variety's sake I'll introduce you to a certain lady I adore. She's called Wisława Szymborska. She's a rare example of an excellent poet and also a true intellectual. Read the poems and, if you like them, I'll send you more.

Kiss you with all my heart,

Your H.

*Still*

Across the country's plains
sealed boxcars are carrying names:
how long will they travel, how far,
will they ever leave the boxcar –
don't ask, I can't say, I don't know.

The name Nathan beats the wall with his fist,
the name Isaac sings a mad hymn,
the name Aaron is dying of thirst,
the name Sarah begs water for him.

Don't jump from the boxcar, name David.
In these lands you're a name to avoid,
you're bound for defeat, you're a sign
pointing out those who must be destroyed.

At least give your son a Slavic name:
he'll need it. Here people count hairs
and examine the shape of your eyelids
to tell right from wrong, "ours" from "theirs."

Don't jump yet. Your son's name will be Lech.
Don't jump yet. The time's still not right.
Don't jump yet. The clattering wheels
are mocked by the echoes of night.

Clouds of people passed over this plain.
Vast clouds, but they held little rain –

just one tear, that's a fact, just one tear.
A dark forest. The tracks disappear.

That's-a-fact. The rail and the wheels.
That's-a-fact. A forest, no fields.
That's-a-fact. And their silence once more,
that's-a-fact, drums on my silent door.*

*Experiment*

As a short subject before the main feature –
in which the actors did their best
to make me cry and even laugh –
we were shown an interesting experiment
involving a head.

The head
a minute earlier was still attached to...
but now it was cut off. Everyone could see
that it didn't have a body.
The tubes dangling from the neck hooked it up to a machine
that kept its blood circulating.
The head
was doing just fine.

Without showing pain or even surprise,
it followed a moving flashlight with its eyes.
It pricked up its ears at the sound of a bell.
Its moist nose could tell
the smell of bacon from odourless oblivion,
and licking its chops with evident relish
it salivated its salute to physiology.

A dog's faithful head,
a dog's friendly head
squinted its eyes when stroked,
convinced that it was still part of a whole
that crooks its back if patted
and wags its tail.

---

* Translation from the Polish by Stanisław Barańczak and Clare Cavanagh in *Poems New and Collected 1957-1997* by Wisława Szymborska. With kind permission of Faber and Faber Ltd.

I thought about happiness and was frightened.
For if that's all life is about,
the head
was happy.*

*Commemoration*

They made love in a hazel grove,
beneath the little suns of dew;
dry leaves and twigs got in their hair
and dry dirt too.

Swallow's heart, have
mercy on them.

They both knelt down on the lakeshore,
they combed the dry leaves from their hair;
small fish, a star's converging rays,
swam up to stare.

Swallow's heart, have
mercy on them.

Reflected in the rippling lake,
trees trembled, nebulous and gray;
o swallow, let them never, never
forget this day.

o swallow, cloud-borne thorn,
anchor of the air,
Icarus improved,
coattails in Assumption,

o swallow, calligraphy,
clockhand minus minutes,
early ornithogothic,
heaven's cross-eyed glance,

o swallow, knife-edged silence,
mournful exuberance,
the aureole of lovers,
have mercy on them.*

---

* Translation from the Polish by Stanisław Barańczak and Clare Cavanagh in *Poems New and Collected 1957-1997* by Wisława Szymborska. With kind permission of Faber and Faber Ltd.

Cumnor, 11.11.79

Darling Funnyface,

You called my last letter 'kind but sad'. I fear this one will be even sadder, because your reply brought out into the open the very thing I find most offensive about myself! This is not an excuse, quite the reverse: we agreed we would write to one another concealing nothing.

I'm talking about this in your letter: 'When in love one thinks only of the other person, about what they feel, what they desire, and what they fear, then one's own happiness rains down as if from heaven.' Darling, that's exactly what I'm incapable of. I've never been able to love my neighbour, I can see that clearly and I reproach myself for it greatly. You've touched the heart of the matter, but you've told me nothing new, I've known about it for years and that's why I've 'withdrawn' and resolved to live alone. At least this solitude won't hurt anyone else, and I've even come to like it. If you want to try to cure me of something then this is it: when I 'love' someone (and I write that in quotation marks because it's hard to call it love), then all I'm after is reciprocity – not to make it good for the other person. If it turns out the other person hasn't rung because of sickness, I'm radiant with relief. Naturally I passionately want their happiness, but I want them to owe it to me: if they're going to be happy with someone else I'd rather they had leukaemia. That's why, in love, I lose all respect for myself because then I'm capable only of cannibalism.

If you cure me of this, I won't care if I love women or boys. Because it's important I love *people*. But the fact is I think this illness is completely incurable. This letter has cost me a lot because it's made me relinquish all of my pride, but I'll send it even though I'm ashamed.

Hug you with all my heart.

Your Andrzej.

PS. How is it that in a country where there are poets like Szymborska they publish J.?

Warsaw, 8.11.79

Darling Andrzej, thank you very much for your frank letter (the one in which you write how badly you feel in my company). Maybe the cause of our unsuccessful meetings is, among others, that we don't work together, or have mutual friends, or share everyday concerns? During my first visit you told me not to talk about my work because it bored you, during my second visit not to talk about Polish matters, or Polish theatre, because it irritated you. You'll willingly talk about the things I write, but I don't write; you'll willingly talk about my experiences, but I don't have any experiences. The only subject which interests us both is you. 'What sort of stories does he like? About himself, because he's *that* sort of Bear.'* But I find it easier to write on this open-ended subject than I do to talk. You expect too much of me, your expectations paralyse me, because when we talk about intelligence and imagination I feel 'like a fly next to the Cathedral of Notre Dame'. I am overcome by mental impotence. Not only do I try – as you write – to 'belittle' myself, but I pretend I'm a little, dead worm, because no one grinds a dead worm down, a dead worm is left in peace. My 'metamorphosis' doesn't please me, either, and I just long to be far from you and to reward your disappointment with a letter. You and my colleague call it 'my form of aggression', but it's only a desperate flight. Maybe in Kafka's *Metamorphosis* the unfortunate Gregor's family also believe that in turning into a nightmarish worm he's acting against them, that 'he's paid them back' as cruelly as he could, but the reader understands why they feel it that way.

You're constantly wanting to renew our unsuccessful meetings, and yet they are doomed to failure from the start!

Let's leave it at writing, let's be joined by this 'bridge over which only one person can cross at a time'…

You wrote that you're difficult in love. And I'm difficult in friendship: I demand sincerity, tolerance, and patience, and if I sense I'm not getting it then I become 'empty and passive'. You say: 'Who'd want to live with Cinderella… ?' But Cinderella stopped being Cinderella when the Good Fairy appeared and showed her some warmth. In Cumnor – she didn't appear. The slipper which I didn't lose – wasn't found by anyone, either. It's a different story that fits in here, not one by the Grimms.' If you like you can try guessing. You like riddles.

Hug you with all my heart,

Your H.

Antwerp, 14.11.79

Darling Funnyface,

I hoped my letter wouldn't make you angry and indeed it didn't. But our own difficulties in mutual contacts are revealing themselves more and more starkly. It's not possible to talk of 'fault' here: firstly because we maintain our friendship to help, not to judge, one another; secondly because how can one blame someone for being themselves?

Unfortunately, in my hurry, I left your last letter at home (it arrived this morning). But I read it three times and I remember it precisely. I agree that the best form of our friendship is this present correspondence. But it doesn't have to be so

---

* The Bear in question is AA Milne's Winnie-the-Pooh and this passage was in English in the letter

for ever. Firstly, because knowledge of a situation changes the situation itself, just as in music – the awareness of certain technical difficulties increases them to begin with, but in the end helps to overcome them. Secondly, we ourselves are changing.

And so from your friends you demand patience, tolerance and warmth. You're right. You're also right that I don't have those qualities. Think what kind of pianist I'd be if I had patience. As for tolerance, my views are decidedly tolerant. I am outraged, for instance, by the treatment of the Indians in Brazil, but it's hard to be tolerant without patience. And though my warmth is passionate and sincere, it is sporadic; it's as if instead of having central heating in your house, your house was burned to the ground every three weeks.

As you see, I agree with all your criticisms. But you're unjust about yourself. After all, you're the one who's writing all those letters which are the basis of my expectations! In your letters, then, you have all the traits I value, but in my presence you're struck down with stage-fright. I am, too, but my fear makes me attack like a bull, while your fear makes you turn into a little worm. What are you afraid of, what am I afraid of? We don't know – surely there's nothing threatening us. Clearly someone has already frightened us to death a long time ago...

I hope that, after this letter, and even more so after the previous one, you'll stop accusing me of a lack of self-knowledge. That hurt me very much because I've been fighting for self-knowledge consciously and stubbornly for years. And that, in fact, was the only one of your letters which was malicious and unjust. I also think that when you visit Basia some time and pay me a 'flying' visit, things will be positively ideal between us, better than ever. Whenever anyone comes to stay with me I'm weighed down by a sense of responsibility. (...) I simply cannot live with people. (...)

And is the story you refer to *Beauty and the Beast*?

Hug you. Your Andrzej.

Cumnor, 21.11.79

Darling Funnyface,

I've just returned from my journey – to *Journey*!* Many thanks; you know how the *The Railway Station in Munich* enchanted me. And recently I finally read *Seduced* and laughed out loud. And the day before yesterday, just as you wished, I gave it to Basia with whom I spent a decidedly pleasant evening...

Maybe, for a change, I could send you something? There is an opportunity because Basia is off to Poland for Christmas. Radu [Lupu] found a tape of my concerto at his place: I'll try to get it copied in time, though that performance

---

* By Stanisław Dygat

and that recording will only give you a fragmentary knowledge of the piece. Furthermore, something very strange has happened: for the first time in my life I've written a short story and not only do I want to send it to you, I also want to dedicate it to you. I think you will understand it particularly well.

I'll have the story typed up and send you a copy. I'm also thinking of sending you two English novels which I positively adore: *Wuthering Heights* by Emily Brontë, and *Till We Have Faces* by C. S. Lewis which even the English don't generally know about.

Bye for now because I've got a terrible cold, my eyes hurt and my nose is running.

Hug you with all my heart,

Your Andrzej.

PS. The strongest argument against our meetings is that I wouldn't get your letters.

Warsaw, 25.11.79

Andrzej, Darling, it's good that you wrote that sad letter though it won't be easy to reply to it.

I don't know where to start. Maybe from the thing which gave rise to the greatest resistance when you were writing it, from your confession: 'If they're going to be happy with someone else I'd rather they had leukaemia.' If you don't believe me, then believe what Shakespeare says. He knew what people were really like and it's not for nothing that Hamlet tells Ophelia to go to a nunnery. After all that's exactly the same thing: I can't have you, so nobody will. You write that, in love, you lose all respect for yourself, and your beloved Dostoevsky replies: 'Can a self-aware human being respect himself even a little?' Hiding behind everything, even behind love, is an expansion of one's own EGO (…).

But at the same time one has to believe that the territory one conquers is safe territory. For you, any 'territory' you wish to conquer, which you'd be glad to be identified with, is a threatening territory. And that is your problem, not a pathological emotional frigidity or a distaste for people. Anyone you start to love immediately becomes a potential enemy because HE can hurt you the most. And can one love a potential enemy with a 'good love'? One can fight him, one can kill him, but one can't identify with him. Do you remember that shattering story of the hunchback? At the trial he said he'd killed the only woman he had ever loved because she was the only one who could hurt him and *she would have done* if he hadn't killed her. That girl knew what he was like but she wanted to be with him despite everything. He, however, did not believe it because he was full of fear and mistrust.

Darling, I'm sorry, but it seems that there isn't much I can do to help, because how could I? To keep repeating 'discard your pride' is like telling a man frozen on the ice: 'Throw off your coat because when you harden yourself you won't feel the cold.' Camus wrote in one of his 'Carnets' [Notebooks]: 'I'm too weak to give up my pride.'

Hug you with all my heart,

Your H.

PS. I'm enclosing some poems by Szymborska again. One so you can understand why I wanted to marry you off – the other so you won't worry that you don't love anyone.

*Portrait of a Woman*

She must be a variety.
Change so that nothing will change.
It's easy, impossible, tough going, worth a shot.
Her eyes are, as required, deep blue, gray,
dark, merry, full of pointless tears.
She sleeps with him as if she's first in line or the only one on earth.
She'll bear him four children, no children, one.
Naïve, but gives the best advice.
Weak, but takes on anything.
A screw loose and tough as nails.
Curls up with Jaspers or *Ladies' Home Journal*.
Can't figure out this bolt and builds a bridge.
Young, young as ever, still looking young.
Holds in her hands a baby sparrow with a broken wing,
her own money for some trip far away,
a meat cleaver, a compress, a glass of vodka.
Where's she running, isn't she exhausted.
Not a bit, a little, to death, it doesn't matter.
She must love him, or she's just plain stubborn.
For better, for worse, for heaven's sake.*

---

* Translation from the Polish by Stanisław Barańczak and Clare Cavanagh in *Poems New and Collected 1957-1997* by Wisława Szymborska. With kind permission of Faber and Faber Ltd.

*Thank-You Note*

I owe so much
to those I don't love.

The relief as I agree
that someone else needs them more.

The happiness that I'm not
the wolf to their sheep.

The peace I feel with them,
the freedom –
love can neither give.
nor take that.

I don't wait for them,
as in window-to-door-and-back.
Almost as patient
as a sundial,
I understand
what love can't,
and forgive
as love never would.

From a rendezvous to a letter
is just a few days or weeks,
not an eternity.

Trips with them always go smoothly,
concerts are heard,
cathedrals visited,
scenery is seen.

And when seven hills and rivers
come between us,
the hills and rivers
can be found on any map.

They deserve the credit
if I live in three dimensions,
in non-lyrical and non-rhetorical space
with a genuine, shifting horizon.

They themselves don't realize
how much they hold in their empty hands.

'I don't owe them a thing,'
would be love's answer
to this open question*

Warsaw, 29.11.79

Darling, I've just received your charming letter. If this continues, there'll be nothing to write about – we agree on everything! (…)

How did the concerts go? You don't write anything about them. Majka, a fan of your work, is with the Chamber Opera and asks if it would be possible to stage your opera there. Does it have a big choral element? They don't have so much in that line.

Szymborska, who is very interested in opera, read Józef Kański's *Opera Guide* and, after perceptive inquiries, discovered that: 'The opera world is ruled by a tough personal politics. Family relationships are controlled by rules which are as unbreakable as those in aboriginal tribes. The soprano has to be the daughter of the bass, the wife of the baritone, the lover of the tenor. A tenor must not father an alto nor have carnal knowledge of a contralto. The baritone-lover is a rarity and he would do better to look for some mezzo. In turn, the mezzo-soprano should beware of tenors – fate usually condemns her to play the role of 'the other woman', or to the even sadder position of being a friend of the soprano. The only woman with a beard in the history of opera (see Stravinsky's *The Rake's Progress*) is a mezzo-soprano and, naturally, does not experience happiness. The basses, apart from fathers, are as a rule cardinals, powers of darkness, prison functionaries and one director of a hospital for the insane.'**

I've copied it out exactly because I'm wondering if *The Merchant* obeys these casting rules fully. You must write and tell me! (…)

A moment ago I received a very funny letter from Jagusia. As you know, Jagusia is an outstanding sociologist and apart from being that writes interesting stories (most recently – about her impressions of America); since she doesn't, however, have confidence in her artistic talents she has strange dreams. She has just described one of them to me: she dreamt that she decided to become a dancer, even though it's a little bit late now; she tries to make up for lost time

---

* Translation from the Polish by Stanisław Barańczak and Clare Cavanagh in *Poems New and Collected 1957-1997* by Wisława Szymborska. With kind permission of Faber and Faber Ltd.

** Wisława Szymborska: *Lektury nadobowiązkowe*, WL, Kraków 1973 (English edition *Nonrequired Reading* Harcourt 2002)

by hard work and she trains diligently. But when the time comes to dance on her toes she notices that, from the knee down, one of her legs is wooden. But even that doesn't discourage her, for she comes to the conclusion that being a professional dancer with an artificial leg is more laudable than one with two good legs! This dream characterises my beloved Jagusia perfectly.

To end with I'll describe a dream of mine which, in turn, characterises me perfectly. Well then, the end of the world was approaching, caused by universal, world-wide starvation. In Poland a patriotic organisation is set up which organises cannibalistic butchers' stalls. I was working on one of those stalls as a 'mincer': I minced and packed human meat. One day I was called into the manager's office and he told me that the supplies hadn't arrived that day and consequently I had to commit suicide. Naturally I agreed (when I say no, I feel guilty). I said: 'Very good, sir, but who will mince me up afterwards?'

Darling, I'll finish now and hug with all my heart.

Your H.

PS. As for the fairy tale, it wasn't *Beauty and the Beast* I had in mind, but Andersen's *The Little Mermaid*. She couldn't have her prince because she was a creature of a different kind. The witch arranged it so she could see him only from time to time, but at what a price! She had to cut her hair (I, too, cut mine), and with every step, with every pace her legs would ache (my legs ached, too). And later, when the prince fell in love and was happy, she dissolved into nothingness. That will probably happen next, but for the time being it is quite pleasant.

With that I'll end this joyful letter.

H.

Cumnor, 5.12.79

My Darling Funnyface,

Yesterday I received two letters from you simultaneously – the one with the new poems by Szymborska, and the one with your cannibalistic dream. Szymborska simply made me cry, just as the Schubert Quintet once did (do you remember?). And her description of the family relationships in opera also brought tears, tears of laughter. I translated it yesterday for Eve and I had to read it three times because it amused us so much we wanted to know every word by heart.

Yes, Szymborska is a genius, but I suspect her of something to which she will probably never confess. I believe in her talent, intelligence, originality, mastery, everything you want me to, but somehow I don't believe in her existence. I am profoundly convinced that Wisława Szymborska is *you*, even though you won't confess to it, either.

*Portrait of a Woman* is, after all, a portrait of you (when I say no, I feel guilty, as you write under your own name). And her genius is your genius: the dream about the butcher's shambles with human meat is not only in Kafka territory, it's of his stature. Simply describe it and publish, and it will be a literary sensation: all you need is to pretend for half a year that you believe in yourself and everyone will believe in you, and in the end even you might, for how would you dare to contradict so many wise people?

Now you really will be afraid to see me. You'll either be shy because you are Szymborska or because you're not Szymborska. Moreover the more you impressed me the greater will be your anticipated disillusionment until you're made speechless and, with aching heart, dissolve into nothingness. But in my view, in this story you're not just the little mermaid, you're also the witch who denies the little mermaid all her natural rights instead of telling her honestly that the man is no prince at all.

I'm very intrigued by your mentioning my 'charming' letter! Truth to tell it's *this* letter that ought to be charming because you're closer to me now than you've ever been before. When you tried to teach me I was fascinated and flattered but only when you wrote: 'Darling, I'm sorry, but it seems that there isn't much I can do to help, because how could I?' To keep repeating 'Discard your pride' is like telling a man frozen on the ice: 'Throw off your coat because when you harden yourself you won't feel the cold.' When you quoted Camus' words: 'I'm too weak to give up my pride' – only then did I sense that you not only understand me, but *accompany* me in my weakness. And that moved me and helped me more than all your bits of advice. I'm enclosing the story (...), it's dedicated to you and if it ever appears in print then it will bear the dedication 'for H'.

If there's anything you don't understand, then show it to Basia because she knows about it. (...) As for the opera, I don't have a piano score. I'm grateful to Majka for wanting to help stage my opera and for believing in me, but it's not a chamber piece; besides a full choir there is a boys' choir (which imitates and persecutes Shylock) and a chamber orchestra on stage, not counting a huge cast and a full orchestra! The only exception to Szymborska's rules is that the counter-tenor is in love with the tenor (the counter-tenor is a male voice which is higher than the tenor, as opposed to a contrabass or a contrabassoon).

The Beethoven Concerto in G major worked surprisingly well – I didn't recognise myself. But since then I've let myself go somewhat: over the weekend I had a visit from Edward and it was wonderful, we explained everything to each other, so only an extreme fanatic would have practised during such an opportunity. But as from tomorrow I'm getting down to work because playing poorly is horribly demoralising. (...)

So bye for now, kisses, and mighty hugs.

Your Andrzej.

Warsaw, 3.1.80

Dearest Darling, I haven't written because I've got Basia here now, as well as a bearded giant, the flu, and toothache. And the bearded giant has diarrhoea and I run round the park with him in the night. Your story is a masterpiece of simplicity and subtlety. In fact we had a terribly animated discussion here about the interpretation of the ending. I feel that, on top of everything else, you'll also become a famous writer!

Your last letters have been kind and dear. I'm ill today and I don't have the strength to write any more. I love you as always, despite everything more than my bearded giant.

Kiss you.

Your H.


POSTCARD: MISHKENOT SHA'ANANIM

Jerusalem, 12.1.80

Darling Funnyface, I'm living here in this colony of artists and thinkers! It's a veritable paradise so I haven't unpacked and I'm waiting for the inevitable banishment.

Forgive me for neglecting you: apart from concerts I'm also teaching a course here, substituting for Lili Kraus! But you'll soon get another card.

Kisses. Your Andrzej.


POSTCARD FROM JERUSALEM: THE JAFFA GATE AND CITADEL

Jerusalem, 14.1.80

Darling Funnyface,

If you could put Shakespeare, Copernicus, Christ, Napoleon and the Marquis de Sade into one human being, the Israelis would ask: 'And why doesn't he play the violin?' You can't impress anyone with anything here. Yesterday, for example, an Arab offered Eve 500 camels, while a postcard seller gave me ten cards free, saying: 'But Bach you must play on the harpsichord.'

Your Andrzej.

Oxford, 21.1.80

Darling Funnyface,

Today I finally sent off the English course with cassettes and texts and I hope it reaches you before your birthday.

Every one of my friends understands my story differently. One day I'll tell you how I understand it, but the fact that I wrote it is by no means a guarantee that I understand it better than others! I only know what I wanted to say. I told Basia the story before I finished writing it. (…)

I'll write again soon.

Meanwhile I hug you and stroke the dog, and give my regards to the bearded giant (or maybe the other way round).

Your Andrzej.

Warsaw, 30.1.80

Andrzej, Darling, you've not been writing me letters lately, but your publishers have recompensed me doubly and now I'm in the middle of writing them a warm epistle. They sent me a cassette in the hope that I'll arrange a performance of the Concerto at the Warsaw Autumn. You mentioned nothing of this to me, so come clean: are you or are you not coming over here with the Concerto?

I'm inviting you warmly, you must come over with Eve. I'll let you have both of my apartments. It's true that in one of them Bisa will be giving birth to several dozen pups, but that's the only unpleasantness that can possibly meet you in Poland.

On the subject of writing letters to publishers, my boss once asked me to write to his publishers in West Germany. The exchange of letters went on for a long time, and my boss understood little of them, until the publisher finished one of the letters: 'Ich küsse dich, Anthony', which he did understand.

I've sent the books. Ask Basia for the Szymanowski LP. Tell me what else you're dreaming of, your dreams are my commands!

Kiss you with all of my heart and let you do the same to Eve.

Your H.

Oxford, 1.2.80

Funnyface dearest,

I'm glad you received and liked my concerto. I also liked it, despite a few misgivings, because it's adventurous and it's intense; in my opinion the most successful part is the scherzo. I also like nearly the whole of the first movement and the cadenza in the last, which I tried to model on the cadenza in Schumann's concerto – I doubt, though, that that can be spotted.

I also think that you'll get to know me better through my compositions than through my words, or my deeds. In life I have a tendency to show off, but in my music I think I'm more serious.

As for my trip to Israel, I'll say only that it exceeded my expectations in every respect. That's except for the concerts themselves, because when something is too important for me, I rehearse too much whereupon I become panic-stricken. At the first concert I played the Rakhmaninov Rhapsody at a speed of a 33 rpm LP being played at 78, but the review (the only one I saw) praised me for my Rakhmaninov and damned me for the Bach F minor concerto ('at best he plays it as if it were Chopin; it's hard to resist wondering how Bach would have played the Tchaikowsky concerto'). I give you these details because you ask for them; they're of no interest to me because for me the personal aspect of the trip gave me a break-through: can you believe it – while I was there I decided I would go to Paris to find, and meet with, my father? I won't let him know in advance, of course, otherwise he would prepare a two-hour speech for the prosecution, or even refuse to see me. But now at last I want to find out who I am, where I come from, and where I belong: a person doesn't choose one's parents; it's not a question of who one wants to be through choice, but of who one is. I'm sure that you'll agree with me, anyway.

I leave for New Zealand on February 14th; you can write to me at the following address: c/o Mr Ian W. Dando, Flat 5, 21 Newbridge Place, Islam, Christchurch 4, New Zealand.

I'll be there till the middle of March, but write as soon as possible because the letter could be a long time wandering round the country.

Big hugs and kisses,

Your Andrzej.


Warsaw, 10.2.80

Dearest Andrzej, I still haven't received a reply to my various silly little letters, but, not disheartened, I write on. Thanks for the English course – it's marvellous! As it turns out, you're marvellous, too, as a violinist from the Philharmonic with whom I play and who listened to your concerto declared. She's been playing in that orchestra for a long time, has played all the Warsaw Autumn Festivals, and she claims that 'apart from Lutosławski' she's never heard anything as good as that. She greatly admired your orchestral imagination and she also said: 'I don't know if that man experienced the war in Poland, but I'm sure he did.' And something else about an atmosphere of Berg and Szymanowski.

And what's happening with you? I'm longing for a letter. Do you know that, at the end of the year, we'll be able to celebrate the silver wedding of our correspondence? If you knew the contents of your first letter to me, you'd fall off your piano stool.

Lots of good wishes.

Your H.


Cumnor, 7.2.80 (Granny's birthday, she would have been 92 today)

My Little Firefly,

Your letter arrived today at the same time as your card. Darling, stop worrying about the Concerto: I simply lied shamelessly to my publisher so he would make a copy and send it to you as quickly as possible. Anyway I warned him yesterday that your influence in the music world has been considerably reduced so he'll stop pestering you with pleas which have nothing to do with our friendship.

Funnyface, you know only too well that whatever happens I won't play that Concerto in Warsaw. Maybe one day someone will, but it certainly won't be me.

A friend I met in Australia five years ago who's now writing stage plays has been living with me for some time now. He came for two days and I invited him to stay as long as he wanted. Just imagine – it's easy and pleasant: I practise, and he writes, each one doing what he wants, and in the evening we talk about literature. I'm telling you about this because that's how I dream your stay with me might be like. Why haven't we managed it yet? Can we ever manage it? I feel I ought to understand something here, I ought to learn something, but so far I've failed. Maybe the reason why everything is so simple is that I have less in common with him?

He hasn't a clue about music, he loves women and eats only smoked sausages so it's not even worth cooking for him… Or maybe it's because he's an Englishman that he feels at home in his own country and isn't dependent on me?

Basia hasn't been in contact lately so your presents will have to wait till my return from New Zealand, but I thank you for them now. But I swear I prefer your letters to presents. (…)

I have an exceptionally busy period ahead (New Zealand, Hong Kong, then Denmark), full of long journeys and multifarious programmes.

Hug you with all my heart, und ich küsse dich!

Andreas.


PS. In the card you write that the bearded giant is a dog, not a lover. How could I have guessed that? The fact that you walked in the park with him when he had diarrhoea is no proof, it's all a question of following one's inclination.

Auckland, 15.3.80

Darling Funnyface, I'm sitting at the airport and waiting for John. We had a terrible storm today (in fact it was a tropical cyclone) and John's plane couldn't land here and flew on to Wellington. The weather has improved now and it's possible that John will get onto a plane there: the chances are not good, however: he's just phoned, they called me to the office, and I promised I'd wait just in case.

Naturally, I very much want this meeting because tomorrow I'm leaving 'for good', which probably means another three years! But something miraculous has occurred, something which has given me peace of mind no matter what happens: John confessed, very shyly, that he loves me, too. You can't imagine how much that cost him! And I seduced him by playing Schubert's Sonata in B flat major at a recital in Christchurch three days ago. He didn't know the piece and was so moved by it that he burst into tears (that rarely happens, too). And since he couldn't thank the composer personally, he projected all the enthusiasm onto me. Actually, I must admit I've never played the sonata so well because I knew John was hearing it for the first time and all those incredible modulations would astonish and enchant him and it wasn't about me but about the beauty of the piece. So naturally I wasn't nervous and every detail was important to me... But I never expected a reward like that, and surely no performer since the juggler of Notre Dame has ever won a prize like it.

16.3.80

I'm on my way to Hong Kong now. In the mean time something extraordinary happened. Having failed to get onto the last plane in Wellington, John rented a car and drove all night so he could spend a few hours with me. He reached me at six in the morning, exhausted but smiling, and for the first time in my life I didn't need any assurances. I advised him to take a nap, I fed him, and finally I bought him a ticket to England and invited him to my place in June. There are two differences between this invitation and the last one: then it was the end of love and neither I nor John wanted another meeting, because I didn't want to spoil a masterpiece, and he had no special reasons to see me – but now it's the beginning of friendship because he's proved everything to me once and for all and all demands have become superfluous, so we simply want to be together a bit, listen to records and enjoy each other's company. In the past John was a bit afraid of seeing me – which is no surprise! – but now he trusts me completely. I know he loves me (though he claims that this love is only germinating, so it must be a baobab!), but I'm just pleased that I love him. I'm as happy, calm, and sure of myself as I've ever been in my life. (…)

Incidentally, John and Basia are very alike – they'll do everything possible or impossible for you, but in their own way and at a time of their own choosing, and that's why it's better not to count on them.

Darling, maybe I will learn to love and understand people after all, and then it will be easier for you to deal with me. It's sometimes hard for me, too, seeing the world distorted like this by my imagination.

Hug you with all my heart.

Your Andrzej,

PS. Oh, Funnyface, I have a favour to ask – a big one. Ian, with whom I stayed in Christchurch, is planning to go to the Warsaw Autumn for which he's received a small grant as a musicologist and a music critic. He's a super person – a little naive, but intelligent, sincere, sensitive, musically sharp and particularly affectionate towards women. (…) He knows no one in Poland, speaks only English, and can't afford anything. Could you try to make his stay there a bit easier? I'm sure you'll like him, and anyway he won't be expecting anything; I'd just want him not to be too lonely.

I thank you in advance and hug you again.

Your Andrzej.

Cumnor, 20.3.80

Darling Funnyface,

I've just returned from New Zealand and Hong Kong and found half your library here! Not only do I not know how to thank you, I don't know which order to do it in.

I can see that Szymborska truly isn't you which not only surprises me, but makes me angry. How dare she? Who does she think she is? She writes like you, the only difference being she's more sure of herself, and then she parades herself under another name and doesn't even thank you. It's just like Gogol's story *The Nose*.

I don't at present have the courage to tackle Wojdowski, I'll do it during the holiday season (the last invitation of the season is for 22 May with Liszt's Concerto in A major in Manchester). Does that mean I'm going to fall into a depression in June? I doubt it because John will probably be here in June. Darling, I feel that I am, after all, learning to love! I've started to think about another human being; if he doesn't want something I lose my desire for it, too.

I think one has to love people like music, carefully and *without trying to change anything*. What do you think: will I have time to learn that?

Hug you with all my heart,

Your grateful and devoted

Andrzej.

PS. I beg you, send me a copy of my first letter to you! You said I'll fall off my piano stool just to arouse my curiosity! You succeeded, so now send me this historic document.

POSTCARD: BODLEIAN LIBRARY, OXFORD.
THE CREATION OF THE ANIMALS

Cumnor, 23.3.80

Darling Funnyface,

Many thanks for the letter; I can't reply at the moment because I'm playing in Chichester today, tomorrow I'm leaving for two concerts in Denmark, and then to Paris for a probable meeting with my father! I'll tell you all about it, because I'm certain that one day you'll write my biography.

For the moment bye, kisses,

Your Andrzej.

PS. I'm reading Szymborska and I'm crying buckets.

Cumnor, 24.3.80

Darling Funnyface,

And yet I am writing to you because I've carved out a moment while I wait for the telephone connection to John.

This is how I understand my short story: Julia was in an impossible position: if she told Ralph she loved him, he'd have taken her, abandoned her after a week and also ridiculed her. So she took the opportunity to confess everything to the fortune-teller and probably received a promise of help from her. The fortune-teller is an excellent actress but in this case she knows everything about Ralph and Julia: therefore, she pretends she knows *less* so as not to arouse his suspicions when she is telling his fortune. Everything would have worked (at least for a little while because they're both too weak to help one another properly) if Julia hadn't been too quick and not betrayed herself by her expression: after all, she wasn't supposed to know what happened in the tent. Ralph sees the fear in her face and that confirms his suspicions. What becomes clear is that she has tricked him not just now, but has been lying to him for months: for instance, she pretended she liked his last poems but she told the fortune-teller what she really thinks of them (that's what would have hurt me the most in his position). Ralph could have been saved only by a strong and brave woman, one who'd say to him: 'I love you, but 1 don't respect you because you don't respect yourself and that's why you're wasting and losing yourself.' But it was Ralph who put Julia into this false position in which she had to hide her love and feign friendship. But I've often been in that situation myself and I know how hard and painful it is. For a long time I thought that telling you or Ann about my problems I was protecting you from this danger. My 'Donjuanerie', which I'm not actually conscious of, stems from a feeling of freedom and sexual safety which leads to the mistaken belief that since I'm not threatened then nothing can threaten others. It's a bit like adding wine to somebody's glass and demanding that they remain sober. I've finally realised all this and decided to stop playing the ostrich. My short story is a consequence of my guilty conscience.

I'm now coming to the heart of the matter. This sense of guilt towards women is a serious obstacle not only in our friendship but in the whole of my emotional life, and you are absolutely right to try and cure me of it! Maybe all my problems spring from that? I learned a long time ago, as long ago as my relationship with my grandmother, that women regard the evocation of feelings of guilt in a man as a consolation prize when they can't get love. And that's the satisfaction I've given to innumerable women. (...) When it was erotic love I told myself 'it's not my fault', but the majority of those relationships were pseudo-maternal. But what was worst of all was that I could never forgive these women those pangs of conscience.

With us it's a vicious circle. The more guilty I feel for not loving you, the more you're afraid of me. The more you're afraid of me, the guiltier I feel. My fury with you stems from the fact that you are one great mute accusation.

Recently I find my relationship with you more and more difficult. You probably do, too.

Apologies and best wishes.

Your

Andrzej.

PS. If I'd 'taken' you, it would have done you less harm: you'd have been bored with me after a week and that would have been that. (...) But I assure you that such relationships weigh me down, too, because I can't do anything here, and so we go round and round in circles like at the end of Wyspiański's *Wesele*.

Warsaw, 31.3.80

Darling, Darling.

I was overjoyed by your letters and your card. Everything came in reverse order, so I read them a bit like Pinter's *Betrayal*. I'm delighted by your internal metamorphosis and by the fact that with John you've found – just as you longed to – a true, reciprocated feeling. Tell me some more about him; after all I know nothing about him and I'll start to suspect that you don't either. (...)

Don't worry about Ian. I'll take care of him and I'll introduce him to a lady who has a very similar name – Ina, which ought to bring them close to each other. The lady is young, charming, and wants to accompany everyone on some instrument because, by profession, she is a painter. To encourage those she wishes to accompany she paints her piano in ever-changing colours. When I was last at her place, the piano was white with little violet windows. Ina also possesses a clavichord and a guitar – she plays all those instruments fluently and with affection. Can Ian sing or do anything where a musical backing would be useful?

As you can guess, I got to know Ina through Basia; incidentally – do you know what's happening with Basia? The latest news were disquieting: she was loved by two gamekeepers simultaneously. I never imagined that London was the place in the world with the largest number of gamekeepers.

You're interested in the beginnings of our correspondence. Your first letter contains only four words: 'I love you, Andrzej.' The second letters starts: 'I love you as I have never loved you before.' Much closer to the truth, however, and astonishingly relevant even now are my letters to you. Here are some fragments: 'You said: "Why should we be bad lovers when we can be good friends?" Darling, that's what I'm longing for! But you, my dear Einstein, imagine that "that's all I'm after", as if your correct violin-playing could be of more interest to someone than the genius of your theory of relativity. You said: "Call me on Monday". I didn't ring. Proust said: "The passion with which people shower each other with unnecessary objects is astonishing. It's the same with feelings." Yes, dear Andrzej, you receive my offers of friendship like embroidered napkins from an elderly aunt – with a gratitude soaked with boredom and irritation. While it seems between us there exists an exceptional possibility of mutual understanding.'

And here's a passage from a letter I could write even today: 'When I am with you, I lose my desire to play because music seems to be a glass mountain. When I listen to you speaking, playing, when I read what you've written, I can no longer speak, play or write myself, I follow you like a shadow. Dull, listless, unintelligent, next to you I change into a resonator which, with time, should resonate better and better. Because, as is well known, the older the resonator, the better the resonance.'

Darling, now to something else. Recently I read an interview with Kurosawa and Iwaszkiewicz's last book about Szymanowski's *Harnasie*. Kurosawa says that pieces which are liked only by the experts are works of art; works which are liked by everyone with the exception of the experts are cheap and trashy; however, masterpieces are those works which are liked by both, 'just like my films', Kurosawa adds modestly. Later, when I was reading about *Harnasie* I understood what causes the creation of masterpieces, not just works of art. I think it's reaching for archetypes. Jung formed the theory of archetypes as a result of his work with schizophrenics. Apparently certain cultural themes which are common to all people, regardless of social class or the country they live in, are to be found in the subconscious of the schizophrenic. So that would be a coded heritage of certain basic meanings which are common to all humanity. It seems that all artists whose work has a wider accessibility reached for archetypes. They were inspired by their own talent, by other creators, but at root there was always something raw and primeval; in music think of Bartók, Ravel, Stravinsky, Szymanowski, Lutosławski. Stephen Bishop is trying to persuade you to write a dance suite; I suspect he's trying to incline you towards a greater simplicity. You're inspired by your talent and the refined music you adore, but you're disgusted by everything which is common or simple.

I'll tell you something which you may interpret as an insult, but then you like my aggression: your music, even though it is emotional, colourful, enticing, betrays the fact that you're cosmopolitan, that you have no roots in any one culture. Great composers raised the quality of their own culture to a supranational culture, not the other way round. Jagusia flew off to San Francisco today; yesterday she was feverishly searching for a record of Szymanowski's Violin Concerto No 1 because the owner of a restaurant there had written a letter begging her to bring this record with her: she had seen *The Maids of Wilko* in Poland (Wajda's film based on Iwaszkiewicz's novella) and she simply had to have the music from that film!

Do you understand what I mean?

Kiss you with all my heart.

Your H.

WARNES HOTEL, WORTHING, SUSSEX

12.4.80

Dear Halinka,

(…) I'm enclosing extracts from your last letter in which you quote your early letters to me. I've marked those letters like a teacher in red pencil so you'll know in future what I never wish to see again!

You'll say they were written a quarter of a century ago. But at the same time you tell me you could have written a similar letter today – in fact I have to admit you still do occasionally. Do you know what I think about that? I suspect more and more that your attitude towards me is partly hostile because it is based not on admiration but on envy. You're constantly jealous of my emotional intensity, of the fact that I'm 'really alive', and because you can't take that from me, you try to spoil it by provoking a sense of guilt in me, or at least of embarrassment. Doing it, you spoil not only my mood, but also our friendship. (…)

Our relationships can only succeed when we don't think about them, or at least don't analyse them. When you criticise my compositions in your letter for their lack of 'roots', I agree with you instantly and I'm grateful for such an accurate and well-meaning criticism (I've been deploring for years the fact that I don't have anything *fundamental* which would help me as much as the Lutheran chorales did Bach and Brahms, or dance music did the Viennese classics). And you call your criticism aggression when it is, in fact, proof of your understanding. What is aggressive are these perpetual attempts to squeeze out of me some reaction to you.

A fish can be seen better in the light of day, but the fish itself feels considerably better in the water. Similarly with friendship: it's like a film which can be developed only in darkness.

I'm sure your head is full of the subtlest commentaries on this, but I'm asking you to spare me them. I warn you that in response to any return to this subject (i.e. our relationship) you'll receive your letter back and it will be returned without any comments at all. Understand that one can try to fight against hostility, but there is no medicine at all for boredom.

You can write about anything else without fear: as Peter the Great used to say: 'Speak fearlessly or I'll strangle you.'…

I'll write to you some time about my two meetings with my father and my half-sister, but first I want you to promise that you'll accept the wish I've expressed in this letter. I'd rather not write about John. I've written to Basia and I thank you for the records in advance.

Best wishes,

Your Andrzej.

Warsaw, 16.4.80

Andrzej my dear, I've just received your letter in which you comment on your story. I would never have guessed that it was an expiation. Why, in God's name, these pangs of conscience? If I or Ann ever had any illusions about winning your affections it was a result of our mythomania and your unconscious Donjuanerie – which was by no means dangerous enough to make every woman fall victim to it. Believe me, only those did who wanted to. For example, never for one moment did it enter Basia's head to capture your love. Basia feels herself tied to you on an astral plane, she doesn't want to 'have' you or change you, it's enough for her that she floats gently over you with her thoughts. So don't accuse yourself: 'He who reaches under the surface does so on his own responsibility.'

A few more words about the short story. First and foremost, the character of Julia is too simplified: contemporary writers simply don't understand women; even women writers play the roles of characters they'd like to be but never showing what they're really like. The last writer who could read the subconscious of women like a book was de Musset, and note that he neither idealised them nor accused them, he simply understood them. (…)

Since you identify yourself with Ralph, all these reflections are of little importance: Ralph is now happily in love and though he is shaking inside with joy – he will create, and it doesn't even matter what. Nietzsche wrote: 'Only out of chaos will a dancing star be born', that's why I'll never say to Ralph: 'You're wasting and losing yourself', because no one has the right to talk like that, it's not a proof of strength, it's just barging into someone's life.

I have to finish off because the dog is dragging me out for a walk.

Your H.

Warsaw, 29.4.80

Darling Andrzej, I've just received your harsh, unpleasant letter. To be honest I was expecting something like it, but I imagined its contents more or less as follows:

Dear Halinka,

I would have been immeasurably grateful for your frankness if one can describe thus your conceited lectures on the subject of 'archetypes', 'cultural roots', 'cosmopolitan art' etc. However, in the sub-text as usual not straight out of these complicated ruminations there lurks a doubt as to whether my compositions are 'masterpieces' or *merely* 'works of art'. To start with, let me assure you I don't care. Secondly, the criterion you give of 'general enthusiasm' is amazingly stupid. Masterpieces – particularly of music and painting – never achieve general approval from their contemporaries since their genius is based on discovery, originality, in other words on something which *cannot* arouse general enthusiasm! And then there's the question of archetypes. First you write that there are themes which are common to all cultures, and therefore independent of the place of residence. Yet on the very next page you reproach me for being a 'cosmopolitan' artist, because I lack the 'roots' which Chopin, Bartók, Ravel etc. all had. I'm not rooted in any culture and that is a fault! So what's the truth of it? What's better: 'archetypes' or 'roots'? I suspect that whichever it is you can't just put it on your head like a hat. Either one needs to reach for certain themes, be they religious, folklorist, historic or cosmic, or one doesn't need to. If Szymanowski was so bewitched by the music of the Tatra highlanders then it was surely his inner choice. He didn't say to himself: 'Maybe it would be fun to write some good music on the basis of some highland pieces?' Armstrong didn't go to themes from black folk or religious music to create hits. Those songs lived within him.

You write that I lack roots. In your last letter, however, you told me that the violinist with whom you play, not knowing if I was a German, Frenchman or an Englishman, young or old, after hearing the cassette of my concerto, said: 'I can hear that this man spent the war in Poland.' I don't know, maybe another of your friends will guess from the concerto that I fought at Stalingrad as a soldier of the Red Army. I know only one thing, that in your 'frankest' assessments you are – as usual basically dishonest. Writing about 'national roots' you don't even suspect what it is you're really after. What you're after is for me to return to Poland, to live and compose there, because then I'd be within your reach...

The beginnings of our correspondence also uncovered certain dishonesties of my own towards you. When I loved John Browning – I wrote that it was you I loved. When I was furious with Edward – you got it in the neck. I think that that's the way I am: if I love someone very much or hate them, it affects my attitude to others. The colouring of the whole world changes in my eyes.

Twenty-five years ago you had doubts about whether we were friends, and now you certainly don't have them, so begging for constant reassurance is pitiful and tiring, good in love but not in friendship. People who say 'I love you' to each other ten times a day – are not ridiculous; friends who say 'we're friends' even three times a day must be idiots.

As for our future meetings, sadly I must agree that you're right – they're pointless since within a tiny moment you change into someone it's impossible to be friends with and I'd gladly throttle!

In my next letter I'll describe my visit to my father. If I see Basia, I'll write about her, too.

Keep well, Your Andrzej.


PS. As you can see, my dear Andrzej, I'm not terrified you're mad at me and don't want to write to me. If you don't write, then I'll write your replies myself.
Hug you with all my heart,

Your H.


Cumnor, 17.5.80

Darling,
Many thanks for the parody of my letters: you know my style considerably better than I do myself. Still, that's not surprising because though I do, of course, send my letters, you have been collecting them for a quarter of a century and reading them like I read Racine: simply out of habit, because you know them all by heart. But you've disarmed me and amused me, and your ingenuity impresses me, as always.

You know what? One day when I'm *not feeling angry* I'll write out everything I have against you – not to re-stoke old misunderstandings, but to banish them completely. I'm waiting here for John to arrive. Naturally, I daren't count on it because it's too important for me. I've got two more performances of Liszt's Concerto in A major left in Manchester, then I'll devote about a month to John (if he comes), and between July and September I'll try to positively drown myself in *The Merchant* and see what comes of it.

Basia was at my recital in London, we'll probably see each other soon. I have the impression that there's no need to be worried about her!

Wish me luck, Darling – this summer I'll be playing for great stakes.

Hug you and kiss you, Your Andrzej.

Warsaw, 11.6.80

Darling Andrzej, I've just come back from Banzin in the GDR where I spent a marvellous holiday. Your letter was waiting for me at home, as was Basia's card which begins with the words: 'I saw Andrzej yesterday. I adore him to the very marrow of his bones.' Darling, I didn't have time to reply to your two letters before I left because I was giving a paper at an important conference which was my professional 'to be or not to be'. Everything went very well, but immediately after it I packed my bags. (…)

I understand your attitude to Julia and Ralph, but not to me. Where does your sense of guilt come from? That's *my* speciality. Every time I leave your house I do it because I feel guilty and it weighs me down so much I have to cut my stay as short as I can; it's simply that every day spent together drives us apart. You promised that you were going to 'tell me off'. Do so quickly and let's get it out of the way.

Bye for now because I've got a thousand things to do.

Kiss you. Your H.

Cumnor, 25.5.80

Darling Halinka,

Yesterday I saw Basia and received your splendid present. I'm quite overwhelmed! Partly by gratitude, partly by the weight of the records. There are many pieces I don't even know (particularly the songs), so you've prepared a positive journey of discovery for me. Szymanowski is, in my view, the most under-rated composer of the 20th century. In his lifetime he was considered in Poland to be too modern (Rytel wrote that his Violin Concerto No.1 was an example of the Jewish-Communist conspiracy in music), and now everyone thinks he's too old-fashioned, so he missed out on being fashionable in two directions at once. But it doesn't matter – fashion will change but he will remain.

Basia is in excellent shape, we spent an enormously pleasant evening together. Each of us did what we do best – I chattered, she listened. She's living near Hyde Park at the moment, in Kasia's old room, in a pleasant artistic-student atmosphere. She's also going for a new job, as a teacher of drawing in a kindergarten. If the management asks me for a reference, I shall write an epic poem about her. Basia confirmed that she does indeed feel 'astrally tied' to me and was surprised that you should have named it so accurately.

Things are a bit hard for me at present. I've got masses of debts and I have to accept concerts from as early as October, and next year I've committed myself to playing throughout the whole season, which worries me. After the excessive number of events in the first quarter, this year I'm very tired emotionally and it's hard for me to start working with any real enthusiasm.

Bye for now, Darling, and many thanks!

Your Andrzej.


Cumnor, 20.7.80

Darling Funnyface,

I came back a fortnight ago from a surprise concert tour in South Africa; I found the letter in which you encourage me to 'get things out of the way'. The fact is it will have to be done one day, because I'm often picking on some trivial details which don't really matter to me and only because I've never told you what I really have against you. Just the thought that I'll tell you someday makes all my objections go away – which is evidence that when I've had it out with you they'll go for good. But at the moment I'm too tired and too demoralised to force myself to do it.

The meeting with John has been called off and in most unpleasant circumstances. Basia will tell you all about it; she happened to ring me at the precise moment and then she came round to cheer me up. I'm enormously grateful to you that I now have in her such a perceptive, good and calming friend. After she left, Terry phoned me and suggested this concert tour to South Africa which some Italian pianist had backed out of. I agreed with relief since I didn't know what to do with myself.

I now have three performances in England. I'm playing Mozart's Concerto in C major K 467, and two recitals, but from the end of July I'm staying at home and working on *The Merchant of Venice*. I doubt if I'll finish it this year – there have been too many breaks and distractions. But I'll do what I can.

Hug you with all my heart,

Your Andrzej.

Warsaw, 1.8.80

Darling Andrzej,

I've re-read the passage from your journal in which you wrote about John. Perhaps you should have stopped there and not tempted reality, because reality is such a master killjoy.

As for 'having it out' with me, don't, at least not at the moment. I'm in a foul mood and what's worse, not because of any love affair. I wrote you a joyful letter after my holiday because I was relaxed and tanned. But apparently during that time there were lots of bad things happening at work and I'm now having to do penance. Before the holiday I had carried out a nationwide sociological survey and I left all the materials to be coded into machines. I came back, paid the encoders enormous sums of money but when I looked through the material I found that the codes were teeming with errors. Now I'm doing everything myself, from scratch. When he heard about it, my boss took pity and said: 'Couldn't you just leave a few errors in?' I smiled and told him a story about my sister when she decided to have a home birth. She called the midwife and asked: 'Are your instruments sterile?' To which the midwife said: 'Lady, I've got every kind of instrument, sterile and non-sterile.' Whereupon my sister leapt to her feet, drove to the hospital and gave birth there. Naturally, my boss didn't understand this illustrative metaphor.

I've grown stupid with all this murderous work and the cheerless mood in the country as a whole, and I've grown sad. I am now an absolutely uninteresting individual and can't write you a nice or wise letter. Forgive me. Send me Basia for a little longer.

Kiss you with all my heart,

Your H.

MIDLAND HOTEL, MANCHESTER

23.7.80

Darling Halinka,

I just happen to have an hour or so free, so I'll try to confess all my old resentments towards you. I'll start from the fact that I truly like you enormously. If you knew how dear you are to me all your fears would vanish and you would laugh at my moods! Because the moods are only variations, but the theme is the personality itself: while you are yourself, and I'm myself, the variations can be *agitato, lugubre* etc. – but it doesn't change our relationship just as foul weather doesn't change the landscape. After all, it's me you like, not my various states of mind. Believe me, I like you in the same way, and after this letter I'll like you even more, because all the resentment I feel from times past will disperse when I tell you about it.

My only fear is that it will lead us once again into some long and complicated analyses which aren't helpful in the spontaneous development of friendship. Darling, please receive this letter without giving a speech for the defence. That sounds unjust because why do I have the right to accuse you and you not have the right to defend yourself? But as far as I'm concerned, this isn't an accusation, it's an explanation and, at the same time, an attempt to liberate myself from the past. Now, after the fiasco with John, I'm especially keen to start my life afresh. Help me in this, please. Feel free to criticise me, but don't let's go back to old subjects; it'll be better if you advise me how I should arrange my future life.

And so by way of a goodbye to old complaints:

Not long ago you wrote that 'you shouldn't barge into someone else's life'. But you see, you did barge into my life frequently, not with your criticisms (which I always receive gratefully), but with your attempts to draw my attention, to 'conquer' me, to inspire feelings in me of which, as you knew, I was incapable. You often put me into a situation where I had to do you wrong, or hurt you at least, and that's where my sense of guilt, and any dislike of you, comes from.

The best example was the Stockholm affair in '62. Of course I couldn't give you a child: it would have been irresponsible to do so because a child with an absent father and a lunatic mother (as your plans then indicated you were) wouldn't have had the remotest chance in life. What's more, I didn't want to ruin your marriage (of course, I didn't know then that nothing could save it anyway). To me, Marek was the man who was prepared to offer you his kidney; at the time, that impressed me enormously and I was certain all I had to do was get out of your path and let him make you happy with his love.

But you demanded that I send you a blank postcard, without a single word save the address, a card which was to indicate that I felt nothing for you, that I found you boring, that I didn't care about you and that you made me sick. Darling, I know very well that card made you unhappy for a long time, and I'm ashamed to be reproaching you for that desperate ultimatum. But believe me, it was incredibly hard for me, too, because you never bored me, you were never a matter of indifference to me and I always liked you very much, so that card was one huge lie. I forced myself to do it only because all the people who had influence over me then – Michael Riddall, George Lyward, and my psychoanalyst – explained vehemently it was the only way I could save your marriage, because the date of your departure for Stockholm was too close for further discussions. Eventually, Michael asked me: 'When it comes to it, what's more important to you – her happiness or her opinion of you?' and that decided it. But I never forgave you for that, even though I know that love often leads to worse things.

A second, similar situation was your proposal in '69. I have one of your letters here in front of me, in which you wrote that I provoked it myself. (First there

194 | ...my guardian demon

were remarks in letters, then you said: 'a solitude like mine is a personal tragedy', then you repeated ten times a day how good it was to have me there and how you'd like to live with me always, and that I still had a special role to play. Added to that were Judy's accounts about how nervous you were before my visit, and the frequent visits to your psychoanalyst). Maybe I really did *subconsciously* provoke that proposal, but, Funnyface, a man who wants to get married doesn't need to provoke a proposal, he simply proposes himself. It's the woman, well, until recently anyway, who kept having to provoke because a woman couldn't even ask a man to dance with her, let alone to marry her. I'm sure that unconsciously I did flirt with you because your admiration always flattered me (especially as I admire you, too). But from that time I've been afraid of showing you any warmth and as soon as I do I retreat so as not to arouse any romantic illusions in you.

Be good and forgive me this letter which you asked for yourself. If you can free yourself, and me, from these former misunderstandings which make you react to every sign of friendship as if it offered the possibility of love, I will be such a friend to you as I've never been, though I've always wanted to be! Let's try to start afresh without any expectations or demands, knowing that we understand and like each other perfectly and that all our petty irritations were the result of a basic problem which we've left behind us.

The fact that our relationship has developed badly is not proof that it has to continue like that. Don't interpret this letter to your disadvantage. On the contrary: think how much I trust you to write about it all so frankly. And remember how brutally and finally I dismissed all the other women who fell in love with me (...). So don't doubt my friendship and for God's sake don't demand any further assurances. But if you must doubt, tell yourself: 'It's not important if he likes me, the most important thing is that I like him'; then both you and I will feel at ease with each other.

Bye for now because this afternoon I'm rehearsing, and in the evening I'm playing Mozart's Concerto in C major K 467. Yesterday I gave a recital, on the whole it was fairly good. Reply quickly so I'll be sure you're not angry.

Hug you with all my heart,

Your Andrzej.

Warsaw, 10.8.80

Darling Andrzej,

Contrary to your expectations, your letter made me very happy. The questions you raise seem so out of date and unimportant that they can't possibly have any meaning now. When you mention 'romantic illusions' it makes me laugh, not hurt me, because lately I've been thinking mainly about what else I'll have time to do before I die.

One other matter did, however, make me uneasy. If you continue to reproach me that dozens of years ago my inappropriate propositions forced you to behave brutally which gave rise to a sense of guilt etc., etc., then I see no end to these resentments. I'll now write to say I feel no bitterness about your frank letter, and you won't believe me, you'll feel guilty, there'll be another wave of disgust and there's no rescue. So I'll try it another way: I'll simply thank you for not wanting to have a child with me, and not wanting to be with me. If I had had two children at that time I'd never have finished my studies, I'd never have got my PhD and I'd have had to spend my whole life teaching piano (it's like forcing you to spend the rest of your life playing only the Jew's harp). I'd have spent years being a nanny and a cook, which I can't bear! And then Daniel would have wandered over to you, just like Basia (your close friend who adores you but doesn't write to me). It's better not to say anything about our marriage. It would have been the worst marriage in the entire United Kingdom! Neither you nor I are made for that form of co-existence. We need another human being from time to time but when they try to settle in for longer, it's like being with Kafka's Gregory – we inspire distaste, a sense of guilt, pity. Then again we sometimes see in them a mortal foe who – as your psychoanalyst said – 'wants to steal our soul'. So my old proposals were designed to make us both unhappy. You successfully prevented that and today, years later, I can only thank you for it!

I'd like to be such a friend to you, too, like I haven't been yet, but I don't really know how to set about it. I don't believe in good advice, and you're asking me how you should live in future. I think you always lived in harmony with your nature and the qualities you value, and maybe that's why you didn't always live in harmony with the people who tried to interfere with that. I think that's the way it'll stay: you'll always live your life to the full in your own way even though you will never cure yourself of your Tonio Kröger complex. A lot can still happen... 'Thy will be done'...

Kiss you, Darling,

Your H.

Cumnor, 22.8.80

My Darling Funnyface,

Well, at last! Now nothing can stand in our way. (...) Enormous thanks for that. But believe me, your fears about me are also out of date now because they arose from the very things which are now over and unimportant. Funnyface, trust me! I'm not concealing any distaste towards you, now we can be friends as if we'd only just met. Bear in mind that of all the ladies about whom I felt guilty (...) you're the only one I haven't broken contact with; more – you were the one who tried to break off (...)

Don't worry about Ian D. He's nice (...) and an expert on music, mountaineering and photography. He assures me he's an expert on women, too – maybe you'll be able to confirm that. He's really looking forward to Warsaw because Lutosławski is his favourite contemporary composer.

Basia is in Scotland, then she's planning to go to Greece. I'm sure that when she gets back we'll see each other again. (...)

Hug you and kiss you,

Your Andrzej.

PS. Yes, marriage to me would be a punishment even Ilsa Koch* didn't deserve! Besides, she's not my type. Think how much more unhappy I'd have made you if I had agreed then.

Warsaw, 28.9.80

My dearest Andrzej!

If you only knew how fond I am of you, you'd forgive me this long silence. Anyway, the fault is your own because you sent me two such magnificent letters I couldn't just scribble any old thing down. The account of the meeting with your father I read together with Piotr, and we were both enraptured. Piotr said you're a second Singer, but even better than Singer, and he would willingly translate your book. Every scene of that account is stunningly written. Believe me, you're an outstanding writer! I was pleased by your account, and I was very pleased by your letter about our friendship. You're so near to me that I feel any misunderstandings very sharply and that's why our final 'reconciliation' is so valuable to me. Iano said that when I've had a few drinks I become very similar to you: I think similarly, I make similar jokes. You were always afraid of older women who mothered you, but with us the paradox is that it was you who shaped me intellectually and you who gave me a sense of security, not the other way round.

You'll probably be surprised by my exaltation, but Iano left me some wonderful Drambuie, and as I write this I'm slowly sipping it and feeling increasingly well disposed towards you.

For the first time in many days I'm alone today. As you know, a lot has been happening lately in Poland, and I'm wholeheartedly involved. At the same time I've been working a great deal. Then Piotr (who's staying with me) and I looked after the birth of Bisa's litter — there were 13 of them! After two days, one of the pups died, and poor Iano, who hadn't anticipated what awaited him in Poland, had to take care of the funeral. But I'll start at the beginning. Bisa was giving birth from three in the afternoon till four the next morning. At

---

* A 'kapo' at Auschwitz, notorious for her cruelty

8 o'clock I went to work. When I got back home I heard the doorbell. No, it wasn't Iano; it was five people who had come (without warning) to arrange a union meeting at my place.* The meeting finished late in the evening and I was, as you can imagine, completely worn out. Piotr went off to Łodź. I was left alone with Bisa and 13 pups. And it was precisely then that Iano appeared. I was so exhausted I had difficulty speaking Polish, let alone English! I wanted to leave him with all those dogs and run away from home. I brought myself under control, however, and set about making supper. Unfortunately, Iano decided to help me and entertained me with conversations about Berg and Schoenberg. This was too much; I asked him to go into the room and lie down on the couch. At the same time I handed him a piece of good, contemporary English prose – your account of your meeting with your father. When we sat down to supper it was clear that Iano was shaken by what he'd read. At the same time, he identified with your father, a father rejected by his child. He was very moved, he talked a lot, and I understood absolutely none of it; I smiled convulsively and waited for a miracle. And the miracle happened: Majka, who lives in the same building, arrived and announced that I had to go down to her place because there was an important telephone call about the dogs. I left Iano, I went to Majka's, I lay down on her couch and said: 'I'm not getting up again.'

Meanwhile Iano finished his supper in solitude and wanted to have a bath. But my bathroom had 11 rags hanging round it, each one covered in blood following Bisa's delivery and your friend meandered round amongst all those rags and dogs, waiting for my return: When I'd come to my senses somewhat, I sent Majka upstairs with a little letter: 'I'm waiting for a long-distance call, I'll come back as soon as possible.' And once again, with relief, I lay down on the couch. A moment later, however, Majka came back... leading Iano in. He was laughing merrily, she was entertaining him in French, with which he is totally unfamiliar. A moment later Iano was splashing in Majka's bath – a bath which, hitherto, had never had knowledge of a New Zealander. Quickly, I ran away to my place in the hope that Majka would fall in love with Iano and keep him with her for the night. This, however, did not happen and Iano reappeared soon after. He was wearing Majka's blue embroidered slippers with little red roses on them. As soon as he was in the doorway he started a lecture on Messiaen's works for the organ.

In the morning came Jagusia, summoned by telegram. I sighed with relief; Jagusia speaks excellent English and she's been dreaming about the concerts of the Warsaw Autumn. (I could not, however, count on her falling for Iano because she was in love at the time with a sociologist who looked like the son of a mafioso).

---

* This was the time of the beginning of the Solidarity movement. The management of the Institute would not allow meetings of the union at work.

Two days later, after a concert, the three of us set off to a wine bar. I didn't want to drink too much. I explained that when I drink I become irresponsible. Surprisingly enough, this declaration pleased Iano. Then I returned home, Iano – as he does every day – took Jagusia home. When, an hour later, I opened the door to let him in, without taking off the rucksack with his film camera, with his coat still on, still standing in the corridor – he put his arms round me and kissed me. And thus, to my amazement, in the midst of Bisa's noisy howls, we kissed and kissed. He with his rucksack on his back, I with a dish cloth in my hand.

Well, I can say all sorts of good things about him and this opinion will be confirmed by the love letters sent by women from various towns and continents, letters which arrive at my address in swarms. After he left three more letters came and I'm sending them on to you; I'll stake my life there's a new woman in love with him! Poor Iano, what's he going to do with all those women? Apparently every one of them has proposed to him. And with all that he's still so innocent!

I learned from your letter to Iano that you're finishing the opera. I'm so pleased; Iano claims it's a great work. You must have played him some themes or shown him fragments of the score? (…)

Darling, I'll end off now. Don't be angry about the long silence.

Write! I'm missing you.

Your H.

PS. I completely forgot to thank you for the marvellous Mozart records!

Cumnor, 3.10.80

My Darling Funnyface,

A letter like that was certainly worth waiting for! I've read it three times even though it only arrived this morning – three times in the course of four hours. Now even Szymborska cannot impress me.

Do you know what occurred to me? I'll tell you boldly even though I'm well aware of the insolence, ridiculousness, and conceit of my request – it's been a long time since those traits of mine surprised you.

Well then, I'd be enormously pleased if you were to write my biography one day. I'll let you have access to all my journals etc., and anyway you know yourself that I have no secrets from you. I'd like you to be ahead of some fool with a diploma in musicology who might want to set about me when I'm no longer in a position to put anything straight…

I assure you, you write a hundred times better in Polish than I do in English. Your admiration for my description of the meeting with my father so amazed me I opened the previous journal and read it through again. Not only do I not see what there is to admire in it, but I even noticed it's full of mistakes.

The whole tone of your letter shows you've forgotten all the fears and uncertainties which divided us, and that makes me happy! Congratulations and encore. If Drambuie has that effect on you, I'll not only feed it to you here, I'll have you bathe in it, too…

Overall, the story with 'Iano' amused me greatly. I wasn't at all surprised, since I know you both (by the way, did he manage to get off with Jagusia, too?). Naturally I guessed straight away from that affectionate nickname – what's he got in common with Iano Buddenbrook? – but I found the details delicious.

I have indeed finished the opera, but where does our mutual friend get the conviction that it's a 'great work' from? The only extract I showed him is not one of the best and what's more I played it like a pudding! But I'm almost faint with relief that, despite everything, after nine years I've finished it, and a whole month before the start of the new season as well. There's the orchestration of the last act and the second half of the epilogue left, but that can be done between concerts, so I'll manage it. But I've put my memoirs to one side. You know, Funnyface, I've completely lost the urge for it. In fact, I've lost all the bitterness which was pushing me to write it. The book was going to be both therapy and revenge – and the therapy turned out so effective that I no longer want revenge. After all, no one harmed me personally and consciously – our whole generation was harmed. If I ever do write that book, then I'll do it for different reasons and maybe only after a time.

Lately I've discovered that I'm not at all indifferent to Poland – I've been sitting with my nose in the television for weeks, fearfully at first, and then joyfully!

What do you think about the affair with John? Lately I've received more letters than I've sent (till now I was always begging for replies and hardly ever getting them). But by and large they're nasty letters, accusing me of indiscretion (rightly, as it happens). I'm disillusioned by this concern for discretion as if that was the most important thing here…

(…) I'm now waiting with amused impatience for Ian's next letter. Perhaps he'll try to conceal something? That, of course, would double the whole humour of the situation. In any case I'm certain it'll be awfully hard for him to return to New Zealand! Everyone speaks English there, so it'll be impossible for him to show off his knowledge of the language, and lectures about contemporary music may not impress all the women there so much. But he is nice, isn't he? I'm already laughing at the thought of our first conversation after his return…

Funnyface, I'd like to ask you a favour. Could you drop in to see Emma Altberg sometime and show her one of my tapes? I got a terribly pitiful letter from her in which she complains about everything in general but also about the fact that she hasn't heard any of my performances or compositions. At the same time she says that, as a result of her poor hearing and advanced old age all music sounds out of tune to her anyway! I assure her it's not old age but the Warsaw Autumn, because music sounds more and more out of tune, including my own, of course.

The other favour is very different: can you get anything other than *The Master and Margarita* by Bulgakov in Poland? I'm most interested in *The Life of Monsieur de Molière* – no one here knows anything about it… Will you try, please?

How do you like this recital programme:

1) Bartók: *Out of Doors*
2) Schubert: Sonata in G major
3) Chopin: 24 Preludes.

I've just started to learn it. What do you say to that?

Try to write back quickly this time, because the foreign tours start on 4 November! This time write 'any old how' if you don't have time for a new masterpiece! Just the sight of your handwriting on the envelope makes me smile…

Kiss, kiss, kiss, Your Andrzej.


Warsaw, 21.10.80

Darling Andrzej,

As you've probably guessed, your letter gave me enormous pleasure, and how it flattered me! It would give me exquisite pleasure to devote the rest of my life to writing your biography, but writing skills aren't as important here as empathy with the other person's nature. I fear that all my little jokes and asides would obscure your personality, the slightly Chaplin-like one – you can laugh and smile with all your heart – I can do it only half-heartedly. I'll pass over the question of your creativity – I wouldn't dare to write one word about it!

At the moment I don't have time even to think about such ambitious undertakings: my life is spent in the middle of a pack of dogs which no-one wants to buy because a newspaper has printed an article about imminent meat rationing. The dogs stuff themselves like pigs, bark like guard dogs and I have to run a soup kitchen for them with one arm in plaster! Yes, yes, while I was protecting someone from an attack by Bisa I dislocated a finger, the index finger of my right hand. Piotr isn't here because he had nowhere to sleep (the dogs used to go into his bed at four in the morning and bite his toes), and he's taking his PhD exams in a week. All my friends have abandoned me, too, because the dogs hung themselves off their coats and dresses as if they were on a merry-go-round. It's a nightmare!

Despite my injury I managed to tape some interesting pieces from the Chopin contest: I've got cassettes of Dang Thai Son and Pogorelić – especially for you.

Ian's opinion of your opera couldn't have been accidental, he spoke with conviction and he really does know about music. I realised that he fell asleep at every concert when they were playing a boring bit but woke instantly whenever there was something interesting to hear! Besides which he was enchanted by my Hofman tape which even Witek didn't appreciate, saying that Hofman plays Chopin like a circus clown. (…)

You ask me what I think about John. I think you're still fascinated, though not without a touch of contempt. Nietzsche wrote: 'What does he know about love who has never despised the object of his love?.' (…)

Yes, you're right, Ian is enormously nice and open, he has this easy-going quality about him which makes it nice and relaxed to be with him. As for Jagusia, I guess that she prefers complicated and over-refined people. I'm terrified by difficulties – she's aroused by them.

I'll carry out all your requests thoroughly as soon as I liberate myself from all these dogs whose own mother has had enough of them.

As you can see, I've replied immediately and with my left hand, too!

Kiss you.

Your H.

Cumnor, 1.11.80

My Darling Funnyface,

Many, many thanks for the birthday telegram which has just arrived, and for your last letter which I still haven't had time to reply to. In fact I don't have time now, either, but I'll send you a page at least.

Yesterday I read Iano the description of your association. He was enraptured, we laughed till half past two in the morning. In fact you fascinated him more than any other woman, so maybe he'll be able to convince you of your worth.

Punctually at midnight Iano handed me four birthday presents which he bought on your advice, so I thank you very much for those, too. And this morning papa phoned with best wishes. I feel sorry for him, but I don't agree with you that my letter to him was a psychological mistake. You see, the difference between you and me is that if someone asks me on Wednesday if it's Sunday, I'll always reply: 'No, it's Wednesday', even if I know he doesn't want to go to work. But you take pity on people and tell them what they want to hear. It seems to me, however, that you'd show them greater respect if you assumed they could take the truth and that's why I'm always so pleased when you criticise me. In my childhood everyone demanded that I lie to them – but you didn't, and you were the first person who accepted my frankness.

It's not that I believe in shoving the truth under people's noses: if someone wants to they have a right to be an ostrich. But if someone asks for the truth then, in my view, there is no choice!

Bye, Funnyface, I have to do some work!

Kisses, your Andrzej.

Warsaw, 12.11.80

My Darling Andrzej,

I keep getting ever nicer letters, either from you or inspired by you (a very engaging letter has just come from Ian). Yes, you've succeeded – you've both convinced me that I truly am a charming old lady. But remember how Janek used to put it? Women, when they are small, love dogs, then their girl friends, then men, then their girl friends again, and eventually they end up loving dogs. That's how it is with me.

Talking of which, I have only five dogs at home now, I sold Camille, Carlo, and Clash, which the girl from the Kennel Club called 'Clap' on the certificate. She obviously had something else on her mind.

Believe it or not, I've managed to finish – in this madhouse – the report on all those awful tests and in December I'll be free and happy.

You're right, I do tell people it's Sunday when it's Wednesday, but you won't believe how convinced I am myself that it is. This faith can sometimes work miracles, but sometimes not. It doesn't work when the person would rather worry about being disillusioned than rejoice at the illusion. There is also a time difference: you can dream for quite a long time, but disillusionment comes once and quickly. Jurek was a congenital mythomane which made him tell lies (driving even me to a rage); he once defended himself saying: 'Yes, I often lie because the truth isn't always the best and it's not always as we desire it. We're condemned to truth anyway, only lies give us a sense of freedom, because we can lie to ourselves and have, even for a moment, the best kind of truth whenever we want it. Besides, there is only one truth, but we can choose the lies we want. Finally: truth is dependent on life because it feeds on reality, but lies are independent because they feed on themselves.' That, more or less, is how my late husband put it, feeding himself lies to the end, and at the very end feeding himself narcotics.

Before your letter came I was reading Heine and I found a splendid poem for Ian:

Das macht den Menschen glücklich
Das macht den Menschen matt,

Wenn er drei schöne Geliebte
Und nur zwei Beine hat.*

It fits him like a glove! Iano asked me if I was planning to marry a third time. I replied: 'If I did it'd only be to please Andrzej – he likes it when I get married.'

Kiss you and kiss you because after all these explanations I can't see any barriers now, can you?

Your H.

Cumnor, 16.11.80

My Darling Funnyface,

You've made me jealous for the first time in my life because Ian's letter from you is longer than mine! (Of course I read them both.) I console myself with the thought that that was precisely why you wrote them that way.

Ian will be here again at the beginning of December, so you can carry on writing with no worries. And I'm off on Wednesday for three and a half weeks to Jerusalem where I'll have a week's rest, then I've promised to visit some conservatoires, and I'll spend any spare time orchestrating *The Merchant* and having interviews with my cousin Halina who spent much time with us in the ghetto and will be able to tell me a lot. But I think the whole of the autobiography will have to be rewritten because its monotonous, persistent sarcasm no longer suits me. For the moment I've resolved simply to listen to Halina (maybe even with a tape-recorder) without provoking or inducing any fresh reactions.

Added to which I now have a new hobby. Do you remember how I complained about Hampton (the author of that play about Rimbaud) because he didn't want to meet me? After two years he decided it was now quite feasible after all and straight away started treating me like an old friend and confidant. We spent the whole afternoon together and he immediately agreed in advance to everything I might want to do with his play. A long time ago I wrote to tell him I intended to interlace his play with Rimbaud's autobiographical poem *Season in Hell*, and Hampton, though he still didn't meet with me, translated many pages of the poem into English for me – whole evenings of work for which no one will ever pay him! But you know what I think about even the most brilliant translations of poetry, they're always going to be a better or worse imitation of the original and the risk is greater when the poetry is excellent. So I came up with another idea: maybe I should do the whole opera in French so

---

* It makes a man happy, It makes a man weak, Chasing three lovers, When he has only two feet

that the Rimbaud texts would be in the original? Once again he agreed straight away, but he warned me that the French translation did not turn out to be very good. 'How is your French?' he asked. So, very excited, I've started to translate *Total Eclipse* into French, a completely new undertaking for me.

I'm not even certain yet I'll go ahead with this opera because the play is so brilliant I can only spoil it! But in any case I want to offer him the translation out of gratitude, as a kind of tribute, and at the same time – why conceal it? – I'd also like to impress him a bit and do a translation which will satisfy him. I'm finding the work very entertaining.

Recently I played the Beethoven Concerto in C major three times in Germany: once well, once appallingly, and once outstandingly. And then I had four recitals in Norway, with Mozart's *Fantasia* and Sonata in C minor, Bartok's suite *Out of Doors* and several pieces of Chopin to whom I've recently been attracted very strongly. Overall it wasn't bad and I enjoyed it.

My relationship with John is now much less tense, there's no longer any question of love but there's a good chance of a permanent friendship. Recently I was amazed to hear John's voice on the telephone: 'Will you invite me over for a bit?' I replied calmly and frankly that I didn't have time. It's hard not to smile, isn't it?

Bye for now and kisses, as always. Darling, write a longer letter. I'm busy, too, but somehow I'll always find time and energy for you…

Hug you, but without a rucksack,

Your Andrzej.

Warsaw, 23.11.80

Darling Andrzej,

I had something important to tell you, but I've forgotten what so I'm writing any old thing just because I feel like it. No, my life hasn't become any easier, on the contrary – all the dogs have been struck down by typhus, they eat nothing and lie motionless one on top of another (a black furry pile) – but a gallows humour has overcome me. You will be jealous of me because, imagine this – I have a lackey! I put up an advertisement and a boy of exceptional charm appeared, aged about twenty and announced that he doesn't need money because his mother lives in New York and sends him dollars; he'd come because he felt the advertisement had been written by a fraternal soul.

It was thanks to the lackey that the dogs fell so terribly ill because while he was peeling carrots all the peel fell onto the floor where the pups gulped them down. Added to which he let them into the room where they tore and swallowed tons of books while he was improvising on the piano. When I'm not at home all he does is make music, when I come back he entertains me with conversations about life. Do you treat life seriously? he asks, because he does. He believes only in music and love. And what do I believe in? etc. The lackey, too, has been ill these last few days so I'm having a bit of a rest from all those philosophical conversations and improvisations. Majka says that I couldn't ever have had any other kind of lackey!

I'm particularly tired today because at midnight some woman came, claiming we knew each other very well and she was a neighbour, though it was the first time I'd ever set eyes on her. Piotr just happened to be spending the night at my place so she started to ask us to go to her apartment and get rid of some man who'd got drunk and didn't want to leave. We have to understand that she has children, two under-age daughters! 'But my dear woman,' I protested from under my bedclothes, 'how can I throw your guests out of your apartment?' 'I beg you!' she shouted and, giving me the number of her apartment, she left. We started to think about it. Finally we decided we'd pretend to be relatives from the provinces who'd just come over to stay the night. We put on furs, scarves, gloves, we took out bags, suitcases and we wandered upstairs. There was a man sleeping on the couch. We made a terrible noise, laughing hysterically and shouting: 'Darling Auntie, we've come, let us stay the night here!' etc. The terrified man leapt up off the couch. My amazement turned to shock: it was the thoroughly charming engineer who lives right next door to me – we walk our dogs together every day. His shock and embarrassment were even greater, he didn't even stop to consider why we'd come up at one in the morning in our furs and scarves and carrying suitcases. The poor man had been afraid to go back to his wife in a state of drunkenness so he'd gone up to his neighbour for a bit to sober up.

We drank a bottle of wine, she kept hugging me for no apparent reason, and he kept excusing himself repeatedly, kissing me on the hand as he did so. Suddenly, Piotr jumped from his chair and introduced himself to the man. More often than not, Piotr does jump up and introduce himself completely unexpectedly. But, as a consequence, the visit became even more surreal. We went back to my place to sober up; then the neighbour suddenly appeared again. She sat down and cried: 'It's hard for me to live without a man' she said. And 'my husband won't be back for a long time because he killed someone and is now in jail.' She likes the engineer very much... She cried such a lot that by three o'clock we realised it had been a mistake to dress up like that and save her from the engineer's embraces. Life is complicated, and women are dishonest with themselves. But I don't need to tell you that, you know it already.

Heaps of best wishes,

Your H.

Cumnor, 26.12.80

My Darling Funnyface,

I came back from Israel recently and found your two enchanting letters. I need a lackey, too; could you send him to me? Surely I deserve some reparation for Iano?

I have lots to tell you but I'm tired and depressed, besides which I'd need to write about 50 pages and I haven't the strength for that! I'll just tell you that, having read Emanuel Ringelblum's Archive of the Warsaw Ghetto during my stay in Israel and half of Wojdowski's book*, I've given up the autobiography. I'll give you the reasons in brief:

1) Fear. After a fortnight's reading I dreamt I was messing about in radioactive clay and, as a result, the skin started to peel off my hands. I showed my hands to a woman standing next to me, and she said: 'That's just the beginning.' I was so terrified that I woke and realised that this dream was a warning and that I can't go on with the work.

2) Shame. You can't even guess how ashamed I am of the few chapters I've written and which I was so proud of. It's not that what I saw, experienced and knew was a drop in the ocean (though it's only now that I realise how effectively my mother shielded me from it, and thanks to that I'm not in an institution). It's just that within the context of the Warsaw Ghetto one can't hurl insults at a contrary aunt nor mock a neurasthenic granny – because it's simply indecent, just like a quarrel at a funeral. And there's something else that's indecent at a funeral, namely, showing off. The whole piece is full of conscious virtuosity; I clearly exploit the collective tragedy to show off my abilities. Both the pride and the bitterness (against Dorka, for instance) are ridiculous, petty and, truth to tell, sordid. All my life I've known I'm an extreme egocentric but it was only then that I came to be ashamed of it.

There are letters and chronicles in the Ringelblum Archive some of which reveal, aside from courage, intelligence and perceptiveness, and quite involuntarily, an exceptional literary talent. Seeing it, I glanced at the footnotes to see who had written such and such a passage. It always turned out that the person had died, and sometimes that it hadn't been possible to establish their identity. Many people of much greater talent than mine died; I have nothing to complain about and nothing to boast of. And note that all these people, despite

---

* Bogdan Wojdowski's book was published in Poland as *Chleb rzucony umarłym* in 1971 and by Northwestern University Press in English as *Bread for the Departed* in 1997

hunger, fear and the inexorable closeness of death, wrote not about themselves but about the situation as a whole.

Once again, therefore, I suggest that you write my biography: I will not do it.

Darling, write to me: that would help me a lot. And I'd be even more grateful if you came here to me, despite fears and previous disappointments. What irritated me about you was superficial: I've now come close to the heart of myself and what I see there I dislike very much. But you accept me and like me through and through with all my cowardice and inability to come out of myself which I now consider to be an affliction... (…)

Lately I've had to get down to some solid practice again because I let myself go completely in Israel and I have a difficult programme of recitals in January. (…) At the same time I'm translating Hampton's play into French and orchestrating the rest of the opera, but only sporadically because it's hard for me to concentrate after four hours of practice.

Well, bye for now, Funnyface. Write back as soon as you can. Hug you with all my heart and you're ever nearer to me. You do believe in our friendship now, don't you?

Your Andrzej.

Warsaw, 19.1.81

Darling, you probably thought I died and you're partly right. This year has exhausted me fatally, because I've never before worked so hard: doing research, union work for Solidarity, and manual work (three months of going round in circles with the pups).

The situation in Poland is exceptionally fascinating, but on a daily basis it entails hellish hard work and constant disputes over every tiny matter. It would be boring for you to read accounts of these endless disputes, but at the moment that is what my life consists of and perhaps that's why I find it hard to write. And generally speaking my attitude to these things isn't as cheerful as yours. Once, Marek P. (you remember the artist who didn't know what to feed his little daughters on) showed me one of his drawings: there was a desert and in it a tiny person; you could see he was about to disappear like an ant amongst the grains of sand. In fact, the desert was white, snowed under, frosty – he would simply freeze to death... Under the drawing Marek had written: 'Oh, yes, when Nikita Sergeyevitch Khrushchev doesn't like someone, he really doesn't like them...'

I received your letters with the startling news about John and about Hampton three weeks ago and I was really pleased.

Many thanks for the copy of *The Merchant* which I'll read with the Polish text at hand. There's been a new translation done by Maciej Słomczyński, who translated Joyce and is the president of an international association concerned with Joyce's work. Słomczyński makes huge sums of money writing detective stories so he can visit all the nooks and crannies described by Joyce. An article where he describes this procedure makes you think he's surrendering to some kind of joyful torture. You will understand it because you do the same thing.

I'm sending you a photo of Pogorelić, and Basia will bring you cassettes of the performances. As for Basia, her emotional life is going along similar lines to yours, so that's probably why you like each other so much…

I've not been in love with anyone for years. Though recently a friend of Tosio's visited me and asked me if I wouldn't be his wife. He explained his desire to marry me by saying that every day between four and six in the afternoon he is overwhelmed by sorrow. I said it would be better for both of us if he just visited me occasionally between those hours. He's been three times now but as a result of these visits I've started to be overwhelmed by sorrow. And anyway he claims I'm a femme fatale because anyone who loves me dies very quickly. Just as well that you at least don't love me!

I'd be very interested to read your reactions to Jerusalem. What were your aunt Halina's accounts of the ghetto like? Did you find out anything new about your mother? What are you doing now and how do you find the world?

I beg you don't be put off by my epistolary impotence and write! I need your letters more than anything in the world.

Kiss you, your H.

Cumnor, 3.2.81

Darling Funnyface,

Though I haven't the time or the energy to write, I want to thank you for the charming letter and the no less charming photo of Pogorelić! And also to inform you that Basia has just phoned and though I vehemently invited her for tomorrow evening she rejected me just as she rejects all her admirers. But we talked very cordially and I was pleased by her return because, despite our rare meetings being spent mainly in silence, your child has become very dear and near to me. As you know, it happened very gradually, in a manner appropriate to Basia's mysteriousness.

Thinking about last year I came to the conclusion that never before has so much happened in a 12-month period. The first trip to Israel; the renewal of the love affair with John; the meeting with my father; the disaster with John; the completion of the opera; and finally the second trip to Israel, whose first impressions I described in a previous letter. No wonder I'm so tired – especially as I've been working all year, am working still, not taking even a week's holiday.

Now I'm trying to reconcile trips and concerts (to Venezuela and Denmark, and between them one recital in England) with the orchestration of my opera. At the same time a very talented lady recommended by Hans Keller, is making a piano score. And since that costs 10 pounds a page, I've mortgaged the house! I now owe everyone money – except my father... So, things aren't easy at the moment, either for me, or for you. But we'll survive, won't we?

Hug you and kiss you with all my heart.

Your Andrzej.

Warsaw, 30.1.81

Dearest Andrzej,

This time your letter took five whole weeks, but now things will probably improve. Lately I've been doing a lot of union work, but a Tarot reading told me I oughtn't to try 'to save the whole of humanity, nor engage in politics because my true vocation is helping *individual* people through psychotherapy and parapsychology'.

But to return to your letter. As far as I know (though I haven't read it), in *The Painted Bird* Kosinski, too, describes the horror of war through a child's story. Or what about *The Diary of Anne Frank*? It's far more moving than statistics, chronicles or historical works about the destruction of the Jews. And who has more moral right to write about it than you?!... A child taken out of the ghetto in a garbage bin. Why did the chapter you wrote about your mother make me cry? She didn't stay in the ghetto with your stepfather because she chose him in preference to you, chose death with him rather than life with you. She was beautiful but her beauty was exceptionally Semitic and she knew it. She knew she could help you in nothing, but she could certainly *damage* you – simply by being close to you. Is that not sufficiently tragic?!

Kiss you, Darling,

Your H.

CARD: CYPRESS TREES

Miami, 22.2.81

Darling Funnyface, I'm thinking about you so much I have no time to write! Unwittingly and by chance I found myself in the middle of the Jewish Renaissance Fair – at first I thought I was back in Golder's Green. Everyone I meet asks me: 'And where were *you* during the war?', which has made me start envying the blacks.

Drop me a line to my house where I'll be in a couple of days and for longer from more or less the 25th of March.

Kisses,

Your Andrzej.

Warsaw, 6.3.81

My Darling Andrzej, thanks for the letter (the one about the difficult year), once again our letters have crossed. Basia has probably reached you with the Pogorelić cassette and you've heard the B flat Sonata. Didn't it seem to you to be the shortest and most emotional sonata in the world?

Lately I've been in a foul mood until suddenly… I fell in love! This love is more hopeless than all your loves put together. To begin with, the object of my love is 15 years younger than me, secondly – she's a girl, and neither of us are lesbians, thirdly – she's leaving the country for good. Can you imagine so many unfavourable circumstances at once? Ewa is small, minute, and has her hair shaved close; she is the personification of grace, intelligence and unusual intuition. Her wonderful energy is infectious: I'm so full of enthusiasm I've written three stories in ten days (each one, progressively worse but that doesn't matter). She initiates all our meetings, which makes it hard for me to give up hope (for what?!!). Ewa claims we are in deep contact with each other and suggests joint sessions of experiencing this and that to get even more deeply in touch with each other (like in the Brahms: *So schnell wie möglich* and then *noch schneller.*)*

Tomorrow, Ewa and I are going to see Tarkovsky's *The Mirror*: Ewa wants me to choose a contemporary novel from which she could make a film. Consequently, I'm reading a new book every day and I'll soon be the best-read person in the country. Has Selimović's *Death and the Dervish* been translated into English? Ewa claims it's a great book, too, but not suitable for film because half its greatness would be lost. So I've given her James Kirkwood's *Good Times, Bad Times* (incidentally, what do you make of the tattered card Peter finds after Jordan's death in the crack of the drawer?).

This letter is completely stupid but that's how things are: anger takes away beauty, and love takes away reason.

Kiss you. H.

---

* As quickly as possible… more quickly still

Warsaw, 8.3.81

Darling Andrzej,

I've just spent two nights without sleep, talking with Ewa. Despite that, or maybe because of it, I feel like chatting to you. After the first conversation Ewa announced that in the morning she felt like a deflowered virgin. Last night I told her about you and she was so fascinated she's resolved to make a film about you. She's determined to meet you!

At the moment we're still debating which book to choose for a screenplay. She judged *Good Times, Bad Times* too primitive and more suited to a Hollywood film with 'stars' (as it happens I don't agree because it's a subtle piece of work and only the translucence of the form makes it appear simple). Ewa's view of Tarkovsky's *Mirror* is that it's a phoney and pretentious film. I agree a bit with that. Because in the film when the dying hero holds a little bird in his hand the colour of the bird echoes the colour of the quilt under which the dead man is lying. There was a child in a Russian village, during the war, sleeping in a hut in a four-poster bed. Ewa expected the child to have a ruby ring on its finger because its mother was drifting round the hut in a ruby-coloured dress. I, in turn, thought the child's dreams in the four-poster would be accompanied by a choir of angels, but the choir didn't arrive till the birth of the sister of the little boy who should have been wearing a ruby ring.

I'm probably boring you, so I'll close now and kiss you.

Your H.

PS. Think about a screenplay for a film about yourself, though Ewa claims that apart from giving permission to shoot the film you don't have to concern yourself with anything. She also says for God's sake don't destroy your autobiography!

Warsaw, 20.3.81

My Darling Andrzej!

Thank you with all my heart for the nice letter you wrote before your visit to Paris. I think your crises are a result of overwork and vernal fluids. Here we're all depressed, we meet and Hamletise... Going to the cinema every day (Ewa has bought tickets for a review of the best films in the world) tires me somewhat instead of cheering me up. Especially as the films make one sad, particularly Tarkovsky's *Stalker* knocks me off my feet...

Ewa has decided to adapt Bulgakov's *Black Snow: A Theatrical Novel*. The novel isn't as good as *The Master and Margarita*, something between Erenburg and the Ilf and Petrov combination, but it's not bad, either...

I read Ewa my story about the alcoholic who hanged himself in hospital during the detoxification programme. Despite sincerely sympathising with him, she said: 'It's great that he hanged himself!' That's what you artists are like… (…)

Darling, I'm probably boring you, but you should thank God I'm not summarising the hundred-page publication I'm just finishing.

Kiss you with all my heart,

Your H.

Cumnor, 30.3.81

My Darling Funnyface,

I came back a few days ago from my trip (Denmark, Germany, Paris) and found both your letters, but I was so tired I didn't, exceptionally, reply at once! It's not work that tires me so much, it's people: work sometimes arouses more energy than it consumes, but conversations with chance acquaintances somehow diffuse all energy and afterwards it takes me some time to recover my concentration. Or maybe it's my hermit's life in Cumnor that's made me unlearn how to be with people?

In Paris I saw my father whose health has deteriorated markedly; he received me very warmly. After the visit his wife told me that when he found out about granny's death he was convinced I would contact him straight away and would return to him; Genie explained that by and large 19-year-old boys prefer to become independent, but my father didn't believe her and for years he waited for a letter or a telephone call! It's only now I understand how big a shock it must have been for him when he sent wife and sister backstage after one of my Paris concerts in '58 and I refused to meet him. And of course I'm sorry for him! After all it's not his fault he understood neither my mother nor me; and that's why he must regard the divorce she demanded and my own breaking off of contacts as a completely undeserved and cruel punishment. But it's only now that I'm capable of understanding that. (…)

Darling, don't be angry but I wrote to Basia to tell her you've fallen in love with a woman, because I'm so proud of you. I don't know if Ewa exists or if you made her up, but I agree with all her attitudes and views. And the film about me will be a great success as long as she never meets me! Eisenstein didn't meet Ivan the Terrible, either, and it proved no handicap…

I don't know Kirkwood's novel, but I'll try to find it in the library. At the moment I'm rushed off my feet: this week I'm playing Beethoven's Concerto in C minor three times. It's an absolutely apocalyptic piece!

In Germany I met Wanda Wiłkomirska and the Varsovia Quartet – they offered to play my 2nd Quartet at the Warsaw Autumn in '82. And Wanda would like to play all the Mozart sonatas with me, but I don't know yet if we'll suit one another…

Funnyface, I'm closing now because I have to get up early tomorrow morning, and for me that's a form of rape!

Kisses, your Andrzej.

Cumnor, 5.4.81

Darling Facekins,

I'm so pleased you're writing more often now! Maybe you'll send me one of your stories, e.g. the one about the alcoholic who hanged himself so splendidly? I much prefer reading you to Bulgakov, especially as I've got the *Theatrical Novel* in English and it didn't grab me, either. If you ever come across *The Life of M. Molière* be good enough to send it to me. I read it in German but then I gave it to Stefan A., and now regret it because it's probably a better subject for an opera than Rimbaud. (I'm still translating Hampton's play, but I get the feeling I'm responding to it like a human being and a lover of literature, not as a musician – so far not one theme has come into my head, and that's surely a dangerous sign).

My depression has passed because I'm less tired and playing better. But you're right, I am overworked and unfortunately will continue to be so. Because of financial difficulties I have to take concerts even in the summer. Besides which I've been invited for the first time in my life to write a composition for a set date: the first performance is to take place on October 16th. They want a piece for four hands to the memory of Bartók, so I'll probably try to write variations on the opening theme of his Viola Concerto (do you know it?). On the 1st of July I'm supposed to play some Mozart concerto in Wales, on the 16th Beethoven's Concerto in C minor in London and three piano quartets in Austria, so I'll have to learn them all simultaneously! There can be no question of a holiday this year.

Next season there's supposed to be the first performance of my Trio, and it's being broadcast on the radio, so of course I'll send you a cassette!

How are things with Ewa? Maybe you'll become a film star yourself? You could, for instance, play me in this biographical film far better than any actor, because you feel as me instinctively and you know me inside out.

At the moment I'm off to London to see an opera and both ballets by Bartók. It's Eve's birthday on Wednesday and I'm taking her to this event, and on Sunday it's my father's birthday. I've lost all my old bitterness and now I only feel sorry for him, you know? He himself lost his wife and his son without understanding how and why. But there's no point in explaining it to him.

Maybe I will write that autobiography some day when I acquire some distance towards those people and those events. But for the moment I'm doing only what I have to.

Anyway I'm never bored unless I'm forced to attend some reception! I have a fascinating job and completely amazing friends – fascinating, honest, devoted and understanding. Nowadays I don't miss love at all.

So you're right when you say I ought to be happy, and besides I frequently am!

Hug you with all of my heart,

Your Andrzej.

Cumnor, 19.4.81

Thanks for the cassettes! Ivo sounds like the young Horowitz.

My Darling Monkey, I'm writing to you while Basia, on the opposite end of the table, is writing to a friend.

I'm writing to remind you of my telephone invitation. Don't wait till July, come over sooner! I've got concerts in July and August, but I'm free in June. You could take turns staying with me and with Basia.

Basia is longing for you to come over with Ewa who has made a great impression on her! I, too, would very much like to meet her.

Yesterday, after the telephone conversation with you, Basia and I listened to Pogorelić playing the Sonata in B flat minor. I understand your excitement because he truly is a demonic guy! But I like the fast parts more because his sound, at least on this cassette, seems to me to be a bit hard and there's a lack of *legato* in it. And the finale sounds, to me, too virtuoso-like – Martha Argerich plays it just as quickly but much more quietly and she finds some hidden polyphony of shades in this unison which is mysterious, virtually unbearable and very disturbing. Ivo plays the third Etude very beautifully, it's full of music and variety, which was lacking a bit in the Sonata.

I'll write you an 'official' invitation on paper you'll be able to show in the appropriate office. I also ought to add that when you're in England you'll bump into Iano who, having become intoxicated with Europe, can't seem to settle in New Zealand! My depression has passed but pianistically speaking I've let myself go and must pull myself together! But I'm tired and find it hard to concentrate.

Hug you, my beloved Funnyface, and await your visit with great impatience.

Your Andrzej.

Warsaw, 19.4.81

Andrzej, I've just read the letter you wrote after your return from Paris. I'm thinking about your father. You just don't know how hard it is to be rejected by your own child, much harder than by a lover, or husband, or wife. Such rejection arouses aggression, which can't be shown so it transforms itself into guilt and distaste for oneself. You can think the most horrible things about your husband, and that gets him out of your hair – he's a stranger, but you can't do that about your child because it is your child. I'm writing this because you equate your relationship with your father with his relationship with your mother.

A few days ago I went away with Ewa for a 10-day rest to Kazimierz. Oh, some rest! It was just like in Cumnor: we came back after four days. I tried to be nice, bewitching, full of charm, but I was boring, polite, silent and depressing. Ewa's nerves couldn't stand it, nor could mine.

As for the film, Ewa claims that the film about Ivan the Terrible was a historical metaphor: it had nothing to do with Ivan, it was about Stalin. That's why the film didn't see the light of day for 12 years and was Eisenstein's swansong. In fact the director conducted numerous conversations with Stalin prior to shooting the film. That's point number one, the second point is: if a condition of making this film is that she never meets you then she'd rather abandon the film.

And what of our Polish situation? As Stalker's wife put it: 'It's becoming a source of everyday unexpected joys.' You acquire a packet of butter and you feel as if you've bought a car, you buy a roll of toilet paper – you're sure you've won the lottery. And what a huge margin of hope! You don't have that there. We're still capable of being pleased by things that no longer cheer you. So who is the richer? And how one pines for this country!... Basia writes: 'Yesterday, at my place, a long party came to an end. There was a great table in the middle of the room. I covered it with the yellow table cloth, the hem-stitched one from granny. When my guests saw the table cloth, they had tears in their eyes, they said they hadn't seen anything like it for years. I also hung up coloured garlands. It was the most beautiful of parties. I danced Polish highland dances with Dolores. Then we listened to the birds fluttering in the park. At the end we had Schubert's Quintet (a record from Andrzej, he loves that Quintet, he cries whenever he hears it). It was very exalted, everyone felt so happy. The party lasted four days. No one wanted to go home.(...)'

I'll finish now because I feel senseless today. I spent half the night with Ewa at a concert of a Negro quartet. Ewa kept plying me with brandy from the buffet and offering me a spliff. When I inhaled deeply it seemed that the quartet was one black cloud issuing thunderclaps (in fact they had a drum as big as a stove).

Kiss you, Darling,

Your H.

CARD: NEW COLLEGE, OXFORD.
CARVINGS ON BELL TOWER

Cumnor, 22.4.81

Darling Halinka, see how miserable I look because I miss you so much! Be good and come to me, all right? I'm free all of June and I've got some free time in July. You can stay at my place or at Basia's because she's got two rooms now. Write quickly to say when you'll be here.

Kisses, Your A.

Warsaw, 21.5.81

Dearest Andrzej, briefly this time. The heat wave here is a nightmare, and my place is the threshold of hell! Ewa is in Łódź editing a film with a Canadian who is as beautiful and silent as an angel. Ewa has fallen in love with the Canadian, which is not surprising.

So: I want to come to you in September, but for a very specific purpose. You once mentioned you wanted me to write your biography, and I said I didn't feel I was capable of it (for various reasons). But I have another idea: we could reconstruct our correspondence, which after all has been going on for a quarter of a century! If you wanted we could supplement some of the letters with extracts from your journal. We'll discuss the idea, and I would look after the collection. I admit it would be better done by someone from outside, who could be objective about certain matters. I have no distance and I could include bits which would be of no interest to anyone. In any case, I'll start it and I want to get down to the work in Cumnor. What would I need? A free room, a typewriter and paper, and apart from that, your materials and suggestions (we'll collect the letters jointly).

So I'm coming, not as a guest but as a collaborator! My letter is short and business-like because that's what a letter from a collaborator should be.

I enclose many laconic kisses.

Your H.

PS. Send me a decent invitation, that card with the gargoyles amused me, but I'm not sure it would amuse the passport officials.

CARD: BODLEIAN LIBRARY, OXFORD.
FUNERAL INVITATION, 1723

Cumnor, 22.5.81

Darling Funnyface, Here's an official invitation, and to my funeral, too! But don't wait for it, just come whenever you can. I'll be touring in August, but you can make yourself at home here! But in June and September I'm comparatively free.

Ian is ill, he's undergoing some hospital tests, so he's not coming here till next year!

Kiss you, your 'Titanic' of sex – Andrzej.

Cumnor, 29.5.81

Darling Funnyface,

Many thanks for the short, perhaps, but nonetheless pleasant and pertinent letter. Your idea of working on our correspondence seems quite promising, in any case it's worth trying! And our relationship will benefit from it because we'll be working together aiming at something we've established in advance, so we won't be wondering how we're feeling in each other's company and why, which will certainly simplify those feelings. (…) I'll put my journals at your disposal, and I've never been mean with my suggestions…

And when will this Ewa come? I feel we'll understand one another perfectly! Her Canadian Marek will also be very welcome. (…)

I'm writing briefly, too, because I'm enormously tired: I've spent the whole day on trains from Glasgow, and the day after tomorrow I have a recital in Bath and tomorrow I'll have to learn the rest of the programme.

On the 31st of August I'm playing Mozart's Concerto in C minor in London: if you're here I'm cordially inviting you and Basia though I daren't promise it'll be any good. And on the 25th I'm giving a charity recital, also in London – perhaps you'll help me learn it?

Kiss you with all my heart,

Your Andrzej.

Warsaw, 1.6.81

Beloved Andrzej, Today is Children's Day so I'm sending you best wishes because the kind of invitations you send me can only be sent by a small, mischievous boy. We'll all come. There will be me, Ewa, her boyfriend Marek, the film crew. I'll be the screenwriter, Marek – the director, Ewa – the editor. (…)

It's a pity to leave Poland just now even though there isn't even any soap. But such excitement instead! You watch the television news like you would a crime thriller. Except that in crime thrillers it's hard to work out the killer, whereas here it's hard to predict the next victim. On one news programme they're shooting at the Pope, on another the Primate dies, on the next ministers commit suicide, the one after that a brave priest uses a judo throw to disarm some bandits, then Wajda brings the Palme d'Or back from Cannes, and someone else kills a passer-by who refused to offer him a cigarette. There's something for everyone here.

I've just received a letter from Iano which made me laugh enormously. Not that the letter was funny: Ian simply invited me for a holiday to Christchurch, but what's funny is that – as I found out from Orbis – the cost of travel from Bangkok to Christchurch is 2500 dollars (you can pay in zlotys only as far as Bangkok). The price of a dollar on the black market is such that I would have to hoard my salary for 50 months to pay for this journey and that's without eating or drinking! (Frozen, no doubt).

But what fabulous perspectives did Ian unfold before me of New Zealand! We'll go swimming, climb mountains, listen to records, drive around in a car with a trailer, play music for four hands etc. I think I probably will freeze myself, but will he still renew the invitation in 5 years?

Kissing and waiting,

Your H.

PS. How is the orchestration of the 3rd act going? When *The Merchant* is finally staged they'll probably give you an official invitation to Poland, as they did with Miłosz. Incidentally, Kałużyński (an amusing film critic) wrote recently that Poland has won the Vatican, the Nobel Prize, the Cannes Palme d'Or – all that's left is to win the next Olympic Games and World War III!

Cumnor, 14.6.81

Darling Funnyface,

(…) I've just got to know Krystian Zimerman and his charming wife Majka. I'm ravished by them! Krys will be staying at my place in August because he has nowhere to practise and I'll be away on tour then. They liked me straight away, too, but they probably like everyone anyway – they're such *sunny* people.

Temporarily I'm not practising, I'm proof-reading the piano score of Act I (this score will ruin me, it's going to cost around 5000 pounds) and I'm finally writing that tango for Stephen which I told you about two years ago! In the first week of September I'll try to write one more dance for this suite. (…)

Kiss you and hug you with all my heart,

Your Andrzej.

Cumnor, 27.6.81

Darling Funnyface,

I had three free weeks so I finally wrote the tango for Stephen's suite, and improved the piano score of the first act, but I strained my eyes and had dizzy spells for a week. Overall, this year has been unusual – instructive, certainly, but totally exhausting emotionally. The depression is gone, but the tiredness remains.

And now my compositions are in demand! I'm enormously pleased by it, naturally. But I fear I won't manage because I write slowly and with difficulty. In my youth I wrote quickly, but I had no critical faculty then; now I have too much. I'll write the suite for Stephen in two versions, for two and four hands, because there are several friends who'd like to record the suite in a version for two pianos in Japan. The Korean violinist Kyung-Wha Chung is pressing me for a cycle of miniatures, the Israeli viola player Atar Arad has been promised a concerto for viola (for which I've some promising ideas and a lot of enthusiasm), the American clarinettist Stephen Bennett has asked me for a concerto – and the third act of *The Merchant* has been set aside because I've not had time to start the instrumentation…

Tomorrow I'm being visited by Mycielski!*, which I'm very pleased about. (…) In October, there's to be an audition of the first two acts of *The Merchant* at the ENO. The lady who's writing the piano score will play the vocal parts on one piano, and I'll play the orchestra on the other. I don't know if this will give anyone any idea of the piece, but the management of the Opera admitted with disarming frankness that, with the possible exception of the conductor, none of them knows how to read a score! That doesn't surprise me since I don't, either, and that's maybe why it takes me so long to write one.

I've started rehearsing again because I've got more concerts starting mid-July – Beethoven's C minor in London, a recital in Oxford playing Chopin's 24 Preludes, which I gave up 20 years ago because they weren't working! If they work this time I'll be very pleased – it may mean that, despite everything, I've matured before getting old. Don't worry about me, Funnyface, or my moods! After all, I always manage somehow in the end, and I do have a lot of joy in my life, more than most of the people I know. What I would ask from you, though, is that when you are here you don't start thinking I'm miserable and impatient because of you! Believe me, and try to help me.

Warm hugs and kisses.

Your Andrzej.

---

* Zygmunt Mycielski, a composer

Cumnor, 30.6.81

Darling Funnyface,

(…) I can't write because I don't have my glasses so instead of a letter I'm sending you a food parcel. I'd very much like to get to know Ewa and Marek. Come, all of you, come!

Kiss you, Andrzej.

Cumnor, 13.7.81

Darling Funnyface,

You can, of course, keep the cassette with my concerto, I'll talk to the publisher. But anyway, you'll see how pleasant it will be for us all! I like solitude during the day: when I've finished work I become relaxed and sociable. When are you coming? Maybe it's not worth writing again? I've got concerts in London the day after tomorrow, 31st of August, and 25th of September. In September I'll be writing a tarantella for the suite for Stephen. I'm waiting, kisses, Darling.

Your Andrzej.

Warsaw, 22.7.81

Darling Andrzej, I've just come back from the mountains from where I sent you thanks for the overwhelming food parcel. The parcel became the chief topic of my life on holiday, and also a source of joy and entertainment because trips were called off by the continuous downpours. I didn't sleep well and I kept having macabre dreams. The most cheerful one concerned Basia: she fell in love with a beautiful youth, became pregnant, the boy proposed marriage. Everything would have turned out well except the boy turned out to be an Italian count; he had a castle in Taormino where he lived with his family; 'I won't go to the castle', Basia cried, 'they'll sneer at me and criticise me.' The count was horrified and announced he would stay with Basia in a squat, take a job as a taxi-driver and marry her instantly. To which Basia said that she hadn't got a divorce from her previous husband. 'Doesn't matter', the count assured her, 'Andrzej will come, he'll testify to your husband's death and be a witness at our wedding.'

I don't know if you did give them that death certificate because I woke up. These weird dreams were probably the result of the protein shock which I must have suffered eating all those little sausages you sent.

I'll write more soon, today I'm dropping off after the journey.

Wishes and kisses,

Your H.

Cumnor, 31.7.81

Darling Funnyface,

Many thanks for the card and the letter. But forgive me, once again I don't want to write! In fact, I don't want to do anything.

I think my life only has meaning when I'm composing. In September I'll try to write a tarantella for Stephen's suite (he chooses and commissions the various dances) and, of course, get down to the orchestration of Act 3 of *The Merchant*, which contains my best music to date. Just the thought of that work improves my mood.

But people tire me. I can't understand how a selfish hermit like me can be so popular! Every day someone phones and invites himself round. I explain I've got a house full of starving Poles, so they offer to help me feed them; I must think up some other excuse.

Actually, by and large, they're very nice people who don't demand anything of me. They simply like my company. But in company I feel I'm diffusing myself, even though I like the people and feel good with them; it's only the next morning that I feel I've lost touch with my own work.

Forgive these complaints! The day after tomorrow I'm going on a tour to Italy and Austria, I'll see the Alps and everything will change. On August 4th I'm playing at the festival in Bardonecchia: a recital with Bach's Toccata in C minor (instead of the Bartók, which I'm bored with now), Schubert's Sonata in G major and Chopin's 24 Preludes. Last week I played this programme in Oxford and I was pleasantly surprised: even the preludes were generally speaking decent. And on the 12th I'm playing three piano quartets in Kitzbühel, which always cheers me up! I like being with people, but I have to *do* something with them, not just chatter! It can, as in this case, be chamber music, jointly learning something, writing a book (your project will be very useful to us) or even cooking supper together. Then conversations, jokes etc. please me, too, but talking on its own tires me quickly. (…)

Funnyface, forgive me this down-in-the-mouth letter: next month everything will be completely different.

Kiss you, Darling,

Your Andrzej.

Warsaw, 15.8.81

Darling Andrzej, it always happens that whenever I send you a letter, a letter from you comes two hours later; I should exploit this parapsychological contact and wait those two hours, but I forget.

Basia's arrival here led to a terrible argument with Ewa. She was awfully thrilled by the idea of Basia coming and she'd planned a joint holiday, but when she found out that Basia was really coming she announced that she hadn't got time, she had to write a screenplay, doing that is the only real rest for her etc. Then I showed her your letter and she went into ecstasies because she was the same as you (she can't bear anyone forcing companionship on her, can't bear planning her holidays etc.). Then she told me I'm wasting my life like stupid Grzesio wasted sand (he carried a bag of sand through the village and 'the sand followed Grzesio, running out through a hole in the sack')* and I'm 'constricted by conventions' etc. (…)

Life here has become so emotionally full it's quite simply difficult to bear. Jean-Marie Drot (who makes films about great contemporary artists with their participation, as it happens – e.g. Giacometti, Zadkine, Chagall) said in an interview that it was Poland that was the European capital of art, that it was here that one had to come. He himself is continually making films here. 'Meetings with your people', he wrote, 'are violent and overwhelming because something is happening in them which will have to happen soon because in Poland tomorrow is so unpredictable. Everywhere else in Europe we know what tomorrow will bring, but here it seems one has to hurry and go straight to the heart of the matter.'

Yes, but permanent 'experiencing' is appallingly tiring. I don't know what the catastrophe will look like, but I'm certain it must happen because the country is disintegrating and the government and Solidarity are like two boxers in a clinch. Do you know the difference between Poland and the Titanic? There is none: even right at the end the band was still playing.

I'm ending this sombre letter and kissing you. Basia's flying in tomorrow.

H.

PS. 16.8.81 – I went to the airport and someone fell into my arms – it was Ewa who was waiting for Basia to arrive! Basia's father was also at the airport. I went up to him and introduced Ewa to him: 'This is our second daughter so let me introduce you.' 'I'm delighted,' he said, greeting her unusually heartily. Nothing but surprises, because even Basia landed at the time predicted!

Cumnor, 27.8.81

My Darling Funnyface,
Your letter about Ewa provoked amazement and jealousy in me. How can she make you lose your equilibrium and I can't? I mean, I was dying trying to provoke you to an explosion. (…) You managed to break off relations with me, but to this day I'm certain you could only do it by letter because in my presence

---

* Reference to a poem for children by Julian Tuwim

you confine your protest to a hunger strike and tranquillizers. A hunger strike in Poland would have passed unnoticed lately, and there are probably no tranquillisers left, so for once in your life you had to show yourself to be a decent human being and tear a strip off someone. Ewa has finally got what she wanted. And what am I – a dog? After all, I'm not that strong, if I were strong I wouldn't yell so much!

But Ewa truly is like me. I, too, plan various escapades and then feel trapped! How many times have I organised a trip to the theatre or the opera for a dozen people but only eleven went because the organiser of the event became terrified and went to bed with a migraine? The best thing to do with such people is to calm them down in advance when they suggest something by saying: 'Very well, we'll see what kind of mood you're in nearer the time.' Then that person will feel they don't have to, and straight away that will make them keen to do it. (…)

Yes, everyone is enthralled by the situation in Poland. I myself am giving two recitals to send you food, one in Brussels and one in London. (…)

Just to cheer you up I'll tell you that Nostradamus forecast the end of mankind for 1999, and he was rarely wrong! For instance, he also predicted the assassination attempt on the Pope for this year, and one can positively teach the history of the French Revolution from his writings even though he lived two centuries earlier…

Kisses without number, Darling

Your Andrzej.

PS. Give Basia a hug if she's still with you.

Note affixed to a cassette, Warsaw, 8.9.81

My dearest Andrzej, I'm sending you some poems by Zbigniew Herbert; they have the same effect on me as Bach. I also like and admire Zbyszek Zapasiewicz, the actor reading the poems. You just believe him like no one else on earth, but acquiring such moving simplicity can't be easy.

H.

PS. I'm sending another cassette, with Bulgakov's play about Molière, through Basia.

Cumnor, 19.9.81

Darling Funnyface,

I'm tired, my eyes hurt, but I want at least to thank you with all my heart for the cassette with Bulgakov. Staś sent me the text so I listened to it with full comprehension. I admit that, in contrast to his excellent biography of Molière, the play seems to be poor – sensationalist, melodramatic and falling apart all over the place! But when you know the situation in which he wrote it and what he couldn't say directly, you understand it rather differently.

If I ever write another opera (which I dare to doubt at this moment), then it may well be based on Molière and in French. But I would base it on the biographical facts which are sufficiently moving without additional dramatising! When you come here I'll tell you about it.

Basia came over and she was bewitching! We had a nice time. Basia says the people in Poland are hungry but cheerful and that's why you've postponed the trip. I've always known you're more afraid of me than you are of death by starvation, so I'm not surprised. I, on the other hand, am not afraid of you, but for you. There was some disturbing news again today – I'm just about to switch the television on to find out more. What will you do if they close the borders?

I recently watched Wajda's *Without Anesthesia* and heard a television interview – he's an impressive guy!

Bye for now, because I'm writing so many notes I haven't the strength to write words.

Kiss you, Funnyface, and I'll see you very soon, surely.

Because you are coming, aren't you?

Your Andrzej.

Cumnor, 28.10.81

My Darling Funnyface,

Many thanks for the letter (the one about Wajda). The letter with the cassette hasn't come yet: I still hope it will come because though a cassette is only an object, I value your letters more than anything else: Shakespeare's sonnets are, possibly, better written, but he addressed them to someone else…

I would indeed like to write something for the Warsaw Autumn. The Varsovia Quartet have offered to play my 2nd Quartet at the Autumn. Is it Guś Bloch* who organises it? I remember him and like him very much. If you know, write and tell me whom my publisher should contact in order to get something performed.

---

\* Augustyn Bloch, Polish composer (1929-2006)

My feelings about Poland are as positive as they can be: on 5th November I'm giving a charity recital in Brussels to feed the Poles, and on 6th December I'll do the same in London. (Perhaps you'll be here then and come to the recital?) They can have my compositions for nothing, too, of course!

I spoke with Basia a couple of days ago, it was very nice though her head was in the clouds as usual and talked mainly about her dreams.

Kantor's *Wielopole* was the hit of the Edinburgh Festival last year; Ian was knocked out with admiration!

Ian writes to me in verse, in German, making up limericks in that language, and I reply in limericks, too.

The audition of the opera has been postponed till 21st December because the piano score wasn't ready on time; it was a great relief because I'll be able to concentrate on my concerts now and on the opera later. I've never been able to combine work in both those areas.

I don't know Gombrowicz's *Operetta* but I'll try to find a copy and read it. Let's talk about Molière when you're here, because it's a fascinating subject! For the moment I'll just say that the principle of this opera would be a stylistic contrast between the author's life treated in a 'contemporary' way, and a baroque version of his life staged. Trust me, Funnyface: I know what I'm doing. Anyway, when I've finished *The Merchant* I intend to give myself a break from opera, to write short pieces and finish them comparatively quickly. I'll start writing the second opera only after I've finished the first in order to learn from the experience.

Today I received a birthday present from my dad: a huge book about Schubert which it is virtually impossible to pick up let alone read! My attitude to my father is also changing by degrees because he makes no demands of me, doesn't reproach me (even though I see him precisely once a year), and sometimes, as now, he shows me his own kindness. A short time ago I dreamt we were walking along in Montmartre, holding hands and talking warmly about our old misunderstandings; I wrote him a letter about it and since then I've wanted to see him and I regret I have to wait till January before I do. Who would have predicted that?

Bye, Funnyface, look after yourself, and I'll try to keep an eye on Basia.

Kisses. Your Andrzej.

CARD: NEW COLLEGE CHAPEL, OXFORD

Cumnor, 12.11.81

Darling Funnyface, I'm writing a card so it will reach you sooner! Yesterday I sent you a food parcel because now, when you're ill, you must eat a lot even if you don't feel like it: 1) to get your health back, 2) to prove that people in Poland do eat...

On 6th December I'm giving a recital to send grub and medicine to Poland. Perhaps you'll be here then? You haven't heard me 'in the flesh' for a quarter of a century. I don't know how it will go, but it will, in any case, help Poland and you'll forgive me, won't you? So try to be here in the first days of December. (…)

Kiss you, get well quickly and see you soonest.

Andrzej.

Cumnor, 23.11.81

Darling little Funnyface, what's happening?

Your 'essential and urgent' operation has terrified me. I spoke to Basia yesterday, but she knows no more than I do, and she's trying to get through to Łódź to find out more.

Today I'm going to Copenhagen, and on Friday to Oslo; I'm coming back here on 2nd December. I don't know what to expect because the last five days I've been suffering from a stomach bug which I brought back from Germany, after a quite successful performance of my concerto (better than the one you know from the cassette). For three days I couldn't practise at all, and for the next two I practised too hard to make up time, and as a consequence the symptoms recurred (to put it bluntly, I got the shits). Don't worry about my health because of course it's nothing serious; I'm worried about the concerts which I won't have time to prepare properly. These last weeks I've had to work wildly because between concerts I've been correcting the second act of the opera, so between writing and practising there's not even been time for a walk.

In addition we have a crisis in our village because the authorities have decided to build 510 houses in Cumnor, of which 15 are at the back of my garden! The whole village was awfully outraged, we had constant meetings, we've been signing petitions, individual protests, letters to the appropriate officials etc. People in Poland must regard all this as ridiculous since you have far more serious things to protest against!

The papers here carry increasingly worrying news from Poland. (…) I've already played one recital for Poland in Brussels in a large and beautiful church which couldn't have been more full if the Pope himself had been preaching there! The church was surrounded by police to prevent acts of terrorism (or maybe just mass hysteria!); inside eight girls in traditional Cracovian costume kept getting in my way offering to help me; and in all this pomp there was no toilet in the church! Well, I was forced to commit blasphemy. In the sacristy I noticed a vase full of beautiful flowers, so I took them out, handed them to the first girl and asked her to present them to me on stage during the recital, and then I disappeared with the vase into a dark corner. But with a Polish Pope I can surely count on getting absolution…

Darling, let me know quickly how the operation went, how you're feeling and if you're fit enough to undertake the trip here. If you haven't the strength to write, then ask Piotr or Majka to. I'll write to Bloch as soon as Majka sends me his address: at the moment I have more pressing matters on my mind, especially as the Warsaw Autumn may not even take place next year...

Kiss you, Funnyface, do what you can to get well again as soon as possible, come here and take advantage of our central heating.

Hug you and kiss you with all my heart.

Your Andrzej.

Cumnor, 4.12.81

My Funnyface, what's going on? You were supposed to be appearing now and in one piece, and here you are letting yourself be cut up into bits and we'll get you in parcels bit by bit. It's nice that you want to return the favour of the parcels you've been getting yourself (albeit rarely), but I'm no Atreus nor even Salome and I'd prefer to swallow you in one gulp like a glass of vodka. I know you don't like to refuse anyone anything, but if they cut too much out you'll have nothing left to give – and what will you do for the rest of your life?

Unfortunately I can't write any longer because the day after tomorrow I'm playing that recital in London for 'Food for Poland', to which I was recently inviting you so ardently (you do refuse me, though... ). But you will hear it because it will be recorded for the radio and transmitted later – perhaps even during your stay here? Anyway, if I can manage it I'll make a cassette of it for you.

I talked to Basia yesterday. She continues to paint little plates and sell them (to exclusive retail establishments, apparently). Generally speaking she's well though she has come out in some spots and the doctor reckons it's an allergy to the paints. She promised to see a dermatologist. It doesn't hinder her in any way. As it happens, she still has to fight off admirers, so nobody, with the exception of the doctor, has noticed the spots...

I don't know Gombrowicz, but ever since you introduced me to Szymborska I go for everything you recommend!

During the first months of the New Year I'll be touring almost constantly, but from 4th March I'll be home for 6 weeks and we'll have a good talk then, shall we?

Let me know as soon as possible what medicines and vitamins I could send you from here.

Masses of heartfelt wishes and kisses,

Your Andrzej.

Warsaw, 8.1.82

Andrzej dearest, I'm writing a short letter because apparently the shorter they are, the quicker they're passed by the censors...

The operation went smoothly, and your latest letters (the last one arrived after martial law was declared) and magnificent parcel helped me get my strength back. After the operation they fed me narcotics which gave me some terrible nightmares. After one of them I made up the following limerick:

A fashion-conscious old girl from Djakarta
Dreamt surgeons had made her a martyr
By filling her innards with spokes;
To her relief when she woke
She found swords in her guts – that's much smarter.

First the doctors told Lili I had cancer, then I didn't – they'd made a mistake. So to begin with everybody loved me terribly, but afterwards they loved me a little less. When I was thinking I probably didn't have long to live I felt like Dudek in Pawlikowska's poem *The Bandit and the Devil*. They wanted to hang Dudek, and he

(...) Didn't fancy hell. Didn't care much for heaven too.
He showed no interest at all. (...)

I spent Christmas Eve with Majka and Wanda Wiłkomirska – Wanda told us masses of things about you and that sad Christmas Eve* became less sad. Ian sent me a pair of magnificent fur gloves for Christmas. I guess my thanks will reach New Zealand in time for next Christmas.

Ewa is getting married to Marek. They'll probably make a film about you in Paris or Canada. I'm writing a novel and hope to get it finished 'before God collects'.

Can you guess who the novel is about?

Andrzej, you have no idea how crazy I am about you!

Masses of kisses and wishes from your old friend.

H.

---

* Christmas Eve was 11 days after the introduction of martial law

Paris, 3.3.82

Darling Funnyface, at last! We've been so worried here! But you're well, letters are getting through, we stopped reading the newspapers, so what's there to worry about? Let me suggest a new game we could play: we'll compare operations. I think I'll probably win that one, because I've had two of them recently, and besides I really did have cancer, and, what's more, a perforated large intestine and peritonitis, so I really do have something to boast about. (What Tchaikowsky won't do to draw attention to himself!) But I don't want to spend a long time writing about it, so I'll just photocopy the appropriate fragments from the journal (about hearing the opera and about the illness) and I'll send you the whole caboodle in a few days.

For the moment I'll just tell you that the surgeon and all the doctors are very optimistic because the cancer hadn't spread so it was possible to get rid of it! I was lucky it had perforated the intestine otherwise it would never have occurred to anyone that I had cancer (I felt very well).

All this happened in West Germany, in Mainz, where I'd gone to teach half-wits to play the piano; I was stuttering in German, they were stuttering on the keyboard. I fell ill the day after I'd finished the course and I was in the clinic for five and a half weeks. Before I left I spoke to Wanda on the telephone; she had just arrived and was as fiery as ever.

I'm in Paris now because the doctors advised me against being alone, so I'm living at my cousins' (...) till mid-April. But since I need solitude like I need air, I'm just spending three days in some friends' empty house. They're pianists, too, they play recitals for four hands and are constantly away so I'll enjoy the pleasure a few times yet.

Despite these operations (or rather because of them) I'm practically the healthiest member of my now quite numerous family. Papa is in hospital with Parkinson's, my cousin has liver cirrhosis, my sister suffers from neuralgia, even the cats at Kazik's need daily injections! I'm looking after the family more than they're looking after me: I took on all of the cooking and that started culinary pilgrimages here undertaken by friends and relations, which flattered me to begin with, but soon got irritating! These three days of isolation have been a veritable salvation.

I paid one visit to my father: he's so apathetic and so depressed by the disease that I don't even know whether he was pleased to see me. (...)

Darling, I must end now because I'm snowed under with letters! Everyone's writing and phoning to find out how I am. I'd never have thought that people like me so much and can be so kind.

I didn't get the cassette with Herbert's poems. What can I send you? What about Ian? A letter from New Zealand has just arrived at Kazik's house – it could be from him...

I'm not back in England till the end of May (I have a long tour before that, 17 concerts in Germany, Holland, Austria and Switzerland, and immediately after that a stay in hospital for observation).

Well, bye, Funnyface. Look after yourself, because at least one of us has to be healthy!

No end of kisses.

Your Andrzej.

Warsaw, 22.2.82

Andrzej, dearest, where are you? How are you feeling? I beg you – write, because I'm going crazy with worry! I've had three letters from Basia, and not one word from you. Every day you come into my dreams with a different part of your body in bandages.

Forgive me for being so hysterical, but you're never ill, I haven't accustomed myself to the thought that it's possible! I've accustomed you to my illnesses: every few years they cut another part of me out and the less there is of me the better I feel. But I don't want there to be less of you, because as far as I'm concerned there's never enough of you… (…)

I went to Emma Altberg with the cassette of your concerto, and she said: 'That is a work to which one can't possibly be indifferent.' Don't send me anything, I can buy everything in the shops but I can't buy your letters.

Kisses, and I'm waiting very impatiently.

Your H.

Postcard: Utrecht, Holland, 16.4.82

Darling Funnyface,

Everything's fine! I spent three days in the clinic in Mainz for tests and the doctors didn't find anything suspicious so there's no reason to cancel the tour. I had my first rehearsal of 1982 (Chopin's Concerto in E minor, the rondo is still a bit wobbly), and the first concert is the day after tomorrow. Till mid-May write to: Bei Herrn H. Hermes, Wielandstrasse 29, 6200 Wiesbaden, West Germany, after that I'll be home.

No end of kisses.

A.

London, 6.7.82

Darling, Darling Mummy,

These last three days have seemed like a nightmare to me. I was hoping I'd wake up. What has happened is so senseless I can't even think about it.

When I came back from Italy I thought I'd visit Andrzej. The telephone was answered by Eve. I thought she was looking after him, but she told me she had some very bad news.

It's so horribly hard for me to write this letter, though you probably know by now. I couldn't say anything to her. I just cried and cried. Now I'm taping a record of Schubert's Quintet for you. They played the adagio at his funeral.

It was only later that I phoned Eve. She told me that they were playing his *Trio Notturno* the next day in Cheltenham. I went down with Terry and his mother. First we drove down to Oxford, which was very sad. Everything was sad. The sight of the boats on the river, seeing the Allisons. And a huge feeling of loss, though everyone was very kind. Then came the concert.

I came back to London with Terry. He told me about the course of the illness. During the concerts in Dusseldorf they discovered there was something wrong after those operations and the doctors realised that the cancer had returned. In May they tried another operation, but the disease was too far advanced. The last hope was that they might prolong his life with chemotherapy. But that, too, proved useless. It worked for a day or two, and then things got worse again. The third time it didn't work at all. And it was probably then that they knew his days were numbered. He said to the doctor: 'I've had it'; and the doctor said: 'I'm afraid so; we've done everything we could.'

All the time he was in hospital he composed for two hours a day. He saw only a handful of friends. He only had four pages of his opera left to orchestrate. He got up on his last day to finish it but he couldn't work any more. They gave him some painkillers and he died in his sleep. It was only after the autopsy that they realised it had been a miracle that, in his state, he'd managed to remain conscious and write his opera.

The funeral took place a week later. First they played the *Trio Notturno*, then Chad* gave the eulogy. Then they played the adagio from the Schubert Quintet. Yesterday I phoned Eve again. Andrzej said you were one of the three people he wanted to write a farewell letter to. He said he'd write them after the chemotherapy, when he was feeling better. But he never did feel better.

Mummy, I'm so worried about you. Half my pain and sadness is because I know how you must be feeling now. I can't forgive myself for not seeing him again. And for not being with him.

I kiss you with all my strength and hug you.

Basia.

---

* The Rev Chad Varah CH, 1911-2007, founder of The Samaritans

London, undated

Harrison Parrot Ltd, 12 Penzance Place, London W11 4PA
Dear Mrs Janowska,
It is with great sadness that we write to you with the news that our great artist and friend André Tchaikowsky died on 26 June at 7 o'clock in the morning. Cancer was diagnosed in January and its spread was so rapid that all treatment proved useless. Over the last eight years it has been my responsibility to look after André's career on the firm's behalf.
His loss has been a painful blow to us all, because we have lost not only an exceptional pianist, but also a magnificent human being and friend. (…)
Respectfully yours,

Angela Kokoszka.


Andrzej Tchaikovsky's last letter, to Zygmunt Mycielski, published in Ruch Muzyczny, September 1982. 17.6.82

30 The Park, Cumnor, Oxford OX2 9QS

Dearest Zygmunt,
My reasons for not writing to Paris are so sad I find it hard to force myself to tell you! I've had three operations for cancer since January, and the last one was in May. They found that the cancer could no longer be removed surgically because it had, between operations, affected the liver and intestines, so it's now incurable and no one knows how much longer I'll survive. The process can often be slowed down by chemotherapy, which I'm given every fortnight. I hope that in my case it works well enough so I have time to write at least what I've got in my head (there's no question, obviously, of performing again). When I discovered how things stand I immediately started to orchestrate the last act of the opera (while I was still in hospital), and I'm only a few pages short now. The next project is a cycle of piano miniatures, and after that, if the therapy really is successful, a concerto for viola.
Death itself doesn't terrify me (old age is hard and besides, the whole of our civilisation is dying), but I'd still like to do something so I could feel I haven't wasted my life.
Write if you feel like it; I'd be very pleased and, if I have the strength, I'll try to reply… (…)

# *Index*

*Where an individual or subject is mentioned extensively only selected page references may be given.*